THE 100 BEST MUTUAL FUNDS YOU CAN BUY 2000

Gordon K. Williamson

Adams Media Corporation
Holbrook, Massachusetts

Also by Gordon K. Williamson

Big Decisions, Small Investor
Low Risk Investing
Making the Most of Your 401(k)

Dedication
This book is dedicated to all of my clients.
I would be nowhere without their trust and support.

Acknowledgments
Special thanks to Cynthia Shaffer for her computer skills. This is a truly
thankless job, and I appreciate everything she has done.

Published by Adams Media Corporation
260 Center Street, Holbrook, MA 02343

ISBN: 1-58062-170-8
ISSN: Pending

Printed in Canada.

J I H G F E D C B A

This book is not designed or intended to provide or replace professional
investment advice. Readers should invest with care, including seeking
specific professional advice, since investments by nature involve significant risk and can result in financial losses. The past performance of the
investments reported in this book does not guarantee or predict future
performance.

The data used to analyze the funds are current through June 30, 1999.

Cover design by Mike Stromberg

*This book is available at quantity discounts for bulk purchases.
For information call 1-800-872-5627.*

Visit our home page at http://www.adamsmedia.com

Contents

I.
About This Book

There are 5.4 million business entities operating in the United States; close to 14,000 of these businesses are publicly held (meaning they have issued stock to the public). Of the 14,000 publicly traded companies, fewer than 4,000 are listed on the New York Stock Exchange (NYSE).

There are over 13,500 mutual funds. There are well over three times as many mutual funds as there are stocks listed on the NYSE! The mutual fund industry is now the second largest financial institution in the nation, with assets exceeding $5 trillion, up from $1 trillion in 1991. Over the past five years, the percentage of U.S. households that invest in mutual funds has risen from 25 percent to 45 percent.

Mutual funds are the *best* investment vehicle that has been developed in the twentieth century. When properly selected, these vehicles combine professional management, ease of purchase and redemption, simple record keeping, risk reduction, and superb performance, all in one type of investment. There are dozens of other types of investments, but none match the overall versatility of mutual funds.

A mutual fund is simply one method of investing. When you invest in a fund, your money is pooled with thousands of other investors' monies. This large pool of money is overseen by the fund's management. These managers invest this pool of money in one or more types of investments. The universe of investments includes common stocks, preferred stocks, corporate bonds, tax-free municipal bonds, U.S. government obligations, zero-coupon bonds, convertible securities, gold, silver, foreign securities, and even real estate. The amount of money invested in one or more of these categories depends upon the fund's objectives and restrictions and on the management's perception of the economy.

The beauty of mutual funds is that once the investor decides upon the *type* of investment desired there are several funds that fulfill that criterion. As an example, someone who needs current income would be attracted to bond funds (or a series of equity-oriented funds coupled with what is known as a "systematic withdrawal plan"—a monthly income program described in Appendix D). A person interested in appreciation would focus on an aggressive growth, growth and income, and/or international stock fund. A person who wanted some current income plus some growth to offset the effects of inflation should consider a balanced fund.

The track records of these funds can easily be obtained, as contrasted to the track records of stockbrokers, who are not ranked at all. A few mutual fund sources even look at a fund's risk-adjusted return, a standard of measurement that has not been sufficiently emphasized in the past.

This book was written to fill a void. There are already several mutual fund books and directories, but none deal exclusively with the very best funds. More important, *none of these publications measure risk properly.*

This is the tenth edition of this book. If you have read one or more of the previous editions, you will notice that this edition includes many funds not previously listed and that several of the previous "100 best" are not included here. This does not mean that you should sell or transfer from a previous recommendation to one that appears in this edition. For the most part, mutual funds described in past editions are still excellent choices and should not be moved. There are a number of reasons why a fund no longer appears in this, or previous, editions. These reasons will be detailed in Chapter 10.

Moving from one fund to another can often spell trouble. Consider a Morningstar study that compared the performance of its growth fund index with the average investor's return during the five-year period ending 5/31/94. While the overall market gained, on average, 12.5 percent a year, the average investor *lost* 2.5 percent a year. Volatility can make it easy for investors to forget about the long-term case for stocks.

Other sources give almost endless numbers and performance statistics for hundreds and hundreds of mutual funds, leaving readers to draw their own conclusions as to what are the best funds. This book will save you a great deal of time because it has taken the over 13,000 existing funds and narrowed them down to the best 100, ranked by specific category and risk level. Even money market funds are included, a category rarely covered by any other publication.

Investors and financial advisors are not concerned with mediocre or poor performers; they simply want the best funds, *given certain parameters*. Personal investment considerations should include (in order of priority) your time horizon, risk tolerance, financial goals, existing portfolio, and tax bracket. Parameters within a given fund category include risk, performance, and consistency.

Current books and periodicals that cover funds focus on how a fund has performed in the past. Studies clearly point out that a fund whose performance is in the top half one year has a 50–50 chance of being in the bottom half the next year, or the year after that. Since there is little correlation between the past and the future when it comes to market returns, this book concentrates on consistency in management and the amount of risk assumed.

The model used to rank the one hundred best is fully described in a later chapter. It is a logical, common-sense approach that cuts through the statistical jargon; it is also easy to understand. As my dad used to say, "There is nothing as uncommon as common sense."

II.
What Is a Mutual Fund?

A mutual fund is an investment company—an entity that makes investments on behalf of individuals and institutions who share common financial goals. The fund pools the money of many people, each with a different amount to invest. Professional money managers then use the pool of money to buy a variety of stocks, bonds, or money market instruments that, in their judgment, will help the fund's shareholders achieve their financial objectives.

Each fund has an investment objective, described in the fund's prospectus, that is important to both the manager and the potential investor. The fund manager uses it as a guide when choosing investments for the fund's portfolio. Prospective investors use it to determine which funds are suitable for their own needs. Mutual funds' investment objectives cover a wide range. Some follow aggressive investment policies, involving greater risk, in search of higher returns; others seek current income from more conservative investments.

When the fund earns money, it distributes the earnings to its shareholders. Earnings come from stock dividends, interest paid by bonds or money market instruments, and gains from the sale of securities in the fund's portfolio. Dividends and capital gains produced are paid out in proportion to the number of fund shares owned. Thus, shareholders who invest a few hundred dollars get the same investment return per dollar as those who invest hundreds of thousands.

Mutual funds remain popular because they are convenient and efficient investment vehicles that give all individuals—even those with small sums to invest—access to a splendid array of opportunities. Mutual funds are uniquely democratic institutions. They can take a portfolio of giant blue-chip companies like IBM, General Electric, and General Motors, and slice it into small enough pieces so that almost anyone can buy.

Mutual funds allow you to participate in foreign stock and bond markets that might otherwise demand too much time, expertise, or expense to be worthwhile. International funds make investing across national borders no more difficult than investing across state lines. Over the next decade, as securities markets develop in the former Iron Curtain countries, mutual funds will no doubt give investors many opportunities to participate in those markets as well.

Mutual funds have opened up a world of fixed-income investing to people who, until recently, had few choices apart from passbook accounts and savings bonds. Through bond funds, shareholders can tap into the interest payments from any kind of fixed-income security you can imagine—and many you have never heard of. The range goes from U.S. Treasury bonds (T-bonds) to collateralized mortgage obligations (CMOs), adjustable-rate preferred stock, floating-rate notes, and even to other countries' debts—denominated both in U.S. dollars and in other currencies.

What is heavily marketed is not necessarily what is appropriate for you to invest in. A global biotechnology fund may be a great investment, but it may not be the right mutual fund for you. Buying what is "hot" rather than what is appropriate is one of the most common mistakes made by investors and an issue that is addressed throughout this book.

III.
How to Invest in a Mutual Fund

Investing in a mutual fund means buying shares of the fund. An investor becomes an owner of shares in the fund just as he or she might be an owner of shares of stock in a large corporation. The difference is that a fund's only business is investing in securities, and the price of its shares is directly related to the value of the securities held by the fund.

Mutual funds continually issue new shares for purchase by the public. The price per share for existing fund investors is not decreased by the ongoing issuance of new shares, since each share created is offset by the amount of new money coming in. Phrased another way, new money that comes into the fund is used to purchase additional securities in order not to dilute the income or value for existing shareholders.

A fund's share price can change from day to day, depending on the daily value of the securities held by the fund. The share price is called the net asset value (NAV), which is calculated as follows. The total value of the fund's investments at the end of the day, after expenses, is divided by the number of shares outstanding.

Newspapers report mutual fund activity every day. An example from the *Wall Street Journal* is shown below.

Everett Funds:			
Evrt r	12.38	NL	−.01
MaxRtn	18.39	NL	+.06
ValTr	12.33	NL	−.01
LtdSl	17.71	NL	−.14
ExtrMid	2.82	2.95	−.02
ExJY p	7.24	7.60	+.01
FBK Gth t	11.06	11.06	..
FJA Funds:			
Capit f	14.67	15.69	−.02
NwHrz	9.65	10.10	..
Permt	12.91	13.81	..
Perrin	20.96	22.42	−.02

The first column in the table is the fund's abbreviated name. Several funds under a single heading indicate a family of funds.

The second column is the net asset value (NAV) per share as of the close of the preceding business day. In some newspapers, the NAV is identified as the sell or the bid price—the amount per share you would receive if you sold your shares. Each mutual fund determines its net asset value every business day by dividing the market value of its total assets, less liabilities, by the number of shares outstanding. On any given day, you can determine the value of your holdings by multiplying the NAV by the number of shares you own.

The third column is usually the offering price or, in some papers, the buy or the asked price—the price you would pay if you purchased shares. The buy price is the NAV plus any sales charges. If there are no sales charges, an NL for no load appears in this column. In such a case, the buy price would be the same as the NAV.

The next column shows the change, if any, in the net asset value (NAV) from the preceding quotation—in other words, the change over the most recent one-day trading period. Thus, if you see a "+.06" in the newspaper next to your fund, *each* of your shares in the fund went up in value by six cents during the previous day.

A *p* following the abbreviated name of the fund denotes a fund that charges a fee that is subtracted from assets for marketing and distribution costs, also known as a 12b-1 plan (named after the federal government rule that permits such an expense). If the fund name is followed by an *r*, the fund has a contingent deferred sales load (CDSL) or a redemption fee. A CDSL is a charge incurred if shares are sold within a certain period; a redemption fee is a cost you would pay *whenever* shares are sold. An *f* indicates a fund that habitually enters the previous day's prices, instead of the current day's. A *t* designates a fund that has both a CDSL or a redemption fee and a 12b-1 plan.

IV.
How a Mutual Fund Operates

A mutual fund is owned by all of its shareholders, the people who purchased shares of the fund. The day-to-day operation of a fund is delegated to a management company.

The management company, often the organization that created the fund, may offer other mutual funds, financial products, and financial services as well. The management company usually serves as the fund's investment advisor.

The investment advisor manages the fund's portfolio of securities. The advisor is paid for its services in the form of a fee that is based on the total value of the fund's assets; fees average 0.5 percent. The advisor employs professional portfolio managers who invest the fund's money by purchasing a number of stocks or bonds or money market instruments, depending on what type of fund it is.

These fund professionals decide where to invest the fund's assets. The money managers make their investment decisions based on extensive, ongoing research into the financial performance of individual companies, taking into account general economic and market trends. In addition, they are backed up by economic and statistical resources. On the basis of their research, money managers decide what and when to buy, sell, or hold for the fund's portfolio, in light of the fund's specific investment objective.

In addition to the investment advisor, the fund may also contract with an underwriter that arranges for the distribution of the fund's shares to the investing public. The underwriter may act as a wholesaler, selling fund shares to security dealers, or it may retail directly to the public.

V.
Different Categories of Mutual Funds

Aggressive Growth. The investment objective of aggressive growth funds is maximum capital gains, with little or no concern for dividends or income of any kind. What makes this category of mutual funds unique is that fund managers often have the ability to use borrowed money (leverage) to increase positions. Sometimes they deal in stock options and futures contracts (commodities). These trading techniques sound, and can be, scary, but such activities represent only a minor portion of the funds' holdings.

Because of their bullish dispositions, these funds will usually stay fully invested in the stock market. For investors, this means better-than-expected results during good (bull) markets and worse-than-average losses during bad (bear) market periods. Fortunately, the average bull market is almost four times as long as the typical bear market.

Do not be confused by economic conditions and stock market performance. There have been eight recessions since World War II. During seven of those eight recessions, U.S. stocks went up. During all eight recessions, stocks posted impressive gains in the second half of every recession. By the same token, do not underestimate the impact of a loss. A 20 percent decline means that you must make 25 percent to break even. A loss of 20 percent does not happen very often to aggressive growth funds, particularly on a calendar year basis, but you should be aware that such extreme downward moves are possible. Often brokers like to focus on the +45 percent and +50 percent years, such as 1980 and 1991, while glossing over a bad year, such as 1984, when aggressive growth funds were down almost 13 percent on average.

One of the great wonders of the stock market is how volatility of returns is reduced when one's holding period is increased. Because of this, aggressive growth funds should only be owned by one of two kinds of investors: those who can live with high levels of daily, monthly, quarterly and/or annual price per share fluctuations and those who realize the importance of a diversified portfolio that cuts across several investment categories—the investor who looks at how the entire package is performing, not just one segment.

The typical price-earnings (p/e) ratio for stocks in this category is 37, a figure that is about 8 percent higher than the S&P 500 Index (which has an average p/e ratio of 35). This group of funds has an average beta of 1.2, making its *market-related* risk 20 percent higher than that of the S&P 500 (which always has a beta of 1.0, no matter what market conditions or levels are).

The standard deviation for aggressive growth funds is 29 percent. This means that one's expected return for any given year may vary either way by 29 percent. In other words, since aggressive growth funds have averaged 13.3 percent over the past three years, annual returns are expected to range from –15.7 percent (13.3 – 29) to 42.3 percent (13.3 + 29). This would represent *one* standard deviation (29 percent in the case of aggressive growth funds). A single standard deviation accounts for what you can expect every two out of three months (67 percent of the time or roughly two out of every three years). If you are looking for greater assurance, then two standard deviations must be used (2 x 29 percent in this case). This means that returns for about 95 percent of the months (two standard deviations) would be 13.3 percent, plus or minus 58 percent. In other words, a range of –44.7 percent to +71.3 percent.

Small-company stocks have an average p/e ratio of 26. (The price-earnings ratio refers to the selling price of a stock in relation to its annual earnings. Thus a fund category that has a p/e ratio of, say, 10 is comprised of mutual funds whose typical stock in the portfolio is selling for ten times what the corporation's earnings are for the year.) Small-company stock funds have a standard deviation of 25 percent and a beta of 1.0 percent, figures that support the view that this category is slightly less volatile than aggressive growth funds.

Historical returns over the past three, five, ten, and fifteen years for aggressive growth and small-company stock funds are shown below. All of the figures shown are average *annual* rates of return (all periods ending 3/31/99).

category	3 years	5 years	10 years	15 years
aggressive growth	13%	16%	14%	13%
small-company stocks	8%	12%	13%	13%
S&P 500	28%	26%	19%	18%
T-bills	5%	5%	5%	6%
CPI (rate of inflation)	2%	2%	3%	3%

The aggressive growth fund category is dominated by technology and service stocks. These two groups represents over 46 percent of the typical aggressive growth fund's portfolio. The other three top sectors are health, financial, and retail stocks. Small-company stocks are also dominated by technology and service issues.

Balanced. This kind of fund invests in common stocks and corporate bonds. The weighting given to stocks depends upon the fund manager's perception of, or belief in, the market. The more bullish the manager is, the more likely the portfolio will be loaded up with equities. Yet no matter how strongly management feels about the stock market, it would be very rare to see stocks equal more than 67 percent of the portfolio. Similarly, no matter how bearish one becomes, it would be unlikely for a balanced fund to have more than 67 percent of its holdings represented by bonds. Often a fund's prospectus will outline the weighting ranges: The fund's managers must stay within these wide boundaries at all times. A small portion of these funds is made up of cash equivalents (T-bills, CDs, commercial paper, etc.) with a very small amount sometimes dedicated to preferred stocks and convertible securities.

Three other categories, "multi-asset global," "convertible," and "asset alloca-tion" have been combined with balanced funds for the purposes of this book. This grouping together is logical; since overall objectives are largely similar, general portfolio composition can be virtually identical in many cases, and the fund man-agers in each of these categories have the flexibility to load up heavily on stocks, bonds, preferreds, or convertible securities.

Multi-asset global funds typically emphasize bonds more than stocks or cash. It is not uncommon to see a multi-asset global fund that has 60 percent of its hold-ings in bonds, with 10 to 20 percent in stocks, and the remainder in foreign equi-ties, preferred stocks, and cash. For the *stock* portion of this category, the p/e ratio is 28 and the standard deviation 12 percent. On the bond side, the average maturity of debt instruments in the portfolio is nine years.

Convertible funds, as the name implies, are made up mostly of convertible preferred stocks and convertible bonds. The conversion feature allows the owner, the fund in this case, to convert or exchange securities for the corporation's common stock. Conversion and price appreciation take place during bull-market periods. Uncertain or down markets make conversion much less likely; instead, management falls back on the comparatively high dividend or interest payments that convertibles enjoy. The typical convertible fund has somewhere between two-thirds and three-quarters of its holdings in convertibles; the balance is in cash, stocks, and preferreds. For the stock portion of this category, the p/e ratio is 27 and the standard deviation is 13 percent. On the bond side, the average maturity of debt instruments in the portfolio is seven years.

Asset allocation funds, like other categories that fall under the broad defini-tion of "balanced," are hybrid in nature, part equity and part debt. These funds have a tendency to emphasize stocks over bonds. A fund manager who wants to take a defensive posture may stay on the sidelines by converting moderate or large parts of the portfolio into cash equivalents. The average asset allocation fund has some-where between 50 and 65 percent of its portfolio in common stocks, with the remainder in bonds, foreign stocks, and cash. For the stock portion of this category, the p/e ratio is 30 and the standard deviation is 12 percent. On the bond side, the average maturity of debt instruments in the portfolio is nine years.

The typical price-earnings (p/e) ratio for stocks in this category is 30, a figure that is lower than that of the S&P 500. This group of funds has an average beta of 0.6, making its *market-related risk* 40 percent less than the S&P 500. Keep in mind that beta refers to a portfolio's *stock market-related* risk—it is not a meaningful way to measure bond or foreign security risk. The typical bond in these funds has an average maturity of nine years.

The standard deviation for balanced funds is 12 percent, well less than half the level of aggressive growth funds. This means that one's expected return for any given year will vary by 12 percent. (For example, if you were expecting an annu-alized return of 14 percent, your actual return would range from 2 percent to 26 percent most of the time.)

Historical returns over the past three, five, ten, and fifteen years for balanced, multi-asset global, convertible, and asset allocation funds are shown below. All of the figures shown are average *annual* rates of return (all periods ending 3/31/99).

category	3 years	5 years	10 years	15 years
balanced	14%	14%	12%	13%
multi-asset global	8%	8%	8%	9%
convertible	12%	12%	12%	12%
asset allocation	14%	14%	12%	11%
Corp./gov't Bond Index	8%	8%	9%	10%

The equity portion of the balanced fund category is dominated by financial and service stocks. These two groups represent a third of the typical balanced fund's stock portfolio. The other four top equity sectors are: technology, industrial cyclicals, health, and retail stocks.

Like other hybrid funds, balanced funds provide an income stream. The average yield of balanced, multi-asset global, and asset allocation funds is under 2.5 percent. The typical yield for convertible securities funds is about 3.5 percent. High-tax-bracket investors who want to invest in these funds should consider using tax-sheltered money, if possible. Balanced, multi-asset global, asset allocation, and convertible bond funds are particularly attractive within an IRA, other qualified retirement plans, or variable annuities. (For more information about both fixed-rate and variable annuities, see two of my other books, *The 100 Best Annuities* and *Getting Started in Annuities*.)

Corporate Bonds. These funds invest in debt instruments (IOUs) issued by corporations, governments, and agencies of the U.S. government. Perhaps the typical corporate bond fund should be called a "government-corporate" fund. Bond funds have a wide range of maturities. The name of the fund will often indicate whether it is made up of short-term or medium-term obligations. If the name of the fund does not include the words "short-term" or "intermediate," then the fund most likely invests in bonds with average maturities over ten years. The greater the maturity, the more the fund's share value can change. There is an inverse relationship between interest rates and the value of a bond; when one moves up, the other goes down.

The weighted maturity date of the bonds within this group averages eight years, with a typical coupon rate of 7.2 percent. (The coupon rate represents what the corporation or government pays out annually on a per-bond basis.) All bonds have a maturity date—a date when the issuer (the government, municipality, or corporation) pays back the *face value* of the bond (which is almost always $1,000 per bond) and stops paying interest. There are often hundreds of different securities in any given bond fund. Each one of these securities (bonds in this case) has a maturity date; these maturity dates can range anywhere from a few days to up to thirty years. "Weighted maturity" refers to the time left until the average bond in the portfolio comes due (matures).

The standard deviation for corporate bonds is 3 percent, less than half the level of balanced funds. This means that one's expected return for any given month, quarter, or year will be more predictable than almost any other category of mutual funds.

Using a beta measurement for bonds is of little value, since beta defines *stock market* risk and has nothing to do with interest-rate or financial risk. Historical returns over the past three, five, ten, and fifteen years for corporate bond funds are shown below. All of the figures shown are average *annual* rates of return (all periods ending 3/31/99).

category	3 years	5 years	10 years	15 years
corporate bond funds	7%	7%	8%	9%
government bond funds	6%	6%	8%	9%
municipal bond funds	6%	7%	7%	8%
world bond funds	6%	6%	8%	10%
CPI (rate of inflation)	2%	2%	3%	3%

Like income funds, corporate funds provide a high yield that is fully taxable and should be sheltered whenever possible. The average yield of these bond funds is just over 6 percent.

Global Stock. This category of mutual funds invests in equities issued by domestic and foreign firms. Fifteen of the twenty largest corporations in the world are located outside of the United States. It makes sense to be able to invest in these and other corporations and industries—to be able to take advantage of opportunities wherever they appear. Global, also known as world, stock funds have the ability to invest in any country. The more countries a fund is able to invest in, the lower its overall risk level will be; often return potential will also increase.

For the purposes of this book, the global stock category includes foreign and international equity funds. When it comes to investing in mutual funds, the words "foreign" and "international" are interchangeable. A foreign, or international, fund invests in securities outside of the United States. Some foreign funds are broadly diversified, including stocks from European as well as Pacific Basin economies. Other international funds specialize in a particular region or country. A global fund invests in domestic as well as foreign securities. The portfolio manager of a global fund generally has more latitude in the securities selected, since either U.S. or foreign securities can end up representing 50 percent or more of the portfolio, depending upon management's view of the different markets, whereas a foreign or international fund may not be allowed to invest in U.S. stocks or bonds.

To get an idea of the return potential of global stocks, take a look at how the United States has fared compared to stock markets in other countries. The table below shows the best-performing market for each of the past twelve years (ending 12/31/97), its total return in U.S. dollars, and performance figures for the U.S. stock market. All of the figures shown below are adjusted for any good or bad foreign currency swings (meaning that these percentage figures reflect those times when the U.S. dollar has been strong or weak).

year	best major market	best emerging market	U.S. returns
1986	Spain (123%)	n/a	+18%
1987	Japan (43%)	n/a	+5%
1988	Belgium (55%)	Indonesia (258%)	+17%
1989	Austria (105%)	Turkey (547%)	+31%
1990	United Kingdom (10%)	Greece (90%)	−3%
1991	Hong Kong (50%)	Argentina (405%)	+31%
1992	Hong Kong (32%)	Jordan (40%)	+8%
1993	Hong Kong (117%)	Poland (754%)	+10%
1994	Finland (52%)	Brazil (66%)	+1%
1995	Switzerland (45%)	Israel (24%)	+37%
1996	Spain (39%)	Venezuela (228%)	+26%
1997	Portugal (47%)	Russia (+209%)	+ 33%

The typical price-earnings (p/e) ratio for stocks in this category is 26, a figure that is virtually identical to that of the S&P 500. This group of funds has an average beta of 0.7, meaning that its *U.S. market-related* risk is about 30 percent less than that of the general market, as measured by the S&P 500. The standard deviation for global stock funds is 11 percent, versus 14 percent for growth funds.

Foreign stock funds, which are exclusive of U.S. investments, have a p/e ratio of 26. Their standard deviation over the past three years has been 12 percent. Pacific Basin funds, a more narrowly focused type of foreign fund, have an average p/e ratio of 26 and a standard deviation of 16 percent. European funds, another type of specialized international fund, have a price-earnings ratio of 24 and a standard deviation of 11 percent.

Historical returns over the past three, five, ten, and fifteen years for global stocks are shown below. All of the figures shown are average *annual* rates of return (all periods ending 3/31/99).

category	3 years	5 years	10 years	15 years
global stock funds	12%	12%	11%	13%
foreign stock funds	8%	7%	8%	12%
S&P 500	28%	26%	19%	18%
world bond funds	6%	6%	8%	10%
CPI (rate of inflation)	2%	2%	3%	3%

The four areas that dominate world stock funds are the United States, Europe, Japan, and the Pacific Rim. Stocks from U.S. and European markets account for over two-thirds of a typical global equity fund's portfolio.

Government Bonds. These funds invest in securities issued by the U.S. government or one of its agencies (or former affiliates), such as GNMA, FHLMC, or FNMA. Investors are attracted to bond funds of all kinds for two reasons. First, bond funds have monthly distributions; individual bonds pay interest only semiannually. Second, effective management can control interest rate risk by varying the average maturity of the fund's portfolio. If management believes that interest rates are moving downward, the fund will load up heavily on long-term obligations. If rates do decline, long-term bonds will appreciate more than their short- and medium-term counterparts. Conversely, if the manager anticipates rate hikes, average portfolio maturity can be pared down so that there will be only modest principal deterioration if rates do go up.

Bond funds have portfolios with a wide range of maturities. Many funds use their names to characterize their maturity structure. Generally, "short term" means that the portfolio has a weighted average maturity of less than five years. "Intermediate" implies an average maturity of five to ten years, and "long term" is over ten years. The longer the maturity, the greater the change in the fund's price per share (your principal) when interest rates change. Longer-term bond funds are riskier than short-term funds but tend to offer higher yields. The top holdings of government bond funds are GNMAs and U.S. Treasury notes (T-notes) of varying maturities.

The weighted maturity date of the bonds within this group averages just under eight years, with a typical coupon rate of 7 percent (the coupon rate represents what is paid out annually on a per bond basis)—figures that are virtually identical to the corporate bond category. These funds have a standard deviation of 4 percent—again the figure is almost identical to that for corporate bonds. This means that corporate and government bonds have similar volatilities.

Historical returns over the past three, five, ten, and fifteen years for government bond funds are shown below (all periods ending 3/31/99).

category	3 years	5 years	10 years	15 years
government bond funds	6%	6%	8%	9%
high-yield bond funds	8%	8%	10%	10%
CPI (rate of inflation)	2%	2%	3%	3%
utility funds	16%	14%	13%	13%
convertible bond funds	12%	12%	12%	12%

Like corporate bond funds, government funds provide a high yield that is fully taxable on the federal level and should be sheltered whenever possible. Interest from direct obligations of the U.S. government—T-bonds, T-notes, T-bills, EE bonds, and HH bonds—are exempt from state and local income taxes. This means that a part of the income you receive from funds that include such securities is exempt from *state* taxes.

Corporate bonds are rated as to their safety. The two major rating services are Moody's and Standard and Poor's. By reading the fund's prospectus or by telephoning the mutual fund company, you can find out how safe a corporate bond fund is. The vast majority of these funds are extremely conservative, and safety (default) is not really an issue. U.S. government bonds are not rated since it is believed that there is no chance of default—unlike a corporation, the federal government can print money.

Growth. These funds seek capital appreciation with dividend income as a distant secondary concern. Indeed, the average annual income stream from growth funds is just 0.5 percent. Investors who are attracted to growth funds are aiming to sell stock at a profit; they are not normally income oriented. If you are interested in current income you will want to look at Appendix D "Systematic Withdrawal Plan."

Growth funds are attracted to equities from large, well-established corporations. Unlike aggressive growth funds, growth funds may end up holding large cash positions during market declines or when investors are nervous about recent economic or market activities. The typical price-earnings (p/e) ratio for stocks in this category is 27, compared to 26 for the S&P 500. This group of funds has an average beta of 1.0, the same as the S&P 500.

The standard deviation for growth funds is 14 percent. This means that one's expected return for any given year will vary by 14 percentage points. As an example, if you were expecting a 15 percent annual return, annual returns would probably range between 1 percent and 29 percent (15 percent plus or minus 14 percent).

Historical returns over the past three, five, ten, and fifteen years for growth and small-company stock funds are shown below. All of the figures shown are average *annual* rates of return (all periods ending 3/31/99).

category	3 years	5 years	10 years	15 years
growth funds	20%	20%	16%	15%
small-company stock funds	8%	12%	13%	13%
S&P 500	28%	26%	19%	18%
growth & income funds	21%	20%	15%	14%
global stock funds	12%	12%	11%	13%

Technology, industrial cyclicals, financial, and service stocks dominate growth funds. The balance is fairly evenly divided up among health, utility, retail, and consumer staple issues.

Growth and Income. With a name like this, one would think that this category of mutual funds is almost equally as concerned with income as it is with growth. The fact is, growth and income funds have an average dividend yield of just one percent. This boost in income is due to the small holdings in bonds and convertibles possessed by most growth and income funds.

The typical price-earnings (p/e) ratio for stocks in this category is 24, versus 26 for the S&P 500. This group of funds has an average beta of just under 0.9, meaning that its *market-related risk* is 10 percent less than that of the general market, as measured by the S&P 500.

The standard deviation for growth and income funds is 12 percent, about 15 percent less than that found with the average growth fund. This means that, as a group, growth and income funds have slightly more predictable returns than growth funds.

For the purposes of this book, a second category, "equity-income funds," has been combined with growth and income. Equity-income funds have a lower standard deviation (10 percent compared to 12 percent for growth and income funds), a higher yield (2.0 percent compared to 1.0 percent), and a lower beta (0.8 percent compared to 0.9 percent for growth and income funds).

The typical growth and income fund is divided as follows: 90 percent in common stocks (5 percent of which is in foreign stock), 6 percent in cash, 2 percent in bonds, and 2 percent in other assets. The average equity-income fund is divided as follows: 83 percent in common stocks (6 percent of which is in foreign stock), 6 percent in cash, 4 percent in bonds, and 7 percent in other assets. The typical price-earnings (p/e) ratio for stocks in this category is 22.

Historical returns over the past three, five, ten, and fifteen years for growth and income funds are shown below. All of the figures shown are average *annual* rates of return (all periods ending 3/31/99).

category	3 years	5 years	10 years	15 years
growth and income funds	21%	20%	15%	14%
equity-income funds	17%	17%	14%	14%
growth funds	20%	20%	16%	15%
balanced funds	14%	14%	12%	13%
foreign stock funds	8%	7%	8%	12%

Industrial cyclicals and financial stocks dominate growth and income funds, representing over a third of the typical portfolio. Service, health, technology, and consumer stocks represent the other major industry groups for this category.

High-Yield. These funds generally invest in lower-rated corporate debt instruments. Bonds are characterized as either "bank quality," also known as "investment grade," or "junk." Investment-grade bonds are bonds rated AAA, AA, A, or BAA; junk bonds are instruments rated less than BAA: BA, B, CCC, CC, C, and D. High-yield bonds, also referred to as junk bonds, offer investors higher yields in exchange for the additional risk of default. High-yield bonds are subject to less *interest-rate risk* than regular corporate or government bonds. However, when the economy slows or people panic, these bonds can quickly drop in value.

The average weighted maturity date of the bonds within this group is eight years, a figure similar to that for high-quality corporate and government bond funds. The typical coupon rate is 9 percent. (The coupon rate represents what the corporation pays out annually on a per bond basis.) When it comes to high-yield bonds, investors would be wise to accept a lower yield in return for more stability of principal and appreciation potential. As with income funds, corporate funds provide a high yield that is fully taxable and should be sheltered whenever possible.

The standard deviation for high-yield bond funds is 4 percent, a figure very similar to that of corporate and government bond funds as a whole but 4 percent less than balanced and global bond funds. Historical returns over the past three, five, ten, and fifteen years for high-yield corporate bond funds are shown below. All of the figures shown are average *annual* rates of return (all periods ending 3/31/99).

category	3 years	5 years	10 years	15 years
high-yield bond funds	8%	8%	10%	10%
corporate bond funds	7%	7%	8%	9%
government bond funds	6%	6%	8%	9%
world bond funds	6%	6%	8%	10%
balanced funds	14%	14%	12%	13%

Metals and Natural Resources. Metals funds invest in precious metals and mining stocks from around the world. The majority of these stocks are located in North America; South Africa and Australia are the only other major players. Most of these companies specialize in gold mining. Some funds own gold and silver bullion outright. Direct ownership of the metal is considered to be a more conservative posture than owning stocks of mining companies; these stocks are more volatile than the metal itself.

Metals funds, also known as gold funds, are the most speculative group represented in this book. They are considered to be a sector or specialty fund, in that they are only able to invest in a single industry or country. Metals funds enjoy international diversification but are still narrowly focused; the limitations of the fund are what make it so unpredictable. Usually, fund management can invest in only three things: mining stocks, direct metal ownership (bullion or coins), and cash equivalents.

Despite their volatile nature, gold funds are included in the book because they can actually reduce portfolio risk. Why? Because gold and other investments often move in opposite directions. For example, when government bonds are moving down in value, gold funds often increase in value. What could otherwise be viewed as a wild investment becomes somewhat tame when included as part of a diversified portfolio.

The typical dividend for metal funds is 0.6 percent. The typical price-earnings (p/e) ratio for stocks in this category is 32, about 20 percent more than the p/e ratio for the S&P 500.

This group of funds has an average beta of 0.6, meaning that its stock market-related risk is modest—but do not let this fool you. We are only talking about *stock market risk*. Beta focuses on that portion of risk that investors cannot reduce by further diversification in U.S. stocks. Metals funds, as shown by their wild track record, are anything but conservative. A 0.6 beta indicates that movement in this category has a fair amount to do with the direction of the S&P 500, and therefore risk can be reduced by further diversification. The standard deviation for metals funds is 23 percent, higher than any other mutual fund category in this book and only 10 percent lower than emerging markets, which has a standard deviation of 26.

Another category, natural resources, has been combined with metals funds for this book. As the name implies, natural resources funds are commodity-driven, just as metals funds are heavily influenced by two commodities, gold and silver. In the case of natural resources funds, the prices of oil, gas, and timber are the driving force. Natural resources funds invest in companies that are involved with the discovery, exploration, development, refinement, storage, and transportation of one or more of these three natural resources. The standard deviation for this group is 17 percent, beta is 0.7, and the p/e ratio is 26.

Historical returns over the past three, five, ten, and fifteen years for metals funds are shown below. All of the figures shown are average *annual* rates of return (all periods ending 3/31/99).

category	3 years	5 years	10 years	15 years
metals funds	–25%	–14%	–5%	–4%
aggressive growth funds	13%	16%	14%	13%
natural resources funds	10%	8%	8%	10%
emerging markets funds	–8%	-7%	2%	6%
CPI (rate of inflation)	2%	2%	3%	3%

Money Market. These funds invest in short-term money market instruments such as bank CDs, T-bills, and commercial paper. By maintaining a short average maturity and investing in high-quality instruments, money market funds are able to maintain a stable $1 net asset value. Since money market funds offer higher yields than a bank's insured money market deposit accounts, they are a very attractive haven for savings or temporary investment dollars. Like bond funds, money market funds come in both taxable and tax-free versions. Reflecting their tax-free status, municipal money market funds pay lower *before-tax* yields than taxable money market funds but can offer higher returns on an *after-tax* basis.

Since the price per share of taxable money market funds always stays at $1, interest is shown by the accumulation of additional shares. (For example, at the beginning of the year, you may have 1,000 shares and by the end of the year 1,050. The 50-share increase, or $50, represents interest.) There are no such things as capital gains or unrecognized gains in a money market fund. The entire return, or yield, is fully taxable (except in the case of a tax-free money market fund, where your gain or return would always be exempt from federal taxes and possibly state income taxes as well).

These funds are designed as a place to park your money for a relatively short period of time, in anticipation of a major purchase such as a car or house, or until conditions appear more favorable for stocks, bonds, and/or real estate. There has only been one, now defunct, money market fund that has ever lost money for its investors (most of whom were bankers).

There are approximately 900 taxable money market funds and 450 tax-exempt money funds. By far the largest money market fund is the Merrill Lynch CMA Money Fund ($41 billion). As of 6/30/98, the ten largest money market funds controlled close to $200 billion and had an average maturity of 64 days. The five highest-yielding taxable money market funds as of the middle of 1997 were: Strong Heritage Money Fund (5.7 percent over the past 12 months), OLDE Premium Plus MM Series (5.6 percent), Strategist Money Market Fund (5.6 percent), E Fund (5.4 percent), and Kiewit Mutual Fund/MMP (5.4 percent).

The standard deviation for money market funds is lower than any other category of mutual funds. Historical returns over the past three, five, ten, and fifteen years for taxable and tax-free money market funds are shown below. All of the figures shown are average *annual* rates of return (all periods ending 12/31/98).

category	3 years	5 years	10 years	15 years
money market funds	5%	5%	5%	6%
tax-free money market funds	3%	3%	3%	4%
prime rate	8%	8%	8%	9%
government bonds	9%	9%	11%	13%
CPI (rate of inflation)	2%	2%	3%	3%

Municipal Bonds. Also known as tax-free, these funds are made up of tax-free debt instruments issued by states, counties, districts, or political subdivisions. Interest from municipal bonds is normally exempt from federal income tax. In almost all states, interest is also exempt from state and local income taxes if the portfolio is made up of issues from the investor's state of residence, a U.S territory (Puerto Rico, the U.S. Virgin Islands, etc.), or the District of Columbia.

Until the early 1980s, municipal bonds were almost as sensitive to interest rate changes as corporate and government bonds. During the last several years, however, tax-free bonds have taken on a new personality. Now when interest rates change, municipal bonds exhibit only one-half to one-third the price change that occurs with similar funds comprised of corporate or government issues. This decreased volatility is due to a smaller supply of municipal bonds and the elimination of almost all tax shelters, which has increased the popularity of tax-free bonds.

Three kinds of events may result in tax liability for every mutual fund except money market funds. The first two events described below cannot be controlled by the investor. The final event is determined solely by you, the shareholder (investor).

First, when bonds or stocks are sold in the fund portfolio for a profit (or loss), a capital gain (or capital loss) occurs. These gains and losses are passed down to the shareholder. Tax-free bond funds are not immune from capital gains taxes (or capital losses).

Second, interest and/or dividends paid by the securities within the fund are also passed on to shareholders (investors). As already mentioned, interest from municipal bonds is free from federal income taxes and, depending on the fund, may also be exempt from state income taxes. Municipal bond funds do not own stocks or convertibles, so they never throw off dividends.

Third, a taxable event may occur when you sell or exchange shares of a fund for cash or to go into another fund. As an example, suppose you bought into the fund at X dollars and cents per share. If shares are sold (or exchanged) by you for X plus Y, then there will a taxable gain (on Y, in this example). If shares are sold or exchanged for a loss (X minus Y), then there will be a capital loss. Municipal bond funds are subject to such capital gains or losses. Fortunately, you are never required to sell off shares in any mutual fund; the decision as to when and how much is always yours.

The standard deviation for municipal bond funds is 5 percent, meaning that this category's volatility is a little greater than that of high-yield bonds and government securities. Historical returns over the past three, five, ten, and fifteen years for municipal funds are shown below. All of the figures shown are average *annual* rates of return (all periods ending 3/31/99).

category	3 years	5 years	10 years	15 years
municipal bond funds	7%	6%	8%	8%
CA municipal bond funds	7%	7%	8%	8%
NY municipal bond funds	7%	6%	8%	8%
government bond funds	7%	6%	8%	9%
municipal bonds (long-term)	8%	7%	9%	11%

Utilities. These funds invest in common stocks of utility companies. A small percentage of the funds' assets are invested in bonds. Investors opposed to or in favor of nuclear power can seek out funds that avoid or buy into such utility companies by reviewing a fund's semiannual report or by telephoning the fund, using its toll-free phone number.

If you like the usual stability of a bond fund but want more appreciation potential, then utility funds are for you. Since these funds are interest-rate sensitive, their performance somewhat parallels that of bonds but is also influenced by the stock market. The large dividend stream provided by utility funds makes them less risky than other categories of stock funds. Recession-resistant demand for electricity, gas, and other utilities translates into a comparatively steady stream of returns.

Since a healthy portion of the total return for utility funds (dividends) cannot be controlled by the investor, these funds are best suited for retirement plans or as part of some other tax-sheltered vehicle. But even if you do not have a qualified retirement plan such as an IRA, pension plan, or TSA, utility funds can be a wise choice to lower overall portfolio volatility. The standard deviation for utility funds is 12 percent, a figure that is about 15 percent lower than that of growth and income funds. Utility funds have a beta of 0.6.

Historical returns over the past three, five, ten, and fifteen years for utilities funds are shown below. All of the figures shown are average *annual* rates of return (all periods ending 3/31/99).

category	3 years	5 years	10 years	15 years
utility funds	16%	14%	13%	13%
convertible funds	12%	12%	12%	12%
multi-asset global funds	8%	8%	8%	9%
asset allocation funds	14%	14%	12%	11%
utility stocks	17%	12%	12%	13%

World Bonds. Although the United States leads the world in outstanding debt, other countries and foreign corporations also issue IOUs as a way of financing projects and operations. As high as our debt seems, it is not out of line when compared to our GNP (now called GDP—gross domestic product). The ratio of our debt to GDP is lower than any other member of the group of seven. (The other G-7 members are: Germany, Japan, Canada, Italy, the United Kingdom, and France.)

International, also known as foreign, bond funds invest in fixed-income securities outside of the United States. Global, or world, bond funds invest around the world, including the United States. Foreign bond funds normally offer higher yields than their U.S. counterparts but also provide additional risk. Global bonds, on the other hand, provide less risk than a pure U.S. bond portfolio and also enjoy greater rates of return.

Global diversification reduces risk because the major economies around the world do not move up and down at the same time. As we climb out of a recession, Japan may be just entering one, and Germany may still be in the middle of one. When Italy is trying to stimulate its economy by lowering interest rates, Canada may be raising its rates in order to curtail inflation. By investing in different world bond markets, you ensure that you will not be at the mercy of any one country's political environment or fiscal policy.

The weighted maturity date of the bonds within this group is nine years, about one year longer than U.S. government bond funds. Global bond funds have an average coupon rate of 8 percent. As with any investment that throws off a high current income, global and foreign bond funds should be part of a qualified retirement plan or variable annuity whenever possible.

The standard deviation for world bond funds is 6 percent, a low figure but one that is still about twice as great as the typical U.S. government bond fund. Historical returns over the past three, five, ten, and fifteen years for world bond funds are shown below. All of the figures shown are average *annual* rates of return (all periods ending 3/31/99).

category	3 years	5 years	10 years	15 years
world bond funds	6%	6%	8%	11%
government bond funds	6%	6%	8%	9%
corporate bond funds	7%	7%	8%	9%
high-yield bond funds	8%	8%	10%	10%
savings bonds (EE)	5%	5%	5%	6%

All Categories. An inescapable conclusion drawn from these different tables is that patience usually pays off. The single-digit performers over the past fifteen years have been emerging markets, government bonds, metals (the only negative category), money market funds, multi-asset global, municipal bond. What the tables do not take into account, moreover, are the tax advantages of certain investments. Government bonds are exempt from state and local income taxes. (Note: this is only true with direct obligations of the United States, it does not apply to GNMAs, FNMAs, or other government-agency issues.) Municipal bonds are exempt from federal income taxes and, depending upon the type of tax-free fund as well as your state of residency, may also be exempt from any state or local taxes.

Money market funds should never be considered an investment. Money market funds, T-bills, and bank CDs should be viewed as places to park your money temporarily. Such accounts are best used to earn interest before you make a major purchase, while you are becoming educated about investing in general, or until market conditions change.

Average Annual Returns for the 15-Year Period Ending 3/31/99

category	15 years	category	15 years
aggressive growth	13%	growth & income	14%
asset allocation	11%	high-yield	10%
balanced	13%	metals (only)	–4%
convertible bond	12%	money market	6%
corporate bond	9%	multi-asset global	9%
emerging markets	6%	municipal bond	8%
equity-income	14%	natural resources	7%
foreign	12%	small company	13%
global equity	13%	utilities	13%
government bond	9%	world bond	10%
growth	15%	average for all categories	10%

A common theme throughout this book is that, given time, equity (the different stock categories) always outperforms debt (the different bond categories). This does not mean that all of your money should be in the equity categories. Not everyone has the same level of patience or time horizon. It does mean that the great majority of investors need to review their portfolios and perhaps begin to emphasize domestic and foreign stocks more.

VI.
Which Funds Are Best for You?

When asked what they are looking for, investors typically say "I want the best." This could mean that they are looking for the most safety and greatest current income or the highest total return. There is no single "best" fund. The top-performing fund may have incredible volatility, causing shareholders to redeem their shares at the first sign of trouble. The "safest" fund may be devastated by risks not previously thought of: inflation and taxes.

As you have already seen, there are several different categories of mutual funds, ranging from tax-free money market accounts to precious metals. During one period or another, each of these categories has dominated some periodical's "ten best funds" list. These impressive scores may only last a quarter, six months, or a year. The fact is that no one knows what will be the *next* best-performing category or individual fund.

For some fund groups, such as international stocks, growth, growth and income, and aggressive growth, the reign at the top may last for several years. For other categories, such as money market, government bond, and precious metals, the glory may last a year or even less. Trying to outguess, chart, or follow a finan-cial guru in order to determine the next trend is a fool's paradise. The notion that anyone has special insights into the marketplace is sheer nonsense. Countless neu-tral and lengthy studies attest to this fact. If this is the case, what should we do?

Step 1: Categories That Have Historically Done Well
First we should look at those generic categories of investments that have histori-cally done well over long periods of time. A time frame of at least fifteen or twenty years is recommended. True, your investment horizon may be a fraction of this, but keep in mind two points. First, fifteen or twenty years includes good as well as bad times. Second, bad results cannot be hidden when you are studying the long term. Even the investor looking at a one- or two-year holding period should ask, "Do I want something that does phenomenally well one out of every five years, or do I want something that has a very good return in eight or nine out of every ten years?" Unless you are a gambler, the answer is obvious.

All investments can be categorized as either debt or equity instruments. Debt instruments in this book include corporate bonds, government bonds, high-yield bonds, international bonds, money market accounts, and municipal bonds. Equity instruments include growth, growth and income, international stocks, metals, and utility funds. Four other categories are hybrid instruments: asset allocation, balanced, convertible, and multi-asset global funds. In this book, these four categories are combined under the heading "balanced."

Throughout history, *equity has outperformed debt*. The longer the time frame reviewed, the better equity vehicles look. Over the past half century, the worst fifteen-year holding period performance for stocks (+4.3 percent a year) was very similar to the average fifteen-year holding period performance for long-term government bonds (+4.9 percent a year). For twenty-year holding periods, the worst period for common stocks has been more than 40 percent better than the average for long-term government bonds. Indeed, stocks have outperformed bonds in every decade. Look at it this way: would you rather have loaned Henry Ford or Bill Gates the money to start their companies, or would you rather have given them money in return for a piece of the action?

Step 2: Review Your Objectives

Decide what you are trying to do with your portfolio. Everyone wants one of the following: growth, current income, or a combination of growth and income. Don't assume that if you are looking for current income your money should go into a bond or money market fund. There is a way to set up an equity fund so that it will give you a high monthly income. This is known as a "systematic withdrawal program" and is discussed in Appendix D. The growth-oriented investor, on the other hand, should consider certain categories of debt instruments or hybrid securities to help add more stability to a portfolio.

Objectives are certainly important, but so is the element of time. The shorter the time frame and the greater the need for assurances, the greater the likelihood that debt instruments should be used. A growth investor who is looking at a single-year time frame and wants a degree of safety is probably better off in a series of bond and/or money market accounts. On the other hand, the longer the commitment, the better equities look. Thus, even a cautious investor who has a life expectancy (or whose spouse has a life expectancy) of ten years or more should seriously consider having at least a moderate portion of his or her portfolio in equities.

A retired couple in their sixties should realize that one or both of them will probably live at least fifteen more years. Since this is the case, and since we know that equities have almost always outperformed bonds when looking at a horizon of ten years or more, their emphasis should be in this area.

The conservative investor may say that stocks are too risky. True, the day-to-day or year-to-year volatility of equities can be quite disturbing. However, it is also true that the medium- and long-term effects of inflation and the resulting diminished purchasing power of a fixed-income investment are even more devastating. At least with an equity there is a better than 50–50 chance that it will go up in value. In the case of inflation, what do you think are the chances that the cost of goods and services will go *down* during the next one, three, five, or ten years? The answer is "not likely."

Step 3: Ascertain Your Risk Level

No investment is worthwhile if you stay awake at night worrying about it. If you do not already know or are uncertain about your risk level, contact your financial advisor. These professionals usually have some kind of questionnaire that you can answer. Your responses will give a good indication of which investments are proper for you and which should be avoided. If you do not deal with a financial advisor, try the test below. Your score, and what it means, are shown at the end of the questionnaire.

Test for Determining Your Risk Level

1. "I invest for the long term, five to ten years or more. The final result is more important than daily, monthly, or annual fluctuations in value."

(10) Totally disagree. (20) Willing to accept some volatility, but not loss of principal. (30) Could accept a moderate amount of yearly fluctuation in return for a good *total return*. (40) Would accept an *occasional* negative year if the final results were good. (50) Agree.

2. Rank the importance of current income.

(10) Crucial, the exact amount must be known. (20) Important, but I am willing to have the amount vary each period. (30) Fairly important, but other aspects of investing are also of concern. (40) Only a modest amount of income is needed. (50) Current income is unimportant.

3. Rank the amount of loss you could tolerate in a single *quarter*.

(10) None. (20) A little, but over a year's time the total value of the investment should not decline. (30) Consistency of total return is more important than trying to get big gains. (40) One or two quarters of negative returns are the price you must pay when looking at the total picture. (50) Unimportant.

4. Rank the importance of beating inflation.

(10) Factors such as preservation of principal and current income are much more important. (20) I am willing to have a slight variance in my returns, *on a quarterly basis only*, in order to have at least a partial hedge against inflation. (30) Could accept some annual volatility in order to offset inflation. (40) I consider inflation to be important, but have mixed feelings about how much volatility I could accept from one year to the next. (50) The long-term effects of inflation are devastating and should not be ignored by anyone.

5. Rank the importance of beating the stock market over any given two-to-three-year period.

(10) Irrelevant. (20) A small concern. (30) Fairly important. (40) Very important. (50) Absolutely crucial.

Add up your score from questions 1 through 5. Your risk, as defined by your total point score, is as follows: 0 –50 points = extremely conservative; 50 –100 points = somewhat conservative; 100 –150 points = moderate; 150 –200 points = somewhat aggressive; 200 –250 points = very aggressive.

Step 4: Review Your Current Holdings

Everyone has heard the expression, "Don't put all your eggs in one basket." This advice also applies to investing. No matter how much we like investment X, if a third of our net worth is already in X, we probably should not add any more to this investment. After all, there is more than one good investment.

Since no single investment category is the top performer every year, it makes sense to diversify into several *fundamentally* good categories. By using *proper* diversification, we have an excellent chance of being number one with a portion of our portfolio every year. Babe Ruth may have hit more home runs than almost anyone, but he also struck out more. As investors, we should be content with consistently hitting doubles and triples.

Trying to hit a homer every time may result in financial ruin. Never lose track of the fact that losses always have a greater impact than gains. An investment that goes up 50 percent the first year and falls 50 percent the next year still has a net loss of 25 percent. This philosophy is emphasized throughout the book.

Step 5: Implementation

There is no such thing as the perfect time to invest. No matter how strongly you or some "expert" individual or publication believes that the market is going to go up or down, no one actually knows.

Once you have properly educated yourself, *now* is the right time to invest. If you are afraid to make the big plunge, consider some form of dollar-cost averaging (see Appendix C). This is a disciplined approach to investing; it also reduces your risk exposure significantly.

Reading investment books and attending classes are encouraged, but some people may be tempted to remain on the sidelines indefinitely. For such people, there is no perfect time to invest. If the stock market drops two hundred points, they are waiting for the next hundred-point drop. If stocks or bonds are up 15 percent, they say things are peaking and they will invest as soon as it drops by 10 percent. If the stock or bond market does drop by that magical figure, these same investors are now certain that it will drop another 10 percent.

The "strategy" described above is frustrating. More important, it is wrong. One can look back in history and find lots of reasons not to have invested. But the fact is that all of the investments in this book have gone up almost every year. The "wait and see" approach is a poor one; the same reasons for not investing will still exist in the present and throughout the future.

Remember, your money is doing something right now. It is invested somewhere. If it is under the mattress, it is being eaten away by inflation. If it is in a "risk-free" investment, such as an insured savings account, bank CD, or U.S.

Treasury bill, it is being subjected to taxation and the cumulative effects of reduced purchasing power. Do not think you can hide by having your money in some safe haven. Once you understand that there can be things worse than market swings, you will become an educated investor who knows there is no such thing as a truly risk-free place or investment.

If you are still not convinced, consider the story of Louie the loser. There is only one thing you can say about Louie's timing: It is *always* awful. So it is no surprise that when he decided to invest $10,000 a year in New Perspective, a fund featured in this book, he managed to pick the *worst* possible times. *Every year* for the past twenty years (1978–1997), he has invested on the very day that the stock market *peaked*. How has he done? He has over $1,158,000, which means his money has grown at an average rate of 15.7 percent a year (a cumulative investment of $200,000; twenty years times $10,000 invested each year).

Yet even by picking the *worst* possible days, Louie still came out way ahead of the $218,000 he would have had if he had put his money in U.S. Treasury bills each year. Even though his timing was terrible, he still fared much better than if he had done what many people are doing today: waiting for the "perfect" time to invest.

After asking you a series of questions, your investment advisor can give you a framework within which to operate. Investors who do not have a good advisor may wish to look at the different sample portfolios below. These general recommendations will provide you with a sense of direction.

The Conservative Investor
   15 percent balanced
   10 percent utilities
   15 percent growth and income
   10 percent world bond
   10 percent international equities
   10 percent money market or short-term bonds
   30 percent intermediate-term municipal or government bonds
      (depending upon your tax bracket)

This portfolio would give you a weighting of 43 percent in equities (stocks) and 57 percent in debt instruments (bonds and cash equivalents). Investors who are not in a high federal income tax bracket may wish to avoid municipal bonds completely and use government bonds instead.

If your tax bracket is such that you are not sure whether you should own tax-free or taxable bonds (if, that is, the after-tax return on government bonds is similar to what a similarly maturing, high-quality municipal bond pays), lean toward a municipal bond fund—they are almost always less volatile than a government bond fund that has the same or a similar average maturity.

The Moderate Investor
> 10 percent small-company growth
> 5 percent balanced/convertibles
> 20 percent growth
> 20 percent growth and income
> 10 percent high yield
> 10 percent world bond
> 20 percent global equities
> 5 percent natural resources

This portfolio would give you a weighting of 80 percent in equities (common stocks) and 20 percent in debt instruments. The figures are a little misleading since high-yield bonds are more of a hybrid investment—part stock and part bond. The price, or value, of high-yield bonds is influenced by economic (macro and micro) news as well as interest rate changes. Whereas government, municipal, and high-quality corporate bonds often react favorably to bad economic news such as a recession, increases in the jobless rate, a slowdown in housing starts, and so on, high-yield bonds have a tendency to view such news positively. Thus, taking into account that high-yield bonds are about halfway between traditional bonds and stocks, the weighting distribution is more in the range of 85 percent equities and 15 percent bonds.

The Aggressive Investor
> 15 percent aggressive growth
> 20 percent small-company growth
> 20 percent growth
> 10 percent growth and income
> 20 percent international equities
> 15 percent emerging markets

This portfolio would give you a weighting of 100 percent in equities. Bond fund categories, with the possible exception of high-yield and international, are not recommended for the aggressive investor because they usually do not have enough appreciation potential.

Readers of the previous editions of this book may notice that this edition weighs equities (the different stock categories) more heavily than it has in the past. This is because bonds cannot experience the appreciation or total return for the balance of the 1990s that they saw in the 1980s and very early 1990s. For the most part, bonds increase in value because of falling interest rates. In 1981, the prime interest rate briefly peaked at 21.5 percent; for more than a dozen years this benchmark figure dropped. During the balance of the 1990s, it would be literally impossible for prime to drop 13 points (it cannot drop below zero).

Stocks, on the other hand, could end up doing worse than bonds, the same, or better. At least conceptually, however, equities have the possibility of exceeding their performance over the past ten years. The 1980s and early 1990s (whatever ten-year period you wish to use during this time horizon) were not the best ten years in a row for stocks. It is certainly possible that the next ten years, or the ten years beginning in 1998 or 1999, will be the best. When you look at the state of the world, the conditions certainly seem more favorable now for tremendous economic and stock market growth for the next several decades.

Step 6: Review

After implementation, it is important that you keep track of how you are doing. One of the beauties of mutual funds is that, if you choose a fund with good management, managers will do their job and you can spend your time on something else. Nevertheless, review your situation at least quarterly. Once you feel comfortable with your portfolio, only semiannual or annual reviews are recommended.

Daily or weekly tracking is pointless. If a particular investment goes up or down 5 percent, that does not mean you should rush out and buy more or sell off. That same investment may do just the opposite the following week or month. By watching your investments too closely, you will be defeating a major attribute of mutual funds: professional management. Presumably these fund managers know a lot more about their particular investments than you do. If they do not, you should either choose another fund or start your own mutual fund.

Step 7: Relax

If you do your homework by reading this book, you will be in fine shape. There are several thousand mutual funds. Some funds are just plain bad. Most mutual funds are mediocre. And, as with everything else in this world, a small portion are truly excellent. This book has taken those thousands of funds and eliminated all of the bad, mediocre, and fairly good. What are left are only excellent mutual funds.

If you would like help in designing a portfolio or picking a specific fund, telephone the Institute of Business and Finance (800/848-2029). The institute will be able to give you the names and telephone numbers of Certified Fund Specialists (CFS) in your area. To become a CFS, one must complete a rigorous, one-year educational program, pass a comprehensive exam, adhere to a professional code of ethics, and meet annual continuing education requirements.

VII.
Fund Features

Advantages of Mutual Funds

Listed below are some of the features of mutual funds—advantages not found in other kinds of investments.

Ease of Purchase. Mutual fund shares are easy to buy. For those who prefer to make investment decisions themselves, mutual funds are as close as the telephone or the mailbox. Those who would like help in choosing a fund can draw upon a wide variety of sources.

Many funds sell their shares through stockbrokers, financial planners, or insurance agents. These representatives can help you analyze your financial needs and objectives and recommend appropriate funds. For these professional services, you may be charged a sales commission, usually referred to as a "load." This charge is expressed as a percentage of the total purchase price of the fund shares. In some cases, there is no initial sales charge, or load, but there may be an annual fee and/or another charge if shares are redeemed during the first few years of ownership.

Other funds distribute their shares directly to the public. They may advertise in magazines and newspapers; most can be reached through toll-free telephone numbers. Because there are no sales agents involved, most of these funds, often called "no loads," charge a much lower fee or no sales commission at all. With these funds it is generally up to you to do your investment homework.

In order to attract new shareholders, some funds have adopted 12b-1 plans (named after a federal government rule). These plans enable the fund to pay its own distribution costs. Distribution costs are those costs associated with marketing the fund, either through sales agents or through advertising. The 12b-1 fee is charged against fund assets and is paid indirectly by existing shareholders. Annual distribution fees of this type usually range between 0.1 percent and 1.25 percent of the value of the account.

Fees charged by a fund are described in the prospectus. In addition, a fee table listing all transactional fees and all annual fund expenses can be found at the front of the prospectus.

Access to Your Money (Marketability). Mutual funds, by law, must stand ready on any business day to redeem any or all of your shares at their current net asset value (NAV). Of course, the value may be greater or less than the price you originally paid, depending on the market.

To sell shares back to the fund, all you need to do is give the fund proper notification, as explained in the prospectus. Most funds will accept such notification by telephone; some funds require a written request. The fund will then send your check promptly. In most instances the fund will issue a check when it receives the notification; by law it must send you the check within seven business days. You receive the price your shares are worth *on the day* the fund gets proper notice of redemption from you. If you own a money market fund, you can also redeem shares by writing checks directly against your fund balance.

Disciplined Investment. The majority of funds allow you to set up what is known as a "check-o-matic plan." Under such a program a set amount of money is automatically deducted from your checking account each month and sent directly to the mutual fund of your choice. Your bank (or credit union) will not charge you for this service. Mutual funds also offer such programs free of charge. Automatic investment plans can be changed or terminated at any time, again at no charge.

Exchange Privileges. As the economy or your own personal circumstances change, the kinds of funds you hold may no longer be the ones you need. Many mutual funds are part of a "family of funds" and offer a feature called an exchange privilege. Within a family of funds there may be several choices, each with a different investment objective, varying from highly conservative funds to more aggressive funds that carry a higher degree of risk. An exchange privilege allows you to transfer all or part of your money from one of these funds to another. Exchange policies vary from fund to fund. The fee for an exchange is nominal, five dollars or less. For the specifics about a fund's exchange privilege, check the prospectus.

Automatic Reinvestment. You can elect to have any dividends and capital gains distributions from your mutual fund investment turned back into the fund, automatically buying new shares and expanding your current holdings. Most shareholders opt for the reinvestment privilege. There is usually no cost or fee involved.

Automatic Withdrawal. You can make arrangements with the fund to automatically send you, or anyone you designate, checks from the fund's earnings or principal. This system works well for retirees, families who want to arrange for payments to their children at college, or anyone needing monthly income checks. See Appendix D for a more detailed example as to how a systematic withdrawal plan (SWP) works.

Detailed Record Keeping. The fund will handle all the paperwork and record keeping necessary to keep track of your investment transactions. A typical statement will note such items as your most recent investment or withdrawal and any dividends or capital gains paid to you in cash or reinvested in the fund. The fund will also report to you on the tax status of your earnings. If you lose any paperwork, the fund will send you copies of current or past statements.

Retirement Plans. Financial experts have long viewed mutual funds as appropriate vehicles for retirement investing; indeed, they are quite commonly used for this purpose. For retirees over the age of seventy and a half, mutual fund companies will recompute the minimum amount that needs to be taken out each year, as dictated by the IRS. Mutual funds are ideal for Keoghs, IRAs, 401(k) plans, and other employer-sponsored retirement plans. Many funds offer prototype retirement plans and standard IRA agreements. Having your own retirement plan drafted by a law firm would cost you thousands of dollars, not to mention what you would be charged for the updates that would be needed every time the laws change. Mutual funds offer these plans and required updates for free.

Accountability. There are literally dozens of sources that track and monitor mutual funds. It is easy for you to determine a fund's track record and volatility over several different time periods. Federal regulatory bodies such as the NASD (National Association of Securities Dealers) and SEC (Securities and Exchange Commission) have strict rules concerning performance figures and what appears in advertisements, brochures, and prospectuses.

Flexibility. Investment choices are almost endless: domestic stocks, foreign debt, international equities, government obligations, money market instruments, convertible securities, short- and intermediate-term bonds, real estate, gold, and natural resources. Your only limitation is the choices offered by the fund family or families you are invested in. And because you can move part or all of your money from one mutual fund to another fund within the same family, usually for only a minimal transfer fee, your portfolio can become more aggressive, conservative, or moderate with a simple phone call.

Economies of Scale. As a shareholder (investor) in a fund, you automatically get the benefit of reduced transaction charges. Since a fund is often buying or selling thousands of shares of stock at a time, it is able to conduct its transactions at dramatically reduced costs. The fees a fund pays are far lower than what you would pay even if you were buying several hundred shares of a stock from a discount broker. The same thing is true when it comes to bonds. Funds are able to add them to their portfolio without any markup. When you buy a bond through a broker, even a discounter, there is always a markup; it is hidden in the price you pay and sell the bond for. The savings for bond investors ranges anywhere from less than 1 percent all the way up to 5 percent.

Risk Reduction: Importance of Diversification

If there is one ingredient to successful investing that is universally agreed upon, it is the benefit of diversification. This concept is also backed by a great deal of research and market experience. The benefit provided by diversification is risk reduction. Risk to investors is frequently defined as volatility of return—in other words, how much an investment's return might vary. Investors prefer returns that are relatively predictable, which is to say, less volatile. On the other hand, they want returns to be high. Diversification eliminates most of the risk without reducing potential returns.

A fund's portfolio manager(s) will normally invest the fund's pool of money in 50 to 150 different securities to spread the fund's holdings over a number of investments. This diversification is an important principle in lessening the fund's overall investment risk. Such diversification is typically beyond the financial capacity of most individual investors. The table below shows the relationship between diversification and investment risk, defined as the variability of annual returns of a stock portfolio.

number of stocks	risk ratio
1	6.6
2	3.8
4	2.4
10	1.6
50	1.1
100	1.0

Note that the variability of return, or risk, associated with holding just one stock is more than six times that of a hundred-stock portfolio. Yet the *increased* potential return found in a portfolio made up of a small number of stocks is minimal.

VIII.
Reading a Mutual Fund Prospectus

The purpose of the fund's prospectus is to provide the reader with full and complete disclosure. The prospectus covers the following key points:

- The fund's investment objective: what the managers are trying to achieve.
- The investment methods it uses in trying to achieve this objective.
- The name and address of its investment advisor and a brief description of the advisor's experience.
- The level of investment risk the fund is willing to assume in pursuit of its investment objective.
- Any investments the fund will *not* make (for example, real estate, options, or commodities).
- Tax consequences of the investment for the shareholder.
- How to purchase shares of the fund, including the cost of investing.
- How to redeem shares.
- Services provided, such as IRAs, automatic investment of dividends and capital gains distributions, check writing, withdrawal plans, and any other features.
- A condensed financial statement (in tabular form, covering the last ten years, or the period the fund has been in existence, if less than ten years) called "Per Share Income and Capital Changes." The fund's performance may be calculated from the information given in this table.
- A tabular statement of any fees charged by the fund and their effect on earnings over time.

IX.
Commonly Asked Questions

Q. Are mutual funds a new kind of investment?
No. In fact, they have roots in eighteenth-century Scotland. The first U.S. mutual fund was organized in Boston in 1924. This fund, Massachusetts Investors Trust, is still in existence today. Several mutual fund companies have been in operation for over half a century.

Q. How much money do you need to invest in a mutual fund?
Literally anywhere from a few dollars to several million. Many funds have no minimum requirements for investing. A few funds are open to large institutional accounts only. The vast majority of funds require a minimum investment of between $250 and $1,000.

Q. Do mutual funds offer a fixed rate of return?
No. Mutual funds invest in securities such as stocks, bonds, and money market accounts whose yields and values fluctuate with market conditions.

Mutual funds can make money for their shareholders in three ways. First, they pay their shareholders dividends earned from the fund's investments. Second, if a security held by a fund is sold at a profit, funds pay their shareholders capital gains distributions. And third, if the value of the securities held by the fund increases, the value of each mutual fund share also increases.

In none of these cases, however, can a return be guaranteed. In fact, it is against the law for a mutual fund to make a claim as to its future performance. Ads quoting returns are based on past performance and should not be interpreted as a fixed rate yield. Past performance should not be taken as a predictor of future earnings.

Q. What are the risks of mutual fund investing?
Mutual funds are investments in financial securities with fluctuating values. The value of the securities in a fund's portfolio, for example, will rise and fall according to general economic conditions and the fortunes of the particular companies that issue those securities. Even the most conservative assets, such as U.S. government obligations, will fluctuate in value as interest rates change. These are risks that investors should be aware of when purchasing mutual fund shares.

Q. How can I evaluate a fund's long-term performance?
You can calculate a fund's performance by referring to the section in the prospectus headed "Per Share Income and Capital Changes." This section will give

you the figures needed to compute the annual rates of return earned by the fund each year for the past ten years (or for the life of the fund if less than ten years). There are also several periodicals that track the performance of funds on a regular basis. You can also telephone the fund, and they will give you performance figures.

Q. What's the difference between *yield* and *total return*?

Yield is the income per share paid to a shareholder from the dividends and interest over a specified period of time. Yield is expressed as a percent of the current offering price per share.

Total return is a measure of the per-share change in total value from the beginning to the end of a specified period, usually a year, including distributions paid to shareholders. This measure includes income received from dividends and interest, capital gains distributions, and any unrealized capital gains or losses. Total return looks at the whole picture: appreciation (or loss) of principal plus any dividends or income. Total return provides the best measure of overall fund performance; *do not be misled by an enticing yield.*

Q. How much does it cost to invest in a mutual fund?

A mutual fund normally contracts with its management company to provide for most of the needs of a normal business. The management company is paid a fee for these services, which usually include managing the fund's investments.

In addition, the fund may pay directly for some of its costs, such as printing, mailing, accounting, and legal services. Typically, these two annual charges average 1.5 percent. In such a fund you would be paying $10 to $15 a year on every $1,000 invested.

Some fund directors have adopted plans (with the approval of the fund's shareholders) that allow them to pay certain distribution costs (the costs of advertising, for example) directly from fund assets. These costs may range from 0.1 percent to 1.25 percent annually.

There may also be other charges involved—for example, in exchanging shares. Some funds may charge a redemption fee when a shareholder redeems his or her shares, usually within five years of purchasing them. All costs and charges assessed by the fund organization are disclosed in its prospectus.

Q. Is the management fee part of the sales charge?

No, the management fee paid by the fund to its investment advisor is for services rendered in managing the fund's portfolio. An average fee ranges from 0.5 percent to 1 percent of the fund's total assets each year. As described above, the management fee and other business expenses generally total somewhere between 1 percent and 1.5 percent. These expenses are paid from the fund's assets and are reflected in the price of the fund shares. In contrast, most sales charges are deducted from your initial investment.

Q. Is my money locked up for a certain period of time in a mutual fund?

Unlike some other types of financial accounts, mutual funds are liquid investments. That means that any shares an investor owns may be redeemed freely on any day the fund is open for business. Since a mutual fund stands ready to buy back its shares at their current net asset value, you always have a buyer for your shares at current market value.

Q. How often do I get statements from a mutual fund?

Mutual funds ordinarily send immediate confirmation statements when an investor purchases or redeems (sells) shares. Statements alerting shareholders to reinvested dividends are sent out periodically. At least semiannually, investors also receive statements on the status of the fund's investments. Tax statements, referred to as "substitute 1099s," are mailed annually. Some funds automatically send out quarterly reports.

Q. I've already purchased shares of a mutual fund. How can I tell how well my investment is doing?

Figuring out how well your fund is faring is a two-step procedure. First you need to know how many shares you *now* own. The "now" is emphasized because if you have asked the fund to plow any dividends and capital gains distributions back into the fund for you, it will do so by issuing you more shares, thereby increasing the value of your investment. Once you know how many shares you own, look up the fund's net assets value (sometimes called the sell or bid price) in the financial section of a major metropolitan daily newspaper. Next, multiply the net asset value by the number of shares you own to figure out the value of your investment as of that date. Compare today's value against your beginning value.

You will need to keep the confirmation statements you receive when you first purchase shares and as you make subsequent purchases in order to compare present value to the original purchase value. You will also need these statements for tax purposes.

Q. Do investment experts recommend mutual funds for IRAs and other qualified plans?

Financial experts view many mutual funds as compatible with the long-term objectives of saving for retirement. Indeed, fund shareholders cite this reason for investing more than any other. Many kinds of funds work best when allowed to ride out the ups and downs of market cycles over long periods of time.

Funds can also offer the owner of an IRA, Keogh, pension plan, 401(k), or 403(b) flexibility. By using the exchange privilege within a family of funds, the investor can shift investments from one kind of security to another in response to changes in personal finances or the economic outlook, or as retirement approaches.

Q. Are money market funds a good investment?

No. If I were to recommend an investment to you that lost money in seventeen of the last twenty-five calendar years (adjusted for income taxes and inflation), you would probably balk. Yet, this is the track record of CDs, money market accounts, and T-bills. Money market funds are an excellent place to park your money for the short-term—some period less than two years.

Q. Why don't more people invest in foreign (international) securities?
Ignorance. The reality is that foreign securities (stocks and bonds), when added to domestic investments, actually reduce the portfolio's level of risk. Stock and bond markets around the world rarely move up and down at the same time. This random correlation is what helps lower risk and volatility: When U.S. stocks (or bonds) are going down, securities in other parts of the world may well be moving sideways or going up.

Q. Is standard deviation the correct way to measure risk?
No. Standard deviation measures volatility (or predictability) of returns. The standard deviation for each of the mutual funds in this book is ranked under the star system next to the heading "predictability of returns." The system used in this book for measuring risk is different, punishing funds for performance that is less than that offered by T-bills, a figure commonly referred to as the "risk-free rate of return." To me this makes more sense than a system that punishes a fund for volatility by translating its high standard deviation figure as "high risk." This is what most financial writers do, whether the volatility the fund experienced was upward or downward volatility. I have yet to meet an investor who is upset that he or she did better than expected. No one minds *upward* volatility.

Q. Why not simply invest in those funds that were the best performers over the past one, three, five, or ten years?
This would be a big mistake. There is little relationship (or correlation) between the performance of one fund or fund category from one year to the next. This, by the way, is the way most investors and advisors select investments—making this one of the biggest and costliest mistakes one could make. Unfortunately, no one knows what the next best performing fund or category will be.

Q. What are you referring to when you talk about "common stocks"?
Whenever you see the words "common stocks," they refer to the Standard & Poor's 500 (S&P 500). The S&P 500 is comprised of 500 of many of the largest corporations in the United States, representing several industry groups. As of the middle of 1998, there had been seventy-five changes made to the S&P 500 since the beginning of 1995. The purpose of changes is to make the index more representative of the U.S. economy and the stock market. As an example, financial stocks now represent 15 percent of the S&P 500 capitalization, up from 8 percent in 1990; technology stocks represent 14 percent, up from 7 percent in 1990 (Microsoft, which was added to the index in 1994, makes up 2.3 percent of the index). In short, the S&P 500 is higher growth, more global, less cyclical, and more diversified than it has ever been (and therefore deserves a higher p/e ratio than in the past).

X.
How the 100 Best Funds Were Determined

With an entry field that numbers over 13,500, it is no easy task to determine the one hundred best mutual funds. Magazines and newspapers report on the "best" by relying on performance figures over a specific period, usually one, three, five, or ten years. Investors often rely on these sources and invest accordingly, only to be disappointed later.

Studies from around the world bear out what investors typically experience: that there is no correlation between the performance of a stock or bond from one year to the next. The same can be said for individual money managers—and sadly, for most mutual funds.

The criteria used to determine the one hundred best mutual funds are unique and far-reaching. In order for a fund to be considered for this book, it must pass several tests. First, all stock and bond funds that have had managers for less than five years were excluded; in the case of money market funds, the only remaining category, the criterion was liberalized since overhead costs have a much greater bearing on net returns than management's expertise.

This first step alone eliminated well over half the contenders. The reasoning for the cutoff is simple: a fund is often only as good as its manager. An outstanding ten-year track record may be cited in a periodical, but how relevant is this performance if the manager who oversaw the fund left a year or two ago? This criterion was liberalized in selecting money market funds because this category of funds normally requires less expertise.

Second, any fund that places in the bottom (worst) half of its *category's* risk ranking is excluded. No matter how profitable the finish line looks, the number of investors will be sparse if the fund demonstrates too much negative activity. In most cases, a little performance was gladly given up if a great deal of risk was eliminated. This reflects the book's philosophy that returns must be viewed in relation to the amount of risk that was taken. In most cases the funds described in the book possess outstanding risk management. Those few selected funds where risk control has been less than stellar have shown tremendous performance, and their risky nature has been highlighted to warn the reader.

Virtually all sources measure risk by something known as *standard deviation*. Determining an investment's standard deviation is not as difficult as you might imagine. First you calculate the asset's average annual return. Usually, the most recent three years are used, updated each quarter. Once an average annual rate of return is determined, a line is drawn on a graph, representing this return.

Next, the monthly returns are plotted on the graph. Since three years is a commonly accepted time period for such calculations, a total of thirty-six individual points are plotted—one for each month over the past three years. After all of these points are plotted, the standard deviation can be determined. Quite simply, standard deviation measures the variance of returns from the norm (the line drawn on a graph).

There is a problem in using standard deviation to determine the risk level of any investment, including a mutual fund. The shortcoming of this method is that standard deviation punishes *good* as well as bad results. An example will help expose the problem.

Suppose there were two different investments, X and Y. Investment X went up almost every month by exactly 1.5 percent but had a few months each year when it went down 1 percent. Investment Y went up only 1 percent most months, but it always went up 6 percent for each of the final months of the year. The standard deviation of Y would be substantially higher than X. It might be so high that we would avoid it because it was classified as "high risk." The fact is that we would love to own such an investment. No one ever minds *upward* volatility or surprises; it is only negative or downward volatility that is cause for alarm.

The system used for determining risk in this book is not widely used, but it is certainly a fairer and more meaningful measurement. The book's method for determining risk is to see how many months over the past three years a fund underperformed what is popularly referred to as a "risk-free vehicle," something like a bank CD or U.S. Treasury bill. The more months a fund falls below this safe return, the greater the fund will be punished in its risk ranking.

Third, the fund must have performed well for the last three and five years. A one- or two-year time horizon could be attributed to luck or nonrecurring events. A ten- or fifteen-year period would certainly be better, if not for the reality that the overwhelming majority of funds are managed by a different person today than they were even six years ago.

Finally, the fund must either possess an excellent risk-adjusted return or have had superior returns with no more than average levels of risk. It is assumed that most readers are equally concerned with risk and reward. Thus, the foundation of the text is based on which mutual funds have the best *risk-adjusted returns*.

Sadly, some funds were excluded, despite their superior performance and risk control, because they were either less than five years old, had new management, or were closed to new investors.

XI
The 100 Best Funds

This section describes the one hundred very best funds out of a universe that now numbers over 13,500. As discussed, the methodology used to narrow down the universe of funds is based on performance, consistency, risk, management, and expenses.

Every one of these one hundred funds is a superlative choice. However, there must still be a means to compare and rank each of the funds within its peer group. Each one of the one hundred funds is first categorized by its investment objective. The category breakdown is as follows:

category of mutual fund	number
aggressive growth	11
balanced	10
corporate bond	6
global equity	8
government bond	5
growth	9
growth & income	11
high-yield bonds	8
metals/natural resources	4
money market	10
municipal bonds	8
utilities	5
world bonds	5
total	100 funds

The funds were ranked based on data through March 31, 1999. They were ranked in five areas: (1) total return, (2) risk/volatility, (3) management, (4) tax minimization (current income in the case of bond, balanced, and money market funds), and (5) expense control. Of these five classifications, management, risk/volatility, and total return are the most important.

The track record of a fund is only as good as its management, which is why extensive space is given to this section for each fund. The areas of concern are management tenure, background and investment philosophy.

The risk/volatility of the fund is the second biggest concern but is more often than not the major screening criteria used in selecting those portfolios that appear in this book. Investors like to be in things that have somewhat predictable results, securities that are not up 60 percent one year and down 25 percent the next. When a highly volatile fund is included in any edition of the book, the risk associated with such a fund is clearly highlighted, informing the prospective investor.

Total return was the third concern. When all is said and done, people like to make lots of money with an acceptable level of risk, or at least get decent returns by taking little, if any, risk. This is also known as the *risk-adjusted return*. So, although the very safest funds within each category were preferred, this safety had to be combined with impressive returns.

The fourth category, current income, was of lesser importance. Income is important to a lot of people but often gets in the way of selecting the proper investment; preservation of capital should also be considered. There is a better way to get current income than to rely on monthly dividend or interest checks. This is known as a systematic withdrawal plan (SWP). A sixty-six-year example of a SWP is shown in Appendix D. Income-oriented investors will truly be amazed when they see how such a system works.

In the case of equity funds, "tax minimization" (how much of the total return is not currently taxed) was substituted for the category "current income." This was done for two reasons. First, there is no reason why a fund whose objective is capital appreciation should be punished simply because it does not throw off a high dividend. Once you are familiar with the benefits of using a systematic withdrawal plan, you will no longer care whether a certain stock fund pays much in the form of dividends. Second, unless your money is sheltered in a qualified retirement plan (IRA, pension plan, etc.), income taxes are a real concern. Funds should be rewarded for minimizing shareholder tax liability. This is why every mutual fund (except money market funds) in the book is rated, one way or another, when it comes to personal income taxes.

Tax-conscious investors want to downplay current income as much as possible. For them, a high current income simply means paying more in taxes. For other categories, such as utilities and balanced funds, a healthy current income stream often translates into lower risk. And for still other categories, such as corporate bonds, government bonds, world bonds, money market, and municipal bonds, current income is, and rightfully should be, a major determinant for selection.

To give you an idea as to how good and bad it gets when it comes to tax minimization, look at the table below. The table shows how five of the most and five of the least tax-efficient funds fared on a pre- and after-tax basis for the three-year period ending February 1998.

tax-efficient funds	pretax return	tax-adjusted return
White Oak Growth Stock	40.6%	40.4%
Montaq & Caldwell Growth	36.9%	36.7%
Baron Growth & Income	33.9%	33.6%
Muhlenkamp	33.2%	32.8%
Depositors of Boston	33.1%	32.6%

tax-inefficient funds	pretax return	tax-adjusted return
Fiduciary Mgmt. Growth	33.1%	19.4%
Mosaic Mid-Cap Growth	15.6%	5.0%
GMO U.S. Sector III	29.6%	19.8%
Dresdner RCM Gr. Equity	25.4%	15.6%
MSDW Inst. Emer. Growth	17.6%	8.1%

"Tax-adjusted return" is what the investor is left with after paying taxes on interest, dividends, and realized gains; it assumes that mutual fund shares have not been sold by the shareholder. The numbers, or percentage figures, are also based on the assumption that all interest, dividends, and capital gains were taxed annually and that additional shares were acquired with these after-tax proceeds. Finally, it is assumed that the investor has not sold any shares.

In this book, "tax minimization" is synonymous with "tax-adjusted return." You will be pleasantly surprised to learn that almost every fund in this book is much more tax-efficient than its peer group average. This means that investors are able to keep more. As a point of comparison, it may be helpful for you to see how tax-efficient funds have been in the past.

Over the past twenty years, from 1979 to the beginning of 1999, growth funds have been 85 percent tax-efficient, while growth and income funds have been able to preserve 83 percent of their total return and taxable bond funds have been 72 percent tax-efficient. Putting this into percentage return figures, over the past two decades, growth funds have have an average annual pretax return of 16.7 percent and an average annual after-tax return of 14.1 percent; growth and income funds were not quite as efficient, with average annual pretax returns of 15.7 percent and 13.0 percent on an after-tax basis.

As expected, taxable bond funds were the worst but still had an impressive efficiency, 9.1 percent on a pretax basis versus an average annual after-tax return of 6.5 percent. What is striking about the 72 percent efficiency of taxable bond funds is the fact that most, if not all, of the long-term total return from a bond fund is its interest payments, which are fully taxable each year. Obviously, municipal bond funds are much more tax-efficient than government, corporate, or world bond funds since their interest payments are exempt from federal income taxes and may also be exempt from state income taxes.

The final category, expenses, rates how effective management is in operating the fund. High expense ratios for a given category mean that the advisors are either too greedy or simply do not know or care about running an efficient operation. The actual expenses incurred by a fund are not directly seen by the client (although there are detailed in the fund's prospectus), but such costs are deducted from the portfolio's gross returns, which is important since such a deduction affects the fund's actual performance, its net return.

In addition to looking at the expense ratio of a fund, the turnover rate is also factored into the rating. The turnover rate shows how often the fund buys and sells its securities; the lower the turnover rate, the less trading in the portfolio. There is a real cost when such a transaction occurs. These transaction costs are borne by the fund and eat into the gross return figure. Expense ratios do not include transaction costs or the spread between the buy and the sell price of any securities being traded. Thus, expense ratios do not tell the whole story. By scrutinizing the turnover rate, the rankings take into account excessive trading. A fund's turnover rate may represent a cost to the investor that is greater than its published expense ratio.

Each fund is ranked in each of these five categories. A rating ranges from zero to five points (stars) in each category. The points can be transcribed as follows: one point = poor, two points = fair, three points = good, four points = very good, and five points = excellent.

All of the rankings for each fund are based on how such a fund fared against its peer group in the book as well as its category average. A fund in the book that is given a low score in one category might still rate as average or even great when compared to the entire universe of funds or even when measured against other funds within the same category but not included in this book.

Do not be fooled by a low rating for any fund in any of the five areas. All 100 of these funds are true winners. Keep in mind that the odds of appearing in the book are less than 1 in 135. The purpose of the ratings is to show the best of the best.

Aggressive Growth Funds

These funds focus strictly on appreciation, with no concern about generating income. Aggressive growth funds strive for maximum capital growth, frequently using such trading strategies as leveraging, purchasing restricted securities, or buying stocks of emerging growth companies. Portfolio composition is almost exclusively U.S. stocks. Aggressive growth funds can go up in value quite rapidly during favorable market conditions. These funds will often outperform other categories of U.S. stocks during bull markets but suffer greater percentage losses during bear markets.

Over the past fifteen years, small stocks, which are included in the aggressive growth category, have *underperformed* common stocks by 7.9 percent per year, as measured by the Standard & Poor 500 Stock Index. From 1984 to 1999, small stocks averaged 11.0 percent, while common stocks averaged 17.9 percent compounded per year. A $10,000 investment in small stocks grew to $48,000 over the past fifteen years; a similar initial investment in the S&P 500 grew to $118,290.

During the past twenty years, there have been sixteen five-year periods (1979–1983, 1980–1984, etc.). The Small Stock Index, made up from the smallest 20 percent of companies listed on the NYSE, as measured by market capitalization, outperformed the S&P 500 in just five of those sixteen five-year periods. During these same twenty years, there have been eleven ten-year periods (1979–1988, 1980–1989, etc.). The Small Stock Index outperformed the S&P 500 in just one of those eleven ten-year periods (1979–1988).

During the past thirty years, there have been eleven twenty-year periods (1969–1988, 1970–1989, etc.). The Small Stock Index outperformed the S&P 500 in every twenty-year period but one (1979–1998).

Over the past fifty years, there have been forty-six five-year periods (1949–1953, 1950–1954, etc.). The Small Stock Index outperformed the S&P 500 in twenty-six of those forty-six five-year periods. Over the past fifty years, there have been forty-one ten-year periods (1949–1958, 1950–1959, etc.). The Small Stock Index outperformed the S&P 500 in twenty-six of those forty-one ten-year periods, the last such period being 1979–1988.

A dollar invested in small stocks for the past fifty years grew to $980 by the end of 1998 (versus $578 for $1 invested in the S&P 500). This translates into an average compound return of 14.8 percent per year for small stocks and 13.6 percent for the S&P 500. Over the past fifty years, the worst year for small stocks was 1973, when a loss of 31 percent was suffered. Two years later these same stocks posted a gain of almost 53 percent in one year. The best year so far has been 1967, when small stocks posted a gain of 84 percent. The best five years in a row for this category were 1975 to 1979, when the rate of return averaged 40 percent per year. The worst five-year period over the past half-century has been 1969 to 1973, when this group lost an average of 11 percent per year. For ten-year periods, the best has been 1975 to 1984 (30 percent per year); the worst has been 1965 to 1974 (3 percent per year).

In order to obtain the kinds of returns described above, investors would have needed quite a bit of patience and understanding. Small company stocks have had a standard deviation (variation of return) of 34 percent, compared to 20 percent for common stocks and 9 percent for long-term government bonds. This means that an investor's return in small stocks over each of the past fifty years would have ranged from +48.9 percent to −19.1 percent two-thirds of the time (14.9 + 34 to 14.9 − 34).

During the past three years (ending 3/31/99), aggressive growth funds have underperformed the S&P 500 by 18.8 percent per year. Over the past five years, this fund category has underperformed the S&P 500 by an average of 13.4 percent per year. Average turnover during the last three years has been 95 percent.

The p/e ratio is 37 for the typical aggressive growth fund, versus 34.8 for the S&P 500. The typical stock in these portfolios is just 4 percent the size of the average stock in the S&P 500. The average beta is 1.1, which means the group has a *market-related risk* that is 10 percent higher than the S&P 500. There is over $120 billion in all aggressive growth funds combined. The average aggressive growth fund throws virtually no annual income stream. The typical annual expense ratio for this group is 1.6 percent.

The p/e ratio for the typical small company fund is 26, a figure about 25 percent lower than the S&P 500. The typical stock in these portfolios is less than 1.5 percent the size of the average stock in the S&P 500. The average beta is 0.9, which means the group's market-related risk is 10 percent less than the S&P 500. There is about $135 billion in all small company funds combined. The average small company growth fund yields an income stream of close to zero annually. The typical annual expense ratio for this group is 1.5 percent.

There are 160 funds that make up the aggressive growth category. The small company stock category, which has 720 funds, has been combined with aggressive growth. Thus, for this section, there were a total of 880 possible candidates. Total market capitalization of these two categories combined is $255 billion.

Over the past three years (ending 3/31/99), aggressive growth funds (which include small company stock funds) have had an average compound return of 9.3 percent per year (8.2 percent for small company stock funds alone). The annual return has been 12.9 percent for the past five years (11.9 percent for small company stock funds), 13.4 percent for the past decade (12.9 percent per year for small company stock funds), and 13.0 percent per year for the past fifteen years (12.9 percent for small company stock funds).

The standard deviation for this combined category (aggressive growth and small company stock) has been 25.9 percent over the past three years. This means that these funds have been more volatile than any other category in the book except metals funds (33 percent standard deviation). Aggressive growth funds are certainly not for the faint of heart.

Aggressive Growth Funds

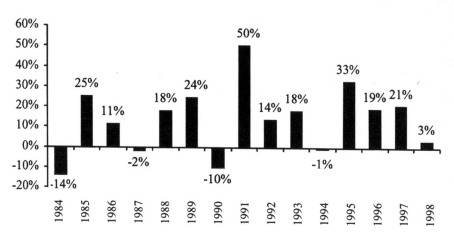

Alger Capital Appreciation B

75 Maiden Lane
New York, NY 10038
800-992-3863

total return	★ ★ ★ ★ ★
risk reduction	★
management	★ ★ ★ ★
tax minimization	★ ★ ★ ★ ★
expense control	★
symbol ACAPX	16 points
up-market performance	excellent
down-market performance	fair
predictability of returns	fair

Total Return   ★ ★ ★ ★ ★

Over the past five years, Alger Capital Appreciation B has taken $10,000 and turned it into $43,236 ($21,011 over three years). This translates into an average annual return of 34 percent over the past five years and 28 percent over the past three years. Over the past five years, this fund has outperformed 99 percent of all mutual funds; within its general category it has done better than 96 percent of its peers. Aggressive growth funds have averaged 13 percent annually over these same five years.

Risk/Volatility   ★

Over the past five years, Alger Capital Appreciation has only been safer than 10 percent of all aggressive growth funds. Over the past decade, the fund has had one negative year, while the S&P 500 has had one (off 3 percent in 1990); the Russell 2000 fell three times (off 20 percent in 1990, 2 percent in 1994, and 3 percent in 1998). The fund has underperformed the S&P 500 and the Russell 2000 three times in the last ten years.

	last 5 years		since inception	
worst year	-2%	1994	-2%	1994
best year	78%	1995	78%	1995

In the past, Alger Capital Appreciation B has done better than 100 percent of its peer group in up markets and outperformed 45 percent of its competition in down markets. Consistency, or predictability, of returns for Alger Capital Appreciation can be described as fair. This fund's risk-adjusted return is fair.

Management   ★ ★ ★ ★

There are fifty stocks in this $310 million portfolio. The average aggressive growth fund today is $290 million in size. Close to 100 percent of the fund's holdings are in stocks. The stocks in this portfolio have an average price-earnings (p/e) ratio of 45 and a median market capitalization of $45 billion. The portfolio's equity holdings can be categorized as large-cap and growth-oriented issues.

David Alger has managed this fund for the past five years. There are eight funds besides Capital Appreciation B within the Alger family. Overall, the fund family's risk-adjusted performance can be described as very good.

Tax Minimization   ★ ★ ★ ★ ★
During the past five years, a $10,000 initial investment grew to $29,960 after taxes, assuming a 39.6 percent income tax bracket (state and federal combined) and a capital gains rate of 28 percent. This means that investors in this fund were able to preserve 91 percent of their total returns. Compared to other equity funds, this fund's tax savings are considered to be excellent.

Expenses   ★
Alger Capital Appreciation B's expense ratio is 2.4 percent; it has also averaged 2.4 percent annually over the past three calendar years. The average expense ratio for the 860 funds in this category is 1.5 percent. This fund's turnover rate over the past year has been 160 percent, while its peer group average has been 95 percent.

Summary
Alger uses over forty analysts to continuously search for possible stock candidates. Prospectus companies are reviewed by the family's four managers who use a bottom-up approach. Stocks are sold if the company's fundamentals deteriorate, the stock becomes overvalued, or a better alternative arises. Alger Capital Appreciation B has high volatility but its returns have certainly rewarded the patient investor. Tax efficiency is also superb. David Alger has always excelled in small cap issues and his stellar performance continues.

Profile
minimum initial investment $1	IRA accounts available . . . . yes
subsequent minimum investment $1	IRA minimum investment $1
available in all 50 states. . . . . yes	date of inception . . . . Oct. 1993
telephone exchanges. . . . . yes	dividend/income paid . . . . annually
number of other funds in family. 8	largest sector weighting . . . technology

Baron Asset
767 Fifth Avenue, 24th Floor
New York, NY 10153
800-992-2766

total return	★ ★ ★ ★ ★
risk reduction	★ ★ ★ ★ ★
management	★ ★ ★ ★ ★
tax minimization	★ ★ ★ ★ ★
expense control	★ ★ ★ ★
symbol BARAX	24 points
up-market performance	excellent
down-market performance	fair
predictability of returns	good

Total Return   ★ ★ ★ ★ ★
Over the past five years, Baron Asset has taken $10,000 and turned it into $27,060 ($15,897 over three years and $44,420 over the past ten years). This translates into an average annual return of 22 percent over the past five years, 17 percent over the past three years, and 16 percent for the decade. Over the past five years, this fund has outperformed 91 percent of all mutual funds; within its general category it has done better than 98 percent of its peers. Aggressive growth funds have averaged 13 percent annually over these same five years.

Risk/Volatility   ★ ★ ★ ★ ★
Over the past five years, Baron Asset has been safer than 95 percent of all aggressive growth funds. Over the past decade, the fund has had one negative year, while the S&P 500 has also had one (off 3 percent in 1990); the Russell 2000 fell three times (off 20 percent in 1990, 2 percent in 1994, and 3 percent in 1998). The fund has underperformed the S&P 500 five times and the Russell 2000 one time in the last ten years.

	last 5 years		last 10 years	
worst year	4%	1998	-18%	1990
best year	35%	1995	35%	1995

In the past, Baron Asset has done better than 95 percent of its peer group in up markets and outperformed 35 percent of its competition in down markets. Consistency, or predictability, of returns for Baron Asset can be described as good. This fund's risk-adjusted return is excellent.

Management   ★ ★ ★ ★ ★
There are eighty-five stocks in this $6 billion portfolio. The average aggressive growth fund today is $290 million in size. Close to 98 percent of the fund's holdings are in stocks. The stocks in this portfolio have an average price-earnings (p/e) ratio of 38 and a median market capitalization of $2 billion. The portfolio's equity holdings can be categorized as mid-cap and growth-oriented issues.

Ronald Baron has managed this fund for the past twelve years. There are two funds besides Asset within the Baron family. Overall, the fund family's risk-adjusted performance can be described as good.

Tax Minimization   ★ ★ ★ ★ ★
During the past five years, a $10,000 initial investment grew to $25,060 after taxes, assuming a 39.6 percent income tax bracket (state and federal combined) and a capital gains rate of 28 percent. This means that investors in this fund were able to preserve 100 percent of their total returns. Compared to other equity funds, this fund's tax savings are considered to be excellent.

Expenses   ★ ★ ★ ★
Baron Asset's expense ratio is 1.3 percent; it has also averaged 1.3 percent annually over the past three calendar years. The average expense ratio for the 860 funds in this category is 1.5 percent. This fund's turnover rate over the past year has been 25 percent, while its peer group average has been 95 percent.

Summary
Baron Asset receives an almost perfect score—24 out of 25 possible points. Ronald Baron knows the value of owning stocks of corporations that have and will benefit from technology. Management uses a bottom-up approach, discovering under-valued stocks that are expected to increase by at least 50 percent over the next couple of years. Frequently, one-third of the fund's holdings are in just ten different equities. This fund is the perfect choice for the small company stock investor.

Profile
minimum initial investment $2,000	*IRA accounts available* . . . . yes
subsequent minimum investment . . . $50	*IRA minimum investment* $2,000
available in all 50 states. . . . . yes	*date of inception.* . . . . June 1987
telephone exchanges. . . . . yes	*dividend/income paid* . . . . annually
number of other funds in family. 2	*largest sector weighting.* . . . . . . services

Citizens Emerging Growth
230 Commerce Way, Suite 300
Portsmouth, NH 03801
800-223-7010

total return	★ ★ ★ ★ ★
risk reduction	★ ★ ★ ★
management	★ ★ ★ ★ ★
tax minimization	★ ★ ★ ★ ★
expense control	★
symbol WAEGX	20 points
up-market performance	very good
down-market performance	very good
predictability of returns	fair

Total Return   ★ ★ ★ ★ ★
Over the past five years, Citizens Emerging Growth has taken $10,000 and turned it into 28,788 ($18,069 over three years). This translates into an average annual return of 24 percent over the past five years and 22 percent over the past three years. Over the past five years this fund has outperformed 95 percent of all mutual funds; within its general category it has done better than 90 percent of its peers. Aggressive growth funds have averaged 13 percent annually over these same five years.

Risk/Volatility   ★ ★ ★ ★
Over the past five years, Citizens Emerging Growth has been safer than 65 percent of all aggressive growth funds. Over the past decade, the fund has not had a negative year, while the S&P 500 has had one (off 3 percent in 1990); the Russell 2000 fell three times (off 20 percent in 1990, 2 percent in 1994, and 3 percent in 1998). The fund has underperformed the S&P 500 two times and the Russell 2000 two times in the last ten years.

	last 5 years		since inception	
worst year	14%	1996	14%	1996
best year	43%	1998	43%	1998

In the past, Citizens Emerging Growth has done better than 85 percent of its peer group in up markets and outperformed 85 percent of its competition in down markets. Consistency, or predictability, of returns for Emerging Growth can be described as very good. This fund's risk-adjusted return is very good.

Management   ★ ★ ★ ★ ★
There are thirty-three stocks in this $110 million portfolio. The average aggressive growth fund today is $290 million in size. Close to 88 percent of the fund's holdings are in stocks. The stocks in this portfolio have an average price-earnings (p/e) ratio of 42 and a median market capitalization of $5.5 billion. The portfolio's equity holdings can be categorized as mid-cap and growth-oriented issues.

Richard D. Little has managed this fund for the past five years. There are three funds besides Emerging Growth within the Citizens family. Overall, the fund family's risk-adjusted performance can be described as very good.

Tax Minimization   ★★★★★

During the past five years, a $10,000 initial investment grew to $24,840 after taxes, assuming a 39.6 percent income tax bracket (state and federal combined) and a capital gains rate of 28 percent. This means that investors in this fund were able to preserve 88 percent of their total returns. Compared to other equity funds, this fund's tax savings are considered to be very good.

Expenses   ★

Citizens Emerging Growth's expense ratio is 2 percent; it has also averaged 2 percent annually over the past three calendar years. The average expense ratio for the 860 funds in this category is 1.5 percent. This fund's turnover rate over the past year has been 245 percent, while its peer group average has been 95 percent.

Summary

Citizens Emerging Growth is a socially conscious fund that favors mid-cap issues that have good earnings momentum. Frequently, stocks are removed from the portfolio if there is an earnings disappointment or manager Little believes there is overvaluation. The fund has made some rather bold moves in the past, greatly overweighing a sector or industry group. Such a concentration has usually paid off handsomely. The fund scores a perfect or near-perfect score in every area but one.

Profile

minimum initial investment $2,500	IRA accounts available . . . . yes
subsequent minimum investment . . . $50	IRA minimum investment $250
available in all 50 states. . . . . yes	date of inception . . . . Feb. 1994
telephone exchanges. . . . . yes	dividend/income paid . . . . annually
number of other funds in family 3	largest sector weighting . . . technology

Evergreen Omega A

237 Park Avenue
New York, NY 10017
800-343-2898

total return	★ ★ ★ ★ ★
risk reduction	★ ★
management	★ ★ ★
tax minimization	★ ★
expense control	★ ★
symbol EKOAX	14 points
up-market performance	very good
down-market performance	excellent
predictability of returns	very good

Total Return   ★ ★ ★ ★ ★

Over the past five years, Evergreen Omega A has taken $10,000 and turned it into $25,639 ($18,509 over three years and $57,427 over the past ten years). This translates into an average annual return of 21 percent over the past five years, 23 percent over the past three years, and 19 percent for the decade. Over the past five years, this fund has outperformed 85 percent of all mutual funds; within its general category it has only done better than 25 percent of its peers. Aggressive growth funds have averaged 13 percent annually over these same five years.

Risk/Volatility   ★ ★

Over the past five years, Evergreen Omega A has been safer than 40 percent of all aggressive growth funds. Over the past decade, the fund has had two negative years, while the S&P 500 has had one (off 3 percent in 1990); the Russell 2000 fell three times (off 20 percent in 1990, 2 percent in 1994, and 3 percent in 1998). The fund has underperformed the S&P 500 six times and the Russell 2000 three times in the last ten years.

	last 5 years		last 10 years	
worst year	-6%	1994	-6%	1994
best year	37%	1995	54%	1991

In the past, Omega has done better than 75 percent of its peer group in up markets and outperformed 90 percent of its competition in down markets. Consistency, or predictability, of returns for Evergreen Omega A can be described as very good. This fund's risk-adjusted return is poor.

Management   ★ ★ ★

There are sixty stocks in this $220 million portfolio. The average aggressive growth fund today is $290 million in size. Close to 92 percent of the fund's holdings are in stocks. The stocks in this portfolio have an average price-earnings (p/e) ratio of 47 and a median market capitalization of $23 billion. The portfolio's equity holdings can be categorized as large-cap and growth-oriented issues.

Maureen Cullinane has managed this fund for the past ten years. There are sixty-seven funds besides Omega A within the Evergreen family. Overall, the fund family's risk-adjusted performance can be described as good.

Tax Minimization   ★ ★
During the past five years, a $10,000 initial investment grew to $18,880 after taxes, assuming a 39.6 percent income tax bracket (state and federal combined) and a capital gains rate of 28 percent. This means that investors in this fund were able to preserve 83 percent of their total returns. Compared to other equity funds, this fund's tax savings are considered to be good.

Expenses   ★ ★
Evergreen Omega A's expense ratio is 1.3 percent; it has also averaged 1.3 percent annually over the past three calendar years. The average expense ratio for the 860 funds in this category is 1.5 percent. This fund's turnover rate over the past year has been 160 percent, while its peer group average has been 95 percent.

Summary
Evergreen Omega A is well diversified by industry sector and size of securities; management particularly likes technology and media. Cullinane uses both a top-down and bottom-up approach to security selection, favoring those companies with a strong management and competitive advantage. This is a particularly attractive choice for mutual fund investors concerned with the downside.

Profile
minimum initial investment . . . . . $1,000   *IRA accounts available* . . . . yes
subsequent minimum investment . . . $50   *IRA minimum investment* $1,000
available in all 50 states. . . . . yes   *date of inception* . . . . April 1968
telephone exchanges. . . . . yes   *dividend/income paid* . . . . annually
number of other funds in family 67   *largest sector weighting* . . . technology

Franklin Small Cap Growth A

777 Mariners Island Boulevard
San Mateo, CA 94403-7777
800-342-5236

total return	★ ★ ★ ★
risk reduction	★ ★ ★ ★ ★
management	★ ★ ★ ★ ★
tax minimization	★ ★ ★
expense control	★ ★ ★ ★ ★
symbol FRSGX	22 points
up-market performance	very good
down-market performance	good
predictability of returns	good

Total Return   ★ ★ ★ ★

Over the past five years, Franklin Small Cap Growth A has taken $10,000 and turned it into $23,258 ($13,982 over three years). This translates into an average annual return of 18 percent over the past five years and 12 percent over the past three years. Over the past five years, this fund has outperformed 90 percent of all mutual funds; within its general category it has done better than 90 percent of its peers. Aggressive growth funds have averaged 13 percent annually over these same five years.

Risk/Volatility   ★ ★ ★ ★ ★

Over the past five years, Franklin Small Cap Growth A has been safer than 85 percent of all aggressive growth funds. Over the past decade, the fund has had one negative year, while the S&P 500 has also had one (off 3 percent in 1990); the Russell 2000 fell three times (off 20 percent in 1990, 2 percent in 1994, and 3 percent in 1998). The fund has underperformed the S&P 500 two times and the Russell 2000 one time in the last ten years.

	last 5 years		since inception	
worst year	-.02%	1998	-.02%	1998
best year	42%	1995	42%	1995

In the past, Small Cap Growth has done better than 85 percent of its peer group in up markets and outperformed 55 percent of its competition in down markets. Consistency, or predictability, of returns for Franklin Small Cap Growth A can be described as good. This fund's risk-adjusted return is excellent.

Management   ★ ★ ★ ★ ★

There are 205 stocks in this $4 billion portfolio. The average aggressive growth fund today is $290 million in size. Close to 90 percent of the fund's holdings are in stocks. The stocks in this portfolio have an average price-earnings (p/e) ratio of 30 and a median market capitalization of $940 million. The portfolio's equity holdings can be categorized as small-cap and growth-oriented issues.

A team has managed this fund for the past five years. There are eighty funds besides Small Cap Growth A within the Franklin-Templeton family. Overall, the fund family's risk-adjusted performance can be described as very good.

Tax Minimization   ★ ★ ★

During the past five years, a $10,000 initial investment grew to $21,230 after taxes, assuming a 39.6 percent income tax bracket (state and federal combined) and a capital gains rate of 28 percent. This means that investors in this fund were able to preserve 93 percent of their total returns. Compared to other equity funds, this fund's tax savings are considered to be excellent.

Expenses   ★ ★ ★ ★ ★

Franklin Small Cap Growth A's expense ratio is .9 percent; it has also averaged .9 percent annually over the past three calendar years. The average expense ratio for the 860 funds in this category is 1.5 percent. This fund's turnover rate over the past year has been 45 percent, while its peer group average has been 95 percent.

Summary

Franklin Small Cap Growth A loves Web-hosting companies and those that help others develop e-commerce. Management uses a blend of computer-driven models plus fundamental analysis for equity selection. The focus is on financial stability, experienced management, and those companies that have a unique niche or competitive edge. This is one of the very best choices for the small company fund investor. The fund has almost a perfect score across the board.

Profile

minimum initial investment $1,000	*IRA accounts available* . . . . yes
subsequent minimum investment . . . $50	*IRA minimum investment* $250
available in all 50 states. . . . . yes	*date of inception* . . . . Feb. 1992
telephone exchanges. . . . . yes	*dividend/income paid.* . . . . semiannually
number of other funds in family 80	*largest sector weighting* . . . technology

Legg Mason Special Investment Trust—Primary Shares

111 South Calvert Street
Baltimore, MD 21203-1476
800-577-8589

total return	★ ★ ★ ★
risk reduction	★
management	★ ★ ★
tax minimization	★
expense control	★ ★ ★
symbol LMASX	12 points
up-market performance	excellent
down-market performance	poor
predictability of returns	fair

Total Return ★ ★ ★ ★

Over the past five years, Legg Mason Special Investment Trust—Primary Shares has taken $10,000 and turned it into $22,387 ($18,613 over three years and $50,677 over the past ten years). This translates into an average annual return of 17 percent over the past five years, 24 percent over the past three years, and 18 percent for the decade. Over the past five years, this fund has outperformed 80 percent of all mutual funds; within its general category it has done better than 55 percent of its peers. Aggressive growth funds have averaged 13 percent annually over these same five years.

Risk/Volatility ★

Over the past five years, Legg Mason Special Investment Trust—Primary Shares has only been safer than 4 percent of all aggressive growth funds. Over the past decade, the fund has had one negative year, while the S&P 500 has also had one (off 3 percent in 1990); the Russell 2000 fell three times (off 20 percent in 1990, 2 percent in 1994, and 3 percent in 1998). The fund has underperformed the S&P 500 four times and the Russell 2000 five times in the last ten years.

	last 5 years		last 10 years	
worst year	-13%	1994	-13%	1994
best year	29%	1996	39%	1991

In the past, Primary Shares has done better than 100 percent of its peer group in up markets and outperformed 30 percent of its competition in down markets. Consistency, or predictability, of returns for Legg Mason Special Investment Trust—Primary Shares can be described as fair. This fund's risk-adjusted return is excellent.

Management   ★ ★ ★

There are forty-five stocks in this $2 billion portfolio. The average aggressive growth fund today is $290 million in size. Close to 86 percent of the fund's holdings are in stocks. The stocks in this portfolio have an average price-earnings (p/e) ratio of 29 and a median market capitalization of $1.7 billion. The portfolio's equity holdings can be categorized as mid-cap and a blend of growth and value stocks.

William Miller III has managed this fund for the past fourteen years. There are fifteen funds besides Primary Shares within the Legg Mason family. Overall, the fund family's risk-adjusted performance can be described as very good.

Tax Minimization   ★

During the past five years, a $10,000 initial investment grew to $19,530 after taxes, assuming a 39.6 percent income tax bracket (state and federal combined) and a capital gains rate of 28 percent. This means that investors in this fund were able to preserve 95 percent of their total returns. Compared to other equity funds, this fund's tax savings are considered to be excellent.

Expenses   ★ ★ ★

Legg Mason Special Investment Trust—Primary Shares' expense ratio is 1.9 percent; it has also averaged 1.9 percent annually over the past three calendar years. The average expense ratio for the 860 funds in this category is 1.5 percent. This fund's turnover rate over the past year has been 30 percent, while its peer group average has been 95 percent.

Summary

Legg Mason Special Investment Trust—Primary Shares has ranked in the top quartile of performance for its peer group for three of the past four years, despite management's bias toward value and small stocks. A good chunk of the portfolio is in computer-service and computer-system equities. Managers Miller and Rapuano use p/e, price-to-cash flow and price-to-book ratios when making their selections. Management is particularly keen on special situations wherein there may be either a capital restructuring or company management changes. Tax efficiency and raw performance are the fund's strongest suits.

Profile

minimum initial investment $1,000
subsequent minimum investment . . $100
available in all 50 states . . . . no
telephone exchanges. . . . . yes
number of other funds in family 15

IRA accounts available . . . . yes
IRA minimum investment $1,000
date of inception. . . . . Dec. 1985
dividend/income paid . . . . annually
largest sector weighting . . . technology

Royce Total Return
1414 Avenue of the Americas
New York, NY 10019
800-221-4268

total return	★ ★ ★
risk reduction	★ ★ ★ ★ ★
management	★ ★ ★
tax minimization	★
expense control	★ ★ ★ ★
symbol RYTRX	16 points
up-market performance	poor
down-market performance	very good
predictability of returns	excellent

Total Return   ★ ★ ★
Over the past five years, Royce Total Return has taken $10,000 and turned it into $19,792 ($14,091 over three years). This translates into an average annual return of 15 percent over the past five years and 12 percent over the past three years. Over the past five years, this fund has outperformed 85 percent of all mutual funds; within its general category it has done better than 95 percent of its peers. Aggressive growth funds have averaged 13 percent annually over these same five years.

Risk/Volatility   ★ ★ ★ ★ ★
Over the past five years, Royce Total Return has been safer than 99 percent of all aggressive growth funds. Over the past decade, the fund has not had a negative year, while the S&P 500 has had one (off 3 percent in 1990); the Russell 2000 fell three times (off 20 percent in 1990, 2 percent in 1994, and 3 percent in 1998). The fund has underperformed the S&P 500 three times and the Russell 2000 one time in the last ten years.

	last 5 years		since inception	
worst year	5%	1998	5%	1998
best year	27%	1995	27%	1995

In the past, Total Return has done better than 20 percent of its peer group in up markets and outperformed 80 percent of its competition in down markets. Consistency, or predictability, of returns for Royce Total Return can be described as excellent. This fund's risk-adjusted return is excellent.

Management   ★ ★ ★
There are fifty stocks in this $240 million portfolio. The average aggressive growth fund today is $290 million in size. Close to 77 percent of the fund's holdings are in stocks. The stocks in this portfolio have an average price-earnings (p/e) ratio of 16 and a median market capitalization of $350 million. The portfolio's equity holdings can be categorized as small-cap and value-oriented issues.

Charles Royce has managed this fund for the past six years. There are nine funds besides Total Return within the Royce family. Overall, the fund family's risk-adjusted performance can be described as very good.

Tax Minimization ★

During the past five years, a $10,000 initial investment grew to $18,910 after taxes, assuming a 39.6 percent income tax bracket (state and federal combined) and a capital gains rate of 28 percent. This means that investors in this fund were able to preserve 87 percent of their total returns. Compared to other equity funds, this fund's tax savings are considered to be very good.

Expenses ★★★★

Royce Total Return's expense ratio is 1.3 percent; it has also averaged 1.3 percent annually over the past three calendar years. The average expense ratio for the 860 funds in this category is 1.5 percent. This fund's turnover rate over the past year has been 66 percent, while its peer group average has been 95 percent.

Summary

Royce Total Return does best at risk reduction; returns have been somewhat lagging in recent years. Still, long-term performance remains quite impressive. Technology is under weighted while natural resource stocks are heavily represented, thereby making returns much more predictable than the fund's peer group. Fundamentals are used for the value security selection; companies with an assets-to-shareholders equity ratio of at least 2:1 are preferred. Risk is further reduced by broad diversification. This fund is a very good choice for the stock investor who is concerned with risk.

Profile

minimum initial investment $2,000
subsequent minimum investment . . . $50
available in all 50 states. . . . . yes
telephone exchanges. . . . . yes
number of other funds in family 9

IRA accounts available . . . . yes
IRA minimum investment $500
date of inception. . . . . Dec. 1993
dividend/income paid . . . . annually
largest sector weighting. . . . . industrial
cyclicals

Selected Special
P.O. Box 1688
Santa Fe, NM 87504
800-243-1575

total return	★ ★ ★ ★
risk reduction	★ ★ ★ ★ ★
management	★ ★ ★ ★
tax minimization	★ ★ ★
expense control	★ ★ ★ ★
symbol SLSSX	20 points
up-market performance	fair
down-market performance	fair
predictability of returns	good

Total Return   ★ ★ ★ ★

Over the past five years, Selected Special has taken $10,000 and turned it into $23,783 ($16,510 over three years and $38,394 over the past ten years). This translates into an average annual return of 19 percent over the past five years, 18 percent over the past three years, and 14 percent for the decade. Over the past five years, this fund has outperformed 85 percent of all mutual funds; within its general category it has done better than 80 percent of its peers. Aggressive growth funds have averaged 13 percent annually over these same five years.

Risk/Volatility   ★ ★ ★ ★ ★

Over the past five years, Selected Special has been safer than 90 percent of all aggressive growth funds. Over the past decade, the fund has had two negative years, while the S&P 500 has had one (off 3 percent in 1990); the Russell 2000 fell three times (off 20 percent in 1990, 2 percent in 1994, and 3 percent in 1998). The fund has underperformed the S&P 500 eight times and the Russell 2000 five times in the last ten years.

	last 5 years		last 10 years	
worst year	-3%	1994	-7%	1990
best year	34%	1995	34%	1995

In the past, Selected Special has done better than 40 percent of its peer group in up markets and outperformed 35 percent of its competition in down markets. Consistency, or predictability, of returns for Special can be described as good. This fund's risk-adjusted return is poor.

Management   ★ ★ ★ ★

There are seventy stocks in this $95 million portfolio. The average aggressive growth fund today is $290 million in size. Close to 93 percent of the fund's holdings are in stocks. The stocks in this portfolio have an average price-earnings (p/e) ratio of 35 and a median market capitalization of $4 billion. The portfolio's equity holdings can be categorized as mid-cap and growth-oriented issues.

Elizabeth Bramwell has managed this fund for the past five years. There are two funds besides Special within the Selected family. Overall, the fund family's risk-adjusted performance can be described as good.

Tax Minimization ★ ★ ★
During the past five years, a $10,000 initial investment grew to $20,390 after taxes, assuming a 39.6 percent income tax bracket (state and federal combined) and a capital gains rate of 28 percent. This means that investors in this fund were able to preserve 88 percent of their total returns. Compared to other equity funds, this fund's tax savings are considered to be very good.

Expenses ★ ★ ★ ★
Selected Special's expense ratio is 1.3 percent; it has averaged 1.4 percent annually over the past three calendar years. The average expense ratio for the 860 funds in this category is 1.5 percent. This fund's turnover rate over the past year has been 50 percent, while its peer group average has been 95 percent.

Summary
Selected Special looks for stocks selling at a discount to their growth rate plus a growth rate that is higher than the S&P 500 Index. Manager Bramwell uses macroeconomics, first looking at the overall growth rate, inflation, and dollar valuation and then determines which industry sectors will best benefit from her near-term conclusions. Individual security selection is based on a company's new products and markets, reduced competition, or cost-cutting efforts. This fund scores very well in every area.

Profile

minimum initial investment $1,000	*IRA accounts available* . . . . yes
subsequent minimum investment . . . $25	*IRA minimum investment* $250
available in all 50 states. . . . . yes	*date of inception.* . . . . May 1939
telephone exchanges. . . . . yes	*dividend/income paid* . . . . annually
number of other funds in family 2	*largest sector weighting* . . . technology

Smith Barney Aggressive Growth A

388 Greenwich Street, 37th Floor
New York, NY 10013
800-451-2010

total return	★ ★ ★ ★ ★
risk reduction	★ ★ ★
management	★ ★ ★ ★
tax minimization	★ ★ ★ ★
expense control	★ ★ ★ ★ ★
symbol SHRAX	21 points
up-market performance	excellent
down-market performance	very good
predictability of returns	poor

Total Return   ★ ★ ★ ★ ★

Over the past five years, Smith Barney Aggressive Growth A has taken $10,000 and turned it into $28,556 ($20,407 over three years and $56,375 over the past ten years). This translates into an average annual return of 23 percent over the past five years, 27 percent over the past three years, and 19 percent for the decade. Over the past five years, this fund has outperformed 90 percent of all mutual funds; within its general category it has done better than 80 percent of its peers. Aggressive growth funds have averaged 13 percent annually over these same five years.

Risk/Volatility   ★ ★ ★

Over the past five years, Smith Barney Aggressive Growth A has been safer than 50 percent of all aggressive growth funds. Over the past decade, the fund has had two negative years, while the S&P 500 has had one (off 3 percent in 1990); the Russell 2000 fell three times (off 20 percent in 1990, 2 percent in 1994, and 3 percent in 1998). The fund has underperformed the S&P 500 six times and the Russell 2000 three times in the last ten years.

	last 5 years		last 10 years	
worst year	-2%	1994	-6%	1990
best year	36%	1995	42%	1991

In the past, Smith Barney Aggressive Growth A has done better than 90 percent of its peer group in up markets and outperformed 75 percent of its competition in down markets. Consistency, or predictability, of returns for Aggressive Growth can be described as poor. This fund's risk-adjusted return is poor.

Management   ★ ★ ★ ★

There are fifty stocks in this $560 million portfolio. The average aggressive growth fund today is $290 million in size. Close to 99 percent of the fund's holdings are in stocks. The stocks in this portfolio have an average price-earnings (p/e) ratio of 41 and a median market capitalization of $13 billion. The portfolio's equity holdings can be categorized as large-cap and growth-oriented issues.

Richard Freeman has managed this fund for the past sixteen years. There are forty-one funds besides Aggressive Growth A within the Smith Barney family. Overall, the fund family's risk-adjusted performance can be described as very good.

Tax Minimization ★ ★ ★ ★
During the past five years, a $10,000 initial investment grew to $22,520 after taxes, assuming a 39.6 percent income tax bracket (state and federal combined) and a capital gains rate of 28 percent. This means that investors in this fund were able to preserve 95 percent of their total returns. Compared to other equity funds, this fund's tax savings are considered to be excellent.

Expenses ★ ★ ★ ★ ★
Smith Barney Aggressive Growth A's expense ratio is 1.2 percent; it has also averaged 1.2 percent annually over the past three calendar years. The average expense ratio for the 860 funds in this category is 1.5 percent. This fund's turnover rate over the past year has been 5 percent, while its peer group average has been 95 percent.

Summary
Smith Barney Aggressive Growth A has ranked in the top performance quartile for each of the past three years; few aggressive growth funds can boost such a record. The fund delivers top marks for performance, tax efficiency, and expense control. Assets are always fully invested in stocks that are expected to be held for the long term. Management prefers undervalued issues in high-growth industries.

Profile

minimum initial investment $1,000	*IRA accounts available* . . . . yes
subsequent minimum investment . . . $50	*IRA minimum investment* $250
available in all 50 states. . . . . yes	*date of inception* . . . . Oct. 1983
telephone exchanges. . . . . yes	*dividend/income paid* . . . . annually
number of other funds in family 41	*largest sector weighting* . . . . health

United New Concepts A
6300 Lamar Avenue
Shawnee Mission, KS 66201-9217
800-366-5465

total return	★ ★ ★ ★ ★
risk reduction	★ ★ ★ ★ ★
management	★ ★ ★ ★ ★
tax minimization	★ ★ ★ ★
expense control	★ ★ ★ ★ ★
symbol UNECX	24 points
up-market performance	very good
down-market performance	good
predictability of returns	good

Total Return   ★ ★ ★ ★ ★
Over the past five years, United New Concepts A has taken $10,000 and turned it into $25,692 ($16,355 over three years and $59,934 over the past ten years). This translates into an average annual return of 21 percent over the past five years, 18 percent over the past three years, and 20 percent for the decade. Over the past five years, this fund has outperformed 95 percent of all mutual funds; within its general category it has done better than 90 percent of its peers. Aggressive growth funds have averaged 13 percent annually over these same five years.

Risk/Volatility   ★ ★ ★ ★ ★
Over the past five years, United New Concepts A has been safer than 85 percent of all aggressive growth funds. Over the past decade, the fund has not had a negative year, while the S&P 500 has had one (off 3 percent in 1990); the Russell 2000 fell three times (off 20 percent in 1990, 2 percent in 1994, and 3 percent in 1998). The fund has underperformed the S&P 500 five times and the Russell 2000 five times in the last ten years.

	last 5 years		last 10 years	
worst year	5%	1996	2%	1990
best year	39%	1998	88%	1991

In the past, United New Concepts A has done better than 85 percent of its peer group in up markets and outperformed 65 percent of its competition in down markets. Consistency, or predictability, of returns for New Concepts can be described as good. This fund's risk-adjusted return is fair.

Management   ★ ★ ★ ★ ★
There are fifty-four stocks in this $975 million portfolio. The average aggressive growth fund today is $290 million in size. Close to 78 percent of the fund's holdings are in stocks. The stocks in this portfolio have an average price-earnings (p/e) ratio of 40 and a median market capitalization of $1.6 billion. The portfolio's equity holdings can be categorized as mid-cap and growth-oriented issues.

Mark Seferovich has managed this fund for the past ten years. There are sixteen funds besides New Concepts A within the United family. Overall, the fund family's risk-adjusted performance can be described as very good.

Tax Minimization ★ ★ ★ ★

During the past five years, a $10,000 initial investment grew to $22,960 after taxes, assuming a 39.6 percent income tax bracket (state and federal combined) and a capital gains rate of 28 percent. This means that investors in this fund were able to preserve 91 percent of their total returns. Compared to other equity funds, this fund's tax savings are considered to be excellent.

Expenses ★ ★ ★ ★ ★

United New Concepts A's expense ratio is 1.3 percent; it has averaged 1.2 percent annually over the past three calendar years. The average expense ratio for the 860 funds in this category is 1.5 percent. This fund's turnover rate over the past year has been 40 percent, while its peer group average has been 95 percent.

Summary

United New Concepts A has recently changed management and investment style. The fund will now favor mid-cap stocks. Management still strongly believes in a long-term, buy-and-hold strategy. Companies with strong management, a well-positioned market niche, as well as those that have been overlooked by Wall Street are potential portfolio candidates. The fund is always looking for industry trends or economic developments that favor specific corporations. With a perfect score of 25 out of 25 possible points, this is the highest-ranked aggressive growth fund in the book. It is also one of only a couple of funds in the entire book that has earned the highest rating.

Profile

minimum initial investment $500	*IRA accounts available* . . . . yes
subsequent minimum investment . . . $50	*IRA minimum investment* $50
available in all 50 states. . . . . yes	*date of inception.* . . . . June 1983
telephone exchanges . . . . no	*dividend/income paid* . . . . annually
number of other funds in family. 16	*largest sector weighting.* . . . . . . services

Value Line Leveraged Growth Investors

220 E. 42nd Street
New York, NY 10017-5891
800-223-0818

total return	★ ★ ★ ★ ★
risk reduction	★ ★
management	★ ★ ★ ★
tax minimization	★ ★ ★ ★
expense control	★ ★ ★ ★ ★
symbol VALLX	20 points
up-market performance	very good
down-market performance	very good
predictability of returns	fair

Total Return   ★ ★ ★ ★ ★

Over the past five years, Value Line Leveraged Growth Investors has taken $10,000 and turned it into $32,573 ($21,753 over three years and $61,866 over the past ten years). This translates into an average annual return of 27 percent over the past five years, 30 percent over the past three years, and 20 percent for the decade. Over the past five years, this fund has outperformed 95 percent of all mutual funds; within its general category it has done better than 70 percent of its peers. Aggressive growth funds have averaged 13 percent annually over these same five years.

Risk/Volatility   ★ ★

Over the past five years, Value Line Leveraged Growth Investors has been safer than only 30 percent of all aggressive growth funds. Over the past decade, the fund has had three negative years, while the S&P 500 has had one (off 3 percent in 1990); the Russell 2000 fell three times (off 20 percent in 1990, 2 percent in 1994, and 3 percent in 1998). The fund has underperformed the S&P 500 five times and the Russell 2000 three times in the last ten years.

	last 5 years		last 10 years	
worst year	-4%	1994	-4%	1994
best year	39%	1998	46%	1991

In the past, Value Line Leveraged Growth Investors has done better than 85 percent of its peer group in up markets and outperformed 75 percent of its competition in down markets. Consistency, or predictability, of returns for Leveraged Growth Investors can be described as fair. This fund's risk-adjusted return is fair.

Management   ★ ★ ★ ★

There are eighty stocks in this $620 million portfolio. The average aggressive growth fund today is $290 million in size. Close to 99 percent of the fund's holdings are in stocks. The stocks in this portfolio have an average price-earnings (p/e) ratio of 44 and a median market capitalization of $39 billion. The portfolio's equity holdings can be categorized as large-cap and growth-oriented issues.

A team has managed this fund for the past twenty-seven years. There are thirteen funds besides Leveraged Growth within the Value Line family. Overall, the fund family's risk-adjusted performance can be described as fair.

Tax Minimization   ★ ★ ★ ★

During the past five years, a $10,000 initial investment grew to $23,190 after taxes, assuming a 39.6 percent income tax bracket (state and federal combined) and a capital gains rate of 28 percent. This means that investors in this fund were able to preserve 83 percent of their total returns. Compared to other equity funds, this fund's tax savings are considered to be good.

Expenses   ★ ★ ★ ★ ★

Value Line Leveraged Growth Investors' expense ratio is .9 percent; it has also averaged .9 percent annually over the past three calendar years. The average expense ratio for the 860 funds in this category is 1.5 percent. This fund's turnover rate over the past year has been 35 percent, while its peer group average has been 95 percent.

Summary

Value Line Leveraged Growth Investors invests in stocks from a universe of 400 possible candidates that are rated either 1 or 2 in Value Line's timeliness rankings. More often than not, these are companies that have a strong earnings growth and share-price momentum. The fund has the ability to leverage itself and be more than 100 percent invested. Management can also short S&P 500 futures when it is bearish. Returns have been extremely good and expenses for the fund are quite low for its category.

Profile

minimum initial investment $1,000	*IRA accounts available* . . . . yes
subsequent minimum investment . . $100	*IRA minimum investment* $1,000
available in all 50 states. . . . . yes	*date of inception* . . . . March 1972
telephone exchanges. . . . . yes	*dividend/income paid* . . . . annually
number of other funds in family. 13	*largest sector weighting* . . . technology

Balanced Funds

The objective of balanced funds, also referred to as total return funds, is to provide both growth and income. Fund management purchases common stocks, bonds, and convertible securities. Portfolio composition is almost always exclusively U.S. securities. The weighting of stocks compared to bonds depends upon the portfolio manager's perception of the stock market, interest rates, and risk levels. It is rare for less than 30 percent of the fund's holdings to be in stocks or bonds.

Balanced funds offer neither the best nor worst of both worlds. These funds will often outperform the different categories of bond funds during bull markets but suffer greater percentage losses during stock market declines. On the other hand, when interest rates are on the rise, balanced funds will typically decline less on a total-return basis (current yield plus or minus principal appreciation) than a bond fund. When rates are falling, balanced funds will also outperform bond funds if stocks are also doing well.

Over the past ten years (ending 3/31/99), the average balanced fund had 73 percent of the return of growth funds with 48 percent less risk. Balanced funds are the perfect choice for the investor who cannot decide between stocks and bonds. This hybrid security is a middle-of-the-road approach, ideal for someone who wants a fund manager to determine the portfolio's weighting of stocks, bonds, and convertibles.

The price-earnings ratio for stocks in a typical balanced fund is 29, a figure that is about 16 percent lower than the S&P 500's p/e ratio. The average beta is 0.6, which means that this group has only 60 percent of the market-related risk of the S&P 500. During the past three years, balanced funds have lagged the performance of the S&P 500 by 15 percent annually. Over the past five years, this benchmark has outperformed balanced funds by an average of 13 percent per year. The figure falls to 7 percent annually for the past decade. Standard deviation for the past three years has been 11.9 percent. Average turnover during the last three years has been 103 percent per annum. Balanced funds throw off an income stream of 2.4 percent annually. The typical annual expense ratio for this group is 1.4 percent.

Over 450 funds make up the balanced category; market capitalization is $200 billion. Three other categories, asset allocation (300 funds, total market capitalization of $80 billion, 11.6 percent standard deviation), multi-asset global (110 funds, total market capitalization of $40 billion, 12.3 percent standard deviation), and convertible (55 funds, total market capitalization of $7 billion, 12.9 percent standard deviation), have been combined with balanced. Thus, for this section, there were a total of 915 possible candidates. Total market capitalization of these four categories combined is $327 billion.

Balanced Funds

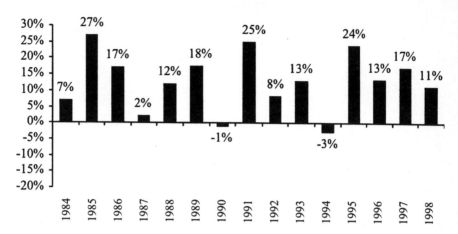

Flex-Funds Muirfield
6000 Memorial Drive
Dublin, OH 43017
800-325-3539

total return	★ ★ ★ ★ ★
risk reduction	★ ★ ★ ★ ★
management	★ ★ ★ ★ ★
current income	★
expense control	★ ★ ★
symbol FLMFX	19 points
up-market performance	very good
down-market performance	excellent
predictability of returns	fair

Total Return   ★ ★ ★ ★ ★

Over the past five years, Flex-Funds Muirfield has taken $10,000 and turned it into $21,589 ($15,348 over three years and $38,629 over the past ten years). This translates into an average annual return of 17 percent over the past five years, 19 percent over the past three years, and 14 percent for the decade. Over the past five years, this fund has outperformed 65 percent of all mutual funds; within its general category it has done better than 95 percent of its peers. Balanced funds have averaged 13 percent annually over these same five years.

During the past five years, a $10,000 initial investment grew to $15,250 after taxes, assuming a 39.6 percent income tax bracket (state and federal combined) and a capital gains rate of 28 percent. This means that investors in this fund were able to preserve 73 percent of their total returns. Compared to other fixed-income funds, this fund's tax savings are considered to be fair.

Risk/Volatility   ★ ★ ★ ★ ★

Over the past five years, Flex-Funds Muirfield has been safer than 90 percent of all balanced funds. Over the past decade, the fund has not had a negative year, while the S&P 500 has had one (off 3 percent in 1990); the Lehman Brothers Aggregate Bond Index also fell once (off 3 percent in 1994). The fund has underperformed the S&P seven times and the Lehman Brothers Aggregate Bond Index three times in the last ten years.

	last 5 years		last 10 years	
worst year	3%	1994	2%	1990
best year	30%	1998	30%	1991

In the past, Flex-Funds Muirfield has done better than 75 percent of its peer group in up markets and outperformed 100 percent of its competition in down markets. Consistency, or predictability, of returns for Flex-Funds Muirfield can be described as fair. This fund's risk-adjusted return is good.

Management ★ ★ ★ ★ ★
The fund is currently 100 percent in cash but normally invests in other mutual funds.

Robert Meeder Jr. has managed this fund for the past eleven years. There are four funds besides Muirfield within the Flex-Funds family.

Current Income ★
Over the past year, Flex-Funds Muirfield had a twelve-month yield of 1.3 percent. During this same twelve-month period, the typical balanced fund had a yield that averaged 2.4 percent.

Expenses ★ ★ ★
Flex-Funds Muirfield's expense ratio is 1.3 percent; it has also averaged 1.3 percent annually over the past three calendar years. The average expense ratio for the 875 funds in this category is 1.4 percent. This fund's turnover rate over the past year has been 395 percent, while its peer group average has been 105 percent.

Summary
Flex-Funds Muirfield has ranked in the top performance quartile over each of the past two years. The fund mostly invests in shares of other equity-oriented mutual funds but has been half, or more, in cash when manager Meeder feels that the market is overvalued. He is highly focused on the relationship between risk and reward. Asset allocation is decided upon by the use of a proprietary market-timing model based on four variables: interest rate forecasting, fundamental analysis, a technical overview, and a composition of market trends. The fund has a perfect score in the three most important categories: return, risk reduction, and management.

Profile
minimum initial investment $2,500	*IRA accounts available* . . . . yes
subsequent minimum investment . . $100	*IRA minimum investment* $500
available in all 50 states. . . . . yes	*date of inception* . . . . Aug. 1988
telephone exchanges. . . . . yes	*dividend/income paid* . . . . quarterly
number of other funds in family 4	*largest sector weighting* . . . . . . services

Gabelli Westwood Balanced Fund—Retail Class

One Corporate Center
Rye, NY 10580-1434
800-937-8966

total return	★ ★ ★ ★
risk reduction	★ ★ ★ ★ ★
management	★ ★ ★ ★
current income	★ ★
expense control	★ ★ ★ ★
symbol WEBAX	19 points
up-market performance	fair
down-market performance	very good
predictability of returns	excellent

Total Return   ★ ★ ★ ★

Over the past five years, Gabelli Westwood Balanced Fund—Retail Class has taken $10,000 and turned it into $21,589 ($15,348 over three years). This translates into an average annual return of 17 percent over the past five years and 15 percent over the past three years. Over the past five years, this fund has outperformed 85 percent of all mutual funds; within its general category it has done better than 95 percent of its peers. Balanced funds have averaged 13 percent annually over these same five years.

During the past five years, a $10,000 initial investment grew to $16,730 after taxes, assuming a 39.6 percent income tax bracket (state and federal combined) and a capital gains rate of 28 percent. This means that investors in this fund were able to preserve 79 percent of their total returns. Compared to other fixed-income funds, this fund's tax savings are considered to be good.

Risk/Volatility   ★ ★ ★ ★ ★

Over the past five years, Gabelli Westwood Balanced Fund—Retail Class has been safer than 85 percent of all balanced funds. Over the past decade, the fund has not had a negative year, while the S&P 500 has had one (off 3 percent in 1990); the Lehman Brothers Aggregate Bond Index also fell once (off 3 percent in 1994). The fund has underperformed the S&P six times and the Lehman Brothers Aggregate Bond Index once in the last ten years.

	last 5 years		since inception	
worst year	0.1%	1994	0.1%	1994
best year	31%	1995	31%	1995

In the past, Gabelli Westwood Balanced Fund—Retail Class has done better than 50 percent of its peer group in up markets and outperformed 75 percent of its competition in down markets. Consistency, or predictability, of returns for Gabelli Westwood Balanced Fund—Retail Class can be described as excellent. This fund's risk-adjusted return is good.

Management   ★ ★ ★ ★

There are fifty stocks and thirty-four fixed-income securities in this $160 million portfolio. The average balanced fund today is $362 million in size. Close to 60 percent of this fund's holdings are in stocks and 34 percent in bonds. The stocks in this portfolio have an average price-earnings (p/e) ratio of 29 and a median market capitalization of $24 billion. The average maturity of the bonds in this account is seven years; the weighted coupon rate averages 6.6 percent. The portfolio's equity holdings can be categorized as large-cap and value-oriented issues. The portfolio's fixed-income holdings can be categorized as intermediate-term, high-quality debt.

Susan Byrne and Patricia Fraze have managed this fund for the past eight years. There are ten funds besides Balanced within the Gabelli-Westwood family. Overall, the fund family's risk-adjusted performance can be described as good.

Current Income   ★ ★

Over the past year, Gabelli Westwood Balanced Fund—Retail Class had a twelve-month yield of 2.1 percent. During this same twelve-month period, the typical balanced fund had a yield that averaged 2.4 percent.

Expenses   ★ ★ ★ ★

Gabelli Westwood Balanced Fund—Retail Class's expense ratio is 1.2 percent; it has also averaged 1.2 percent annually over the past three calendar years. The average expense ratio for the 875 funds in this category is 1.4 percent. This fund's turnover rate over the past year has been 77 percent, while its peer group average has been 105 percent.

Summary

Gabelli Westwood Balanced Fund—Retail Class ranked in the top performance quartile every year from 1993 through 1997; recent performance has still been attractive and risk-adjusted returns are stellar. On the equity side, software, telecommunications, and pharmaceuticals are favored; debt instruments are the kind that benefits when there is a "flight to quality." Management uses a top-down approach (e.g., interest rates, inflation, corporate profits, etc.) to help determine the mix between stocks and bonds. The fund tries to strive for a 60/40 stock-to-bond mix.

Profile

minimum initial investment $1,000	*IRA accounts available* . . . . yes
subsequent minimum investment . . . $50	*IRA minimum investment* $1,000
available in all 50 states. . . . . yes	*date of inception* . . . . Oct. 1991
telephone exchanges. . . . . yes	*dividend/income paid* . . . . quarterly
number of other funds in family 10	*largest sector weighting* . . . . financials

Invesco Total Return

P.O. Box 173706
Denver, CO 80217-3706
800-525-8085

total return	★ ★ ★ ★
risk reduction	★ ★ ★ ★ ★
management	★ ★ ★ ★
current income	★ ★ ★
expense control	★ ★ ★ ★ ★
symbol FSFLX	21 points
up-market performance	poor
down-market performance	very good
predictability of returns	very good

Total Return ★ ★ ★ ★

Over the past five years, Invesco Total Return has taken $10,000 and turned it into $21,469 ($15,400 over three years and $36,267 over the past ten years). This translates into an average annual return of 17 percent over the past five years, 15 percent over the past three years, and 14 percent for the decade. Over the past five years, this fund has outperformed 85 percent of all mutual funds; within its general category it has done better than 95 percent of its peers. Balanced funds have averaged 13 percent annually over these same five years.

During the past five years, a $10,000 initial investment grew to $19,080 after taxes, assuming a 39.6 percent income tax bracket (state and federal combined) and a capital gains rate of 28 percent. This means that investors in this fund were able to preserve 90 percent of their total returns. Compared to other fixed-income funds, this fund's tax savings are considered to be excellent.

Risk/Volatility ★ ★ ★ ★ ★

Over the past five years, Invesco Total Return has been safer than 85 percent of all balanced funds. Over the past decade, the fund has had one negative year, while the S&P 500 has had one (off 3 percent in 1990); the Lehman Brothers Aggregate Bond Index also fell once (off 3 percent in 1994). The fund has underperformed the S&P six times and the Lehman Brothers Aggregate Bond Index once in the last ten years.

	last 5 years		last 10 years	
worst year	3%	1994	-3%	1990
best year	29%	1995	29%	1995

In the past, Invesco Total Return has done better than 25 percent of its peer group in up markets and outperformed 85 percent of its competition in down markets. Consistency, or predictability, of returns for Invesco Total Return can be described as very good. This fund's risk-adjusted return is good.

Management

There are ninety-nine stocks and sixty-two fixed-income securities in this $3.2 billion portfolio. The average balanced fund today is $362 million in size. Close to 68 percent of this fund's holdings are in stocks and 29 percent in bonds. The stocks in this portfolio have an average price-earnings (p/e) ratio of 22 and a median market capitalization of $13.8 billion. The average maturity of the bonds in this account is nine years; the weighted coupon rate averages 6.7 percent. The portfolio's equity holdings can be categorized as large-cap and value-oriented issues. The portfolio's fixed-income holdings can be categorized as intermediate-term, high-quality debt.

A team has managed this fund for the past five years. There are thirty-one funds besides Total Return within the Invesco family. Overall, the fund family's risk-adjusted performance can be described as very good.

Current Income   ★ ★ ★

Over the past year, Invesco Total Return had a twelve-month yield of 2.6 percent. During this same twelve-month period, the typical balanced fund had a yield that averaged 2.4 percent.

Expenses

Invesco Total Return's expense ratio is .8 percent; it has also averaged .8 percent annually over the past three calendar years. The average expense ratio for the 875 funds in this category is 1.4 percent. This fund's turnover rate over the past year has been 17 percent, while its peer group average has been 105 percent.

Summary

Invesco Total Return excels at risk reduction and expense control—two very important ingredients for a balanced fund. Management currently favors mid-cap and smaller large-cap companies for the stock portion and quality bonds that have very similar characteristics to the Lehman Brothers Government/Corporate Index.

Profile

minimum initial investment $1,000	*IRA accounts available* . . . . yes
subsequent minimum investment . . . $50	*IRA minimum investment* $250
available in all 50 states. . . . . yes	*date of inception* . . . . Sept. 1987
telephone exchanges. . . . . yes	*dividend/income paid* . . . . quarterly
number of other funds in family 31	*largest sector weighting.* . . . . . industrial cyclicals

Oppenheimer Quest Opportunity Value Fund A
P.O. Box 5270
Denver, CO 80217-5270
800-525-7048

total return	★ ★ ★ ★ ★
risk reduction	★ ★ ★ ★
management	★ ★ ★ ★
current income	★
expense control	★ ★ ★
symbol QVOPX	17 points
up-market performance	poor
down-market performance	very good
predictability of returns	good

Total Return   ★ ★ ★ ★ ★
Over the past five years, Oppenheimer Quest Opportunity Value Fund A has taken $10,000 and turned it into $24,237 ($15,090 over three years and $47,945 over the past ten years). This translates into an average annual return of 19 percent over the past five years, 15 percent over the past three years, and 17 percent for the decade. Over the past five years, this fund has outperformed 95 percent of all mutual funds; within its general category it has done better than 75 percent of its peers. Balanced funds have averaged 13 percent annually over these same five years.

During the past five years, a $10,000 initial investment grew to $21,560 after taxes, assuming a 39.6 percent income tax bracket (state and federal combined) and a capital gains rate of 28 percent. This means that investors in this fund were able to preserve 91 percent of their total returns. Compared to other fixed-income funds, this fund's tax savings are considered to be excellent.

Risk/Volatility   ★ ★ ★ ★
Over the past five years, Oppenheimer Quest Opportunity Value Fund A has been safer than 75 percent of all balanced funds. Over the past decade, the fund has had one negative year, while the S&P 500 has had one (off 3 percent in 1990); the Lehman Brothers Aggregate Bond Index also fell once (off 3 percent in 1994). The fund has underperformed the S&P six times and the Lehman Brothers Aggregate Bond Index twice in the last ten years.

	last 5 years		last 10 years	
worst year	5%	1994	-10%	1990
best year	42%	1995	51%	1991

In the past, Oppenheimer Quest Opportunity Value Fund A has done better than 15 percent of its peer group in up markets and outperformed 75 percent of its competition in down markets. Consistency, or predictability, of returns for Oppenheimer Quest Opportunity Value Fund A can be described as good. This fund's risk-adjusted return is poor.

Management   ★ ★ ★ ★
There are forty-two stocks in this $1.9 billion portfolio. The average balanced fund today is $362 million in size. Close to 90 percent of this fund's holdings are in stocks and 5 percent in bonds. The stocks in this portfolio have an average price-earnings (p/e) ratio of 25 and a median market capitalization of $33 billion.

Richard Glasebrook II has managed this fund for the past eight years. There are forty-three funds besides Quest Opportunity Value within the Oppenheimer family. Overall, the fund family's risk-adjusted performance can be described as very good.

Current Income   ★
Over the past year, Oppenheimer Quest Opportunity Value Fund A had a twelve-month yield of .8 percent. During this same twelve-month period, the typical balanced fund had a yield that averaged 2.4 percent.

Expenses   ★ ★ ★
Oppenheimer Quest Opportunity Value Fund A's expense ratio is 1.5 percent; it has averaged 1.6 percent annually over the past three calendar years. The average expense ratio for the 875 funds in this category is 1.4 percent. This fund's turnover rate over the past year has been 45 percent, while its peer group average has been 105 percent.

Summary
Oppenheimer Quest Opportunity Value Fund A has frequently been in the top quartile of performance since its 1989 inception. Manager Glasebrook emphasizes stocks over bonds and is often fond of value issues. He is a "hands on" type of guy who personally visits a large number of companies each year. The fund is very interested in companies that respond to shareholder concerns.

Profile
minimum initial investment $1,000	*IRA accounts available* . . . . yes
subsequent minimum investment . . . $25	*IRA minimum investment* $250
available in all 50 states. . . . . yes	*date of inception* . . . . Jan. 1989
telephone exchanges. . . . . yes	*dividend/income paid* . . . . annually
number of other funds in family 43	*largest sector weighting.* . . . . . industrial cyclicals

Preferred Asset Allocation
P.O. Box 8320
Boston, MA 02266-8320
800-662-4769

total return	★ ★ ★ ★ ★
risk reduction	★ ★ ★ ★ ★
management	★ ★ ★ ★ ★
current income	★ ★ ★
expense control	★ ★ ★ ★ ★
symbol PFAAX	23 points
up-market performance	very good
down-market performance	excellent
predictability of returns	very good

Total Return   ★ ★ ★ ★ ★

Over the past five years, Preferred Asset Allocation has taken $10,000 and turned it into $24,217 ($17,419 over three years). This translates into an average annual return of 19 percent over the past five years, and 20 percent over the past three years. Over the past five years, this fund has outperformed 85 percent of all mutual funds; within its general category it has done better than 95 percent of its peers. Balanced funds have averaged 13 percent annually over these same five years.

During the past five years, a $10,000 initial investment grew to $18,550 after taxes, assuming a 39.6 percent income tax bracket (state and federal combined) and a capital gains rate of 28 percent. This means that investors in this fund were able to preserve 81 percent of their total returns. Compared to other fixed-income funds, this fund's tax savings are considered to be very good.

Risk/Volatility   ★ ★ ★ ★ ★

Over the past five years, Preferred Asset Allocation has been safer than 85 percent of all balanced funds. Over the past decade, the fund has had one negative year, while the S&P 500 has had one (off 3 percent in 1990); the Lehman Brothers Aggregate Bond Index also fell once (off 3 percent in 1994). The fund has under-performed the S&P five times and has outperformed the Lehman Brothers Aggregate Bond Index every year for the last ten years.

	last 5 years		since inception	
worst year	-3%	1994	-3%	1994
best year	33%	1995	33%	1995

In the past, Preferred Asset Allocation has done better than 85 percent of its peer group in up markets and outperformed 100 percent of its competition in down markets. Consistency, or predictability, of returns for Preferred Asset Allocation can be described as very good. This fund's risk-adjusted return is excellent.

Management   ★ ★ ★ ★ ★

There are 505 stocks and 33 fixed-income securities in this $230 million portfolio. The average balanced fund today is $362 million in size. Close to 44 percent of this fund's holdings are in stocks and 31 percent in bonds. The stocks in this portfolio have an average price-earnings (p/e) ratio of 34 and a median market capitalization of $65 billion. The average maturity of the bonds in this account is twenty-two years; the weighted coupon rate averages 8.3 percent. The portfolio's equity holdings can be categorized as large-cap and a blend of growth and value stocks. The portfolio's fixed-income holdings can be categorized as long-term, high-quality debt.

Thomas Hazuka has managed this fund for the past seven years. There are six funds besides Asset Allocation within the Preferred family. Overall, the fund family's risk-adjusted performance can be described as very good.

Current Income   ★ ★ ★

Over the past year, Preferred Asset Allocation had a twelve-month yield of 2.6 percent. During this same twelve-month period, the typical balanced fund had a yield that averaged 2.4 percent.

Expenses   ★ ★ ★ ★ ★

Preferred Asset Allocation's expense ratio is .9 percent; it has averaged 1 percent annually over the past three calendar years. The average expense ratio for the 875 funds in this category is 1.4 percent. This fund's turnover rate over the past year has been 28 percent, while its peer group average has been 105 percent.

Summary

Preferred Asset Allocation frequently waffles between the first and second quartile when it comes to performance in its peer group. Overall, it scores a near perfect score of 23 out of 25 points, making it the number one choice for the balanced, total return, or asset allocation fund investor. Management is very risk conscious and it is not uncommon for the fund to have only a modest weighting in equities. This fund is highly recommended.

Profile

minimum initial investment $1,000	*IRA accounts available* . . . . yes
subsequent minimum investment . . . $50	*IRA minimum investment* $250
available in all 50 states. . . . . yes	*date of inception.* . . . . June 1992
telephone exchanges. . . . . yes	*dividend/income paid* . . . . quarterly
number of other funds in family 6	*largest sector weighting* . . . technology

Stagecoach Asset Allocation A
111 Center Street
Little Rock, AR 72201
800-222-8222

total return	★ ★ ★ ★
risk reduction	★ ★ ★
management	★ ★ ★ ★
current income	★
expense control	★ ★ ★ ★
symbol PFAAX	16 points
up-market performance	very good
down-market performance	good
predictability of returns	good

Total Return   ★ ★ ★ ★

Over the past five years, Stagecoach Asset Allocation A has taken $10,000 and turned it into $23,004 ($17,297 over three years and $38,934 over the past ten years). This translates into an average annual return of 18 percent over the past five years, 20 percent over the past three years, and 15 percent for the decade. Over the past five years, this fund has outperformed 80 percent of all mutual funds; within its general category it has done better than 85 percent of its peers. Balanced funds have averaged 13 percent annually over these same five years.

During the past five years, a $10,000 initial investment grew to $17,040 after taxes, assuming a 39.6 percent income tax bracket (state and federal combined) and a capital gains rate of 28 percent. This means that investors in this fund were able to preserve 79 percent of their total returns. Compared to other fixed-income funds, this fund's tax savings are considered to be good.

Risk/Volatility   ★ ★ ★

Over the past five years, Stagecoach Asset Allocation A has been safer than 50 percent of all balanced funds. Over the past decade, the fund has had one negative year, while the S&P 500 has had one (off 3 percent in 1990); the Lehman Brothers Aggregate Bond Index also fell once (off 3 percent in 1994). The fund has underperformed the S&P eight times and the Lehman Brothers Aggregate Bond Index three times in the last ten years.

	last 5 years		last 10 years	
worst year	-3%	1994	-3%	1994
best year	29%	1995	29%	1995

In the past, Stagecoach Asset Allocation A has done better than 85 percent of its peer group in up markets and outperformed 65 percent of its competition in down markets. Consistency, or predictability, of returns for Stagecoach Asset Allocation A can be described as good. This fund's risk-adjusted return is good.

Management   ★ ★ ★ ★

There are 503 stocks and 24 fixed-income securities in this $1.4 billion portfolio. The average balanced fund today is $362 million in size. Close to 70 percent of this fund's holdings are in stocks and 22 percent in bonds. The stocks in this portfolio have an average price-earnings (p/e) ratio of 33 and a median market capitalization of $61 billion. The average maturity of the bonds in this account is twenty-three years; the weighted coupon rate averages 7.6 percent. The portfolio's equity holdings can be categorized as large-cap and a blend of growth and value stocks. The portfolio's fixed-income holdings can be categorized as high-quality, long-term debt.

A team has managed this fund for the past eleven years. There are twenty-five funds besides Asset Allocation within the Stagecoach family. Overall, the fund family's risk-adjusted performance can be described as good.

Current Income   ★

Over the past year, Stagecoach Asset Allocation A had a twelve-month yield of 1.5 percent. During this same twelve-month period, the typical balanced fund had a yield that averaged 2.4 percent.

Expenses   ★ ★ ★ ★

Stagecoach Asset Allocation A's expense ratio is 1 percent; it has averaged .9 percent annually over the past three calendar years. The average expense ratio for the 875 funds in this category is 1.4 percent. This fund's turnover rate over the past year has been 51 percent, while its peer group average has been 105 percent.

Summary

Stagecoach Asset Allocation A has ranked in the top performance quartile for each of the past several years. Well-known large-cap stocks are emphasized; the modest to moderate debt portion is mostly in T-bills and T-notes. These short-term instruments lower overall risk more than most investors realize.

Profile

minimum initial investment $1,000	*IRA accounts available* . . . . yes
subsequent minimum investment . . $100	*IRA minimum investment* $250
available in all 50 states. . . . . yes	*date of inception* . . . . Nov. 1986
telephone exchanges. . . . . yes	*dividend/income paid* . . . . quarterly
number of other funds in family 25	*largest sector weighting* . . . . financials

Value Line Asset Allocation
220 East 42nd Street
New York, NY 10017-5891
800-223-0818

total return	★ ★ ★ ★ ★
risk reduction	★ ★
management	★ ★ ★ ★
current income	★
expense control	★ ★
symbol PFAAX	14 points
up-market performance	excellent
down-market performance	poor
predictability of returns	poor

Total Return   ★ ★ ★ ★ ★

Over the past five years, Value Line Asset Allocation has taken $10,000 and turned it into $27,755 ($18,100 over three years). This translates into an average annual return of 23 percent over the past five years, and 22 percent over the past three years. Over the past five years, this fund has outperformed 95 percent of all mutual funds; within its general category it has done better than 97 percent of its peers. Balanced funds have averaged 13 percent annually over these same five years.

During the past five years, a $10,000 initial investment grew to $20,300 after taxes, assuming a 39.6 percent income tax bracket (state and federal combined) and a capital gains rate of 28 percent. This means that investors in this fund were able to preserve 75 percent of their total returns. Compared to other fixed-income funds, this fund's tax savings are considered to be good.

Risk/Volatility   ★ ★

Over the past five years, Value Line Asset Allocation has been safer than 25 percent of all balanced funds. Over the past decade, the fund has not had a negative year, while the S&P 500 has had one (off 3 percent in 1990); the Lehman Brothers Aggregate Bond Index also fell once (off 3 percent in 1994). The fund has underperformed the S&P three times and has outperformed the Lehman Brothers Aggregate Bond Index every year for the last ten years.

	last 5 years		since inception	
worst year	3%	1994	3%	1994
best year	36%	1995	36%	1995

In the past, Value Line Asset Allocation has done better than 90 percent of its peer group in up markets and outperformed 30 percent of its competition in down markets. Consistency, or predictability, of returns for Value Line Asset Allocation can be described as poor. This fund's risk-adjusted return is fair.

Management   ★ ★ ★ ★
There are 306 stocks and 10 fixed-income securities in this $175 million portfolio. The average balanced fund today is $362 million in size. Close to 85 percent of this fund's holdings are in stocks and 7 percent in bonds. The stocks in this portfolio have an average price-earnings (p/e) ratio of 35 and a median market capitalization of $2.6 billion. The average maturity of the bonds in this account is ten years; the weighted coupon rate averages 6.2 percent. The portfolio's equity holdings can be categorized as mid-cap and growth-oriented issues. The portfolio's fixed-income holdings can be categorized as intermediate-term, high-quality debt.

A team has managed this fund for the past six years. There are thirteen funds besides Asset Allocation within the Value Line family. Overall, the fund family's risk-adjusted performance can be described as fair.

Current Income   ★
Over the past year, Value Line Asset Allocation had a twelve-month yield of .1 percent. During this same twelve-month period, the typical balanced fund had a yield that averaged 2.4 percent.

Expenses   ★ ★
Value Line Asset Allocation's expense ratio is 1.2 percent; it has averaged 1.3 percent annually over the past three calendar years. The average expense ratio for the 875 funds in this category is 1.4 percent. This fund's turnover rate over the past year has been 139 percent, while its peer group average has been 105 percent.

Summary
Value Line Asset Allocation invests in high-quality bonds, much like its peer group, but strays from the crowd when it comes to equities, focusing on small- and mid-cap issues. Manager Grant uses a quantitative modeling system that helps sort out the best price momentum and earnings trends. Stocks that fall out of favor are quickly dumped. The allocation to stocks has been as high as 90 percent or more in the past. This is one fund that is not afraid to overweight equities when it feels the market is hot. Management's calls have usually been correct as evidenced by the fund's excellent track record.

Profile
minimum initial investment $1,000	*IRA accounts available* . . . . yes
subsequent minimum investment . . $100	*IRA minimum investment* $1,000
available in all 50 states. . . . . yes	*date of inception* . . . . Aug. 1993
telephone exchanges. . . . . yes	*dividend/income paid* . . . . annually
number of other funds in family 13	*largest sector weighting* . . . technology

Vanguard Asset Allocation
Vanguard Financial Center
P.O. Box 2600
Valley Forge, PA 19482
800-662-7447

total return	★ ★ ★ ★ ★
risk reduction	★ ★ ★
management	★ ★ ★ ★ ★
current income	★
expense control	★ ★ ★ ★ ★
symbol PFAAX	19 points
up-market performance	very good
down-market performance	very good
predictability of returns	good

Total Return   ★ ★ ★ ★ ★

Over the past five years, Vanguard Asset Allocation has taken $10,000 and turned it into $25,884 ($18,154 over three years and $45,464 over the past ten years). This translates into an average annual return of 21 percent over the past five years, 22 percent over the past three years, and 16 percent for the decade. Over the past five years, this fund has outperformed 95 percent of all mutual funds; within its general category it has done better than 97 percent of its peers. Balanced funds have averaged 13 percent annually over these same five years.

During the past five years, a $10,000 initial investment grew to $19,920 after taxes, assuming a 39.6 percent income tax bracket (state and federal combined) and a capital gains rate of 28 percent. This means that investors in this fund were able to preserve 81 percent of their total returns. Compared to other fixed-income funds, this fund's tax savings are considered to be very good.

Risk/Volatility   ★ ★ ★

Over the past five years, Vanguard Asset Allocation has been safer than 60 percent of all balanced funds. Over the past decade, the fund has had one negative year, while the S&P 500 has had one (off 3 percent in 1990); the Lehman Brothers Aggregate Bond Index also fell once (off 3 percent in 1994). The fund has underperformed the S&P eight times and the Lehman Brothers Aggregate Bond Index once in the last ten years.

	last 5 years		last 10 years	
Worst year	-2%	1994	-2%	1994
best year	35%	1995	35%	1995

In the past, Vanguard Asset Allocation has done better than 75 percent of its peer group in up markets and outperformed 85 percent of its competition in down markets. Consistency, or predictability, of returns for Vanguard Asset Allocation can be described as good. This fund's risk-adjusted return is excellent.

Management   ★ ★ ★ ★ ★
There are 504 stocks and 23 fixed-income securities in this $7.4 billion portfolio. The average balanced fund today is $362 million in size. Close to 50 percent of this fund's holdings are in stocks and 40 percent in bonds. The stocks in this portfolio have an average price-earnings (p/e) ratio of 34 and a median market capitalization of $65 billion. The average maturity of the bonds in this account is twenty-two years; the weighted coupon rate averages 8.4 percent. The portfolio's equity holdings can be categorized as large-cap and a blend of growth and value stocks. The portfolio's fixed-income holdings can be categorized as long-term, high-quality debt.

William Fouse & Thomas Loeb have managed this fund for the past eleven years. There are sixty-eight funds besides Asset Allocation within the Vanguard family. Overall, the fund family's risk-adjusted performance can be described as very good.

Current Income   ★
Over the past year, Vanguard Asset Allocation had a twelve-month yield of 2.9 percent. During this same twelve-month period, the typical balanced fund had a yield that averaged 2.4 percent.

Expenses   ★ ★ ★ ★ ★
Vanguard Asset Allocation's expense ratio is .5 percent; it has also averaged .5 percent annually over the past three calendar years. The average expense ratio for the 875 funds in this category is 1.4 percent. This fund's turnover rate over the past year has been 60 percent, while its peer group average has been 105 percent.

Summary
Vanguard Asset Allocation tries to maintain a weighting of 60 percent equities and 40 percent in bonds, but states that it could go up to 100 percent in either category. It is the asset mix, not so much individual stock selection, that most concerns management—equities typically mirror the return and risk characteristics of the S&P 500. Management earns a rating of exceptional, partially due to its keen eye on expenses and turnover. Returns have also been superb for an asset allocation or balanced fund.

Profile
minimum initial investment $3,000	*IRA accounts available* . . . . yes
subsequent minimum investment . . $100	*IRA minimum investment* $1,000
available in all 50 states. . . . . yes	*date of inception* . . . . Nov. 1988
telephone exchanges. . . . . yes	*dividend/income paid.* . . . . semiannually
number of other funds in family. 68	*largest sector weighting* . . . technology

Vanguard Balanced Index
Vanguard Financial Center
P.O. Box 2600
Valley Forge, PA 19482
800-662-7447

total return	★★★★
risk reduction	★★★★
management	★★★★★
current income	★★★★
expense control	★★★★★
symbol VBINX	22 points
up-market performance	very good
down-market performance	good
predictability of returns	very good

Total Return   ★★★★

Over the past five years, Vanguard Balanced Index has taken $10,000 and turned it into $22,000 ($16,351 over three years). This translates into an average annual return of 18 percent over the past five years and 17 percent over the past three years. Over the past five years, this fund has outperformed 80 percent of all mutual funds; within its general category it has done better than 85 percent of its peers. Balanced funds have averaged 13 percent annually over these same five years.

During the past five years, a $10,000 initial investment grew to $17,810 after taxes, assuming a 39.6 percent income tax bracket (state and federal combined) and a capital gains rate of 28 percent. This means that investors in this fund were able to preserve 86 percent of their total returns. Compared to other fixed-income funds, this fund's tax savings are considered to be very good.

Risk/Volatility   ★★★★

Over the past five years, Vanguard Balanced Index has been safer than 75 percent of all balanced funds. Over the past decade, the fund has had one negative year, while the S&P 500 has had one (off 3 percent in 1990); the Lehman Brothers Aggregate Bond Index also fell once (off 3 percent in 1994). The fund has under-performed the S&P six times and has outperformed the Lehman Brothers Aggregate Bond Index every year for the last ten years.

	last 5 years		since inception	
worst year	-2%	1994	-2%	1994
best year	29%	1995	29%	1995

In the past, Vanguard Balanced Index has done better than 75 percent of its peer group in up markets and outperformed 65 percent of its competition in down markets. Consistency, or predictability, of returns for Vanguard Balanced Index can be described as very good. This fund's risk-adjusted return is good.

Management ★ ★ ★ ★ ★

There are 2,800 stocks and 1,060 fixed-income securities in this $2.1 billion portfolio. The average balanced fund today is $362 million in size. Close to 60 percent of this fund's holdings are in stocks and 40 percent in bonds. The stocks in this portfolio have an average price-earnings (p/e) ratio of 33 and a median market capitalization of $38 billion. The average maturity of the bonds in this account is nine years; the weighted coupon rate averages 7.4 percent. The portfolio's equity holdings can be categorized as large-cap and a blend of growth and value stocks. The portfolio's fixed-income holdings can be categorized as intermediate-term, high-quality debt.

A team has managed this fund for the past seven years. There are sixty-eight funds besides Balanced Index within the Vanguard family. Overall, the fund family's risk-adjusted performance can be described as very good.

Current Income ★ ★ ★ ★

Over the past year, Vanguard Balanced Index had a twelve-month yield of 2.9 percent. During this same twelve-month period, the typical balanced fund had a yield that averaged 2.4 percent.

Expenses ★ ★ ★ ★ ★

Vanguard Balanced Index's expense ratio is .2 percent; it has also averaged .2 percent annually over the past three calendar years. The average expense ratio for the 875 funds in this category is 1.4 percent. This fund's turnover rate over the past year has been 25 percent, while its peer group average has been 105 percent.

Summary

Vanguard Balanced Index ranks as the second best fund within its category and misses out on first place by only one point. Like the several other Vanguard offerings in this book, management ensures that turnover, expenses, and taxation are at a bare minimum. Management's goal is to duplicate Wilshire 500 Index returns for the roughly 60 percent in equities and the Lehman Brothers Aggregate Bond Index for the remaining 40 percent of the portfolio.

Profile

minimum initial investment $3,000	*IRA accounts available* . . . . yes
subsequent minimum investment . . $100	*IRA minimum investment* $1,000
available in all 50 states. . . . . yes	*date of inception* . . . . Sept. 1992
telephone exchanges. . . . . yes	*dividend/income paid* . . . . quarterly
number of other funds in family 68	*largest sector weighting* . . . technology

Vanguard Wellington
Vanguard Financial Center
P.O. Box 2600
Valley Forge, PA 19482
800-662-7447

total return	★★★★
risk reduction	★★★
management	★★★★
current income	★★★★★
expense control	★★★★★
symbol VWELX	21 points
up-market performance	poor
down-market performance	very good
predictability of returns	very good

Total Return   ★★★★

Over the past five years, Vanguard Wellington has taken $10,000 and turned it into $22,094 ($15,548 over three years and $35,823 over the past ten years). This translates into an average annual return of 17 percent over the past five years, 16 percent over the past three years, and 14 percent for the decade. Over the past five years, this fund has outperformed 85 percent of all mutual funds; within its general category it has done better than 95 percent of its peers. Balanced funds have averaged 13 percent annually over these same five years.

During the past five years, a $10,000 initial investment grew to $18,600 after taxes, assuming a 39.6 percent income tax bracket (state and federal combined) and a capital gains rate of 28 percent. This means that investors in this fund were able to preserve 88 percent of their total returns. Compared to other fixed-income funds, this fund's tax savings are considered to be very good.

Risk/Volatility   ★★★

Over the past five years, Vanguard Wellington has been safer than 55 percent of all balanced funds. Over the past decade, the fund has had two negative years, while the S&P 500 has had one (off 3 percent in 1990); the Lehman Brothers Aggregate Bond Index also fell once (off 3 percent in 1994). The fund has underperformed the S&P seven times and the Lehman Brothers Aggregate Bond Index once in the last ten years.

	last 5 years		last 10 years	
worst year	-0.5%	1994	-3%	1990
best year	33%	1995	33%	1995

In the past, Vanguard Wellington has done better than 25 percent of its peer group in up markets and outperformed 85 percent of its competition in down markets. Consistency, or predictability, of returns for Vanguard Wellington can be described as very good. This fund's risk-adjusted return is fair.

Management   ★ ★ ★ ★

There are 105 stocks and 226 fixed-income securities in this $26 billion portfolio. The average balanced fund today is $362 million in size. Close to 57 percent of this fund's holdings are in stocks and 37 percent in bonds. The stocks in this portfolio have an average price-earnings (p/e) ratio of 25 and a median market capitalization of $23 billion. The average maturity of the bonds in this account is seventeen years; the weighted coupon rate averages 7.1 percent. The portfolio's equity holdings can be categorized as large-cap and value-oriented issues. The portfolio's fixed-income holdings can be categorized as long-term, high-quality debt.

Paul Kaplan and Ernst von Metzsch have managed this fund for the past five years. There are sixty-eight funds besides Wellington within the Vanguard family. Overall, the fund family's risk-adjusted performance can be described as very good.

Current Income   ★ ★ ★ ★ ★

Over the past year, Vanguard Wellington had a twelve-month yield of 3.7 percent. During this same twelve-month period, the typical balanced fund had a yield that averaged 2.4 percent.

Expenses   ★ ★ ★ ★ ★

Vanguard Wellington's expense ratio is .3 percent; it has also averaged .3 percent annually over the past three calendar years. The average expense ratio for the 875 funds in this category is 1.4 percent. This fund's turnover rate over the past year has been 29 percent, while its peer group average has been 105 percent.

Summary

Vanguard Wellington has more investment flexibility than most other Vanguard offerings but the fund is still characterized by the company's near-legendary concern over expenses, turnover, and tax efficiency. Equities typically represent 60–70 percent of the fund's holdings, a smart move since stocks historically have dramatically outperformed bonds and other debt instruments. Management uses a fundamental value approach when selecting equities and prefers large-cap issues. Bond duration is long.

Profile

minimum initial investment $3,000
subsequent minimum investment . . $100
available in all 50 states. . . . . yes
telephone exchanges. . . . . yes
number of other funds in family. 68

IRA accounts available . . . . yes
IRA minimum investment $1,000
date of inception . . . . July 1929
dividend/income paid . . . . quarterly
largest sector weighting. . . . . industrial
                                        cyclicals

Corporate Bond Funds

Traditionally, bond funds are held by investors who require high current income and low risk. Interest income is normally paid on a monthly basis. Corporate bond funds are made up primarily of bonds issued by domestic corporations; government securities often represent a moderate part of these funds. Portfolio composition is almost always exclusively U.S. issues.

Bonds are normally purchased because of their income stream; one's principal in a bond fund fluctuates. The major influence on bond prices, and therefore the value of the fund's shares, is interest rates. There is an inverse relationship between interest rates and bond values; whatever one does, the other does the opposite. If interest rates rise, the price per share of a bond fund will fall, and vice versa.

The amount of appreciation or loss of a corporate bond fund primarily depends upon the average maturity of the bonds in the portfolio; the cumulative amount of interest rate movement and the typical yield of the bonds in the fund's portfolio are distant secondary concerns. Short-term bond funds, made up of debt instruments with an average maturity of five years or less, are subject to very little interest rate risk or reward. Medium-term bond funds, with maturities averaging between six and ten years, are subject to one-third to one-half the risk level of long-term funds. A long-term corporate bond fund will average roughly an 8 percent increase or decrease in share price for every cumulative 1 percent change in interest rates.

Often investors can tell what kind of corporate bond fund they are purchasing by its name. Unless the fund includes the term "short" in its title, chances are that it is a medium- or long-term bond fund. Investors would be wise to contact the fund or counsel with an investment advisor to learn more about the portfolio's average maturity; most bond funds will dramatically reduce their portfolio's average maturity during periods of interest-rate uncertainty.

The average weighted maturity for the bonds in these funds is just over eight years, the average coupon rate is 6.9 percent, and the average weighted price is $1,035 (meaning that the bonds are worth $35 more than face value, on average). A price, or value, of par ($1,000 per bond) means that the bonds in a portfolio are worth face value and are not currently being traded at a discount (a price less than $1,000 per bond) or at a premium (some figure above $1,000). The portfolio of the "average" corporate bond fund is made up of securities purchased at a $35 per-bond premium ($1,035 vs. $1,000 for bonds bought at face value). A portfolio manager purchases bonds at a premium for one of two reasons: to increase the portfolio's current income, or to decrease the fund's volatility slightly (the higher the coupon rate, the less susceptible a bond is to the effects of interest-rate changes).

During the past three, five, and ten years, corporate bond funds have underperformed the Lehman Brothers Aggregate Bond Index by 1 percent per year. Average turnover during the last three years has been 149 percent, a surprisingly high figure given the general belief that stocks are traded (turned over) much more frequently than bonds. (The typical growth fund has a turnover rate of 94 percent annually.) The average corporate bond fund throws off an annual income stream of about 5.7 percent. The typical annual expense ratio for this group is 0.9 percent.

Over the past fifteen years, individual corporate bonds have underperformed common stocks by over 9 percent per year. From 1984 to 1999, long-term corporate bonds averaged 9.5 percent compounded per year, compared to 18.5 percent for common stocks and 13.0 percent for small stocks. A $10,000 investment in corporate bonds grew to $56,360 over the past fifteen years; a similar initial investment in common stocks grew to $118,290 and just $47,960 for small stocks.

Over the past half century, corporate bonds have outpaced inflation only on a pretax basis. A dollar invested in corporate bonds at the beginning of 1949 grew to $20.20 by the end of 1998. This translates into an average compound return of 6.2 percent per year. During this same period, $1 inflated to $6.80; this translates into an average annual inflation rate of 3.9 percent. Assuming an *historical* combined state and federal income tax bracket of 50 percent, 6.2 percent becomes 3.1 percent after taxes, a figure less than the 3.9 percent rate of inflation. Over the past fifty years, the worst year for long-term corporate bonds, on a total return basis (yield plus or minus principal appreciation or loss), was 1969, when a loss of 8 percent was suffered. The best year so far has been 1982, when corporate bonds posted a gain of 43 percent.

Over 830 funds make up the corporate bonds category. Total market capitalization of this category is $230 billion. Over the past three and five years, corporate bond funds have had an average compound return of 6.7 percent per year. For the decade, corporate bond funds have averaged 8.2 percent per year and 9.5 percent per annum for the past fifteen years (all figures ending 3/31/99). All of these figures represent total returns. This means that bond appreciation (or depreciation) was added (or subtracted) from current yield.

The standard deviation for corporate bond funds has been 3.5 percent over the past three years. As you may recall, a low standard deviation means a greater predictability of returns (fewer surprises, for better or worse). If a fund, or fund category, such as corporate bonds, has an average annual return of 10 percent and a standard deviation of 3.5 percent, this means that returns for every two out of three years should be roughly 10 percent, plus or minus 3.5 percent (one standard deviation). If you want to increase certainty of returns, then you must look at two standard deviations. This means that returns, for about 95 percent of the time, would be 10 percent plus or minus 7.0 percent (or +3.0 percent to +17.0 percent). These funds have been less volatile than any equity fund and have shown similar return variances (volatility) as government bond funds.

Corporate Bond Funds

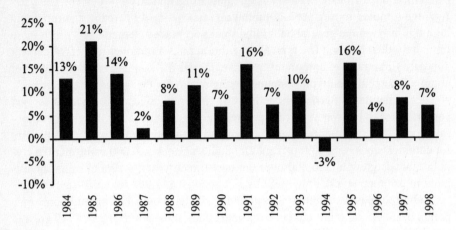

Fremont Bond

50 Beale Street, Suite 100
San Francisco, CA 94105
800-548-4539

total return	★ ★ ★ ★
risk reduction	★ ★ ★
management	★ ★ ★
current income	★ ★ ★ ★ ★
expense control	★ ★
symbol FBDFX	17 points
up-market performance	good
down-market performance	excellent
predictability of returns	good

Total Return   ★ ★ ★ ★

Over the past five years, Fremont Bond has taken $10,000 and turned it into $15,260 ($13,022 over three years). This translates into an average annual return of 8 percent over the past five years and 8 percent over the past three years. Over the past five years, this fund has outperformed 60 percent of all mutual funds; within its general category it has done better than 99 percent of its peers. Corporate bond funds have averaged 7 percent annually over these same five years.

During the past five years, a $10,000 initial investment grew to $12,880 after taxes, assuming a 39.6 percent income tax bracket (state and federal combined) and a capital gains rate of 28 percent. This means that investors in this fund were able to preserve 87 percent of their total returns. Compared to other fixed-income funds, this fund's tax savings are considered to be excellent.

Risk/Volatility   ★ ★ ★

Over the past five years, Fremont Bond has been safer than 50 percent of all corporate bond funds. Over the past decade, the fund has had one negative year, while the Lehman Brothers Aggregate Bond Index has had one (off 3 percent in 1994); the Lehman Brothers Corporate Bond Index also fell once (off 4 percent in 1994). The fund has underperformed the Lehman Brothers Aggregate Bond Index once and the Lehman Brothers Corporate Bond Index once in the last ten years.

	last 5 years		since inception	
worst year	-4%	1994	-4%	1994
best year	21%	1995	21%	1995

In the past, Fremont Bond has done better than 65 percent of its peer group in up markets and outperformed 90 percent of its competition in down markets. Consistency, or predictability, of returns for Fremont Bond can be described as good. This fund's risk-adjusted return is excellent.

Management   ★ ★ ★

There are seventy-four fixed-income securities in this $230 million portfolio. The average corporate bond fund today is $265 million in size. Close to 100 percent of the funds holdings are in bonds. The average maturity of the bonds in this account is seven years; the weighted coupon rate averages 6.9 percent. The portfolio's fixed-income holdings can be categorized as intermediate-term, high-quality debt.

William Gross has managed this fund for the past five years. There are eleven funds besides Bond within the Fremont family. Overall, the fund family's risk-adjusted performance can be described as good.

Current Income   ★ ★ ★ ★ ★

Over the past year, Fremont Bond had a twelve-month yield of 6.9 percent. During this same twelve-month period, the typical corporate bond fund had a yield that averaged 5.7 percent.

Expenses   ★ ★

Fremont Bond's expense ratio is .6 percent; it has also averaged .6 percent annually over the past three calendar years. The average expense ratio for the 850 funds in this category is 1.0 percent. This fund's turnover rate over the past year has been 250 percent, while its peer group average has been 150 percent.

Summary

Fremont Bond has placed in the top performance quartile for each of the past four calendar years—something that few of its peers have been able to accomplish. Legendary manager Bill Gross keeps the portfolio's duration within a year or so of the Lehman Brothers Aggregate Index's. Gross looks at a number of economic and interest rate indicators in order to determine which sector (e.g., mortgage-backed, high quality, high yield, etc.) to favor. This fund will appeal to anyone looking for current income with little risk.

Profile

minimum initial investment $2,000	*IRA accounts available* . . . . yes
subsequent minimum investment . . $100	*IRA minimum investment* $1,000
available in all 50 states. . . . . yes	*date of inception* . . . . April 1993
telephone exchanges. . . . . yes	*dividend/income paid*. . . . . monthly
number of other funds in family 11	*average credit quality*. . . . . AA

Invesco Select Income

P.O. Box 173706
Denver, CO 80217-3706
800-525-8085

total return	★ ★ ★ ★
risk reduction	★ ★ ★ ★ ★
management	★ ★ ★ ★ ★
current income	★ ★ ★ ★ ★
expense control	★ ★ ★
symbol FBDSX	
up-market performance	22 points
down-market performance	very good
predictability of returns	poor
	good

Total Return   ★ ★ ★ ★

Over the past five years, Invesco Select Income has taken $10,000 and turned it into $15,274 ($12,801 over three years and $24,311 over the past ten years). This translates into an average annual return of 9 percent over the past five years, 9 percent over the past three years, and 9 percent for the decade. Over the past five years, this fund has outperformed 65 percent of all mutual funds; within its general category it has done better than 90 percent of its peers. Corporate bond funds have averaged 7 percent annually over these same five years.

During the past five years, a $10,000 initial investment grew to $12,860 after taxes, assuming a 39.6 percent income tax bracket (state and federal combined) and a capital gains rate of 28 percent. This means that investors in this fund were able to preserve 86 percent of their total returns. Compared to other fixed-income funds, this fund's tax savings are considered to be excellent.

Risk/Volatility   ★ ★ ★ ★ ★

Over the past five years, Invesco Select Income has been safer than 98 percent of all corporate bond funds. Over the past decade, the fund has had one negative year, while the Lehman Brothers Aggregate Bond Index has had one (off 3 percent in 1994); the Lehman Brothers Corporate Bond Index also fell once (off 4 percent in 1994). The fund has underperformed the Lehman Brothers Aggregate Bond Index three times and the Lehman Brothers Corporate Bond Index three times in the last ten years.

	last 5 years		last 10 years	
worst year	-1%	1994	-1%	1994
best year	21%	1995	21%	1995

In the past, Invesco Select Income has done better than 75 percent of its peer group in up markets and outperformed 25 percent of its competition in down markets. Consistency, or predictability, of returns for Invesco Select Income can be described as good. This fund's risk-adjusted return is excellent.

Management   ★ ★ ★ ★ ★

There are 112 fixed-income securities in this $550 million portfolio. The average corporate bond fund today is $265 million in size. Close to 97 percent of the funds holdings are in bonds. The average maturity of the bonds in this account is nine years; the weighted coupon rate averages 7.9 percent. The portfolio's fixed-income holdings can be categorized as intermediate-term, medium-quality debt.

Jerry Paul has managed this fund for the past five years. There are thirty-one funds besides Select Income within the Invesco family. Overall, the fund family's risk-adjusted performance can be described as very good.

Current Income   ★ ★ ★ ★ ★

Over the past year, Invesco Select Income had a twelve-month yield of 6.5 percent. During this same twelve-month period, the typical corporate bond fund had a yield that averaged 5.7 percent.

Expenses   ★ ★ ★

Invesco Select Income's expense ratio is 1.1 percent; it has averaged 1 percent annually over the past three calendar years. The average expense ratio for the 850 funds in this category is 1.0 percent. This fund's turnover rate over the past year has been 140 percent, while its peer group average has been 150 percent.

Summary

Invesco Select Income has ranked in the top performance quartile for five of the past six years. Manager Paul is most concerned with an issuer's credit and trying to find mispriced bonds; he is not sensitive to interest-rate sensitivity. Nevertheless, his intermediate-term holdings provide the best risk-adjusted returns possible. A larger weighting in high-yield issues has certainly paid off and is one of the things that makes this fund different from its peers. The fund's risk-adjusted returns over the past three, five, and ten years have been outstanding.

Profile

minimum initial investment $1,000	*IRA accounts available* . . . . yes
subsequent minimum investment . . . $50	*IRA minimum investment* $250
available in all 50 states. . . . . yes	*date of inception* . . . . Nov. 1976
telephone exchanges. . . . . yes	*dividend/income paid.* . . . . monthly
number of other funds in family 31	*average credit quality.* . . . . BBB

Lebenthal Taxable Municipal Bond

120 Broadway
New York, NY 10271
800-221-5822

total return	★ ★ ★ ★
risk reduction	★ ★ ★ ★
management	★ ★ ★ ★ ★
current income	★ ★ ★ ★ ★
expense control	★ ★ ★ ★ ★
symbol N/A	23 points
up-market performance	poor
down-market performance	excellent
predictability of returns	fair

Total Return   ★ ★ ★ ★

Over the past five years, Lebenthal Taxable Municipal Bond has taken $10,000 and turned it into $15,071 ($12,975 over three years). This translates into an average annual return of 9 percent over the past five years and 9 percent over the past three years. Over the past five years, this fund has outperformed 60 percent of all mutual funds; within its general category it has done better than 95 percent of its peers. Corporate bond funds have averaged 7 percent annually over these same five years.

During the past five years, a $10,000 initial investment grew to $13,330 after taxes, assuming a 39.6 percent income tax bracket (state and federal combined) and a capital gains rate of 28 percent. This means that investors in this fund were able to preserve 88 percent of their total returns. Compared to other fixed-income funds, this fund's tax savings are considered to be excellent.

Risk/Volatility   ★ ★ ★ ★

Over the past five years, Lebenthal Taxable Municipal Bond has been safer than 75 percent of all corporate bond funds. Over the past decade, the fund has had one negative year, while the Lehman Brothers Aggregate Bond Index has had one (off 3 percent in 1994); the Lehman Brothers Corporate Bond Index also fell once (off 4 percent in 1994). The fund has underperformed the Lehman Brothers Aggregate Bond Index once and the Lehman Brothers Corporate Bond Index twice in the last ten years.

	last 5 years		since inception	
worst year	-5%	1994	-5%	1994
best year	22%	1995	22%	1995

In the past, Lebenthal Taxable Municipal Bond has done better than 20 percent of its peer group in up markets and outperformed 100 percent of its competition in down markets. Consistency, or predictability, of returns for Lebenthal Taxable Municipal Bond can be described as fair. This fund's risk-adjusted return is very good.

Management   ★ ★ ★ ★ ★

There are forty-eight fixed-income securities in this $20 million portfolio. The average corporate bond fund today is $265 million in size. Close to 100 percent of the funds holdings are in bonds. The average maturity of the bonds in this account is eleven years; the weighted coupon rate averages 7.2 percent. The portfolio's fixed-income holdings can be categorized as long-term, high-quality debt.

James Gammon has managed this fund for the past five years. There are two funds besides Taxable Municipal Bond within the Lebenthal family. Overall, the fund family's risk-adjusted performance can be described as poor.

Current Income   ★ ★ ★ ★ ★

Over the past year, Lebenthal Taxable Municipal Bond had a twelve-month yield of 6.6 percent. During this same twelve-month period, the typical corporate bond fund had a yield that averaged 5.7 percent.

Expenses   ★ ★ ★ ★ ★

Lebenthal Taxable Municipal Bond's expense ratio is .7 percent; it has also averaged .7 percent annually over the past three calendar years. The average expense ratio for the 850 funds in this category is 1.0 percent. This fund's turnover rate over the past year has been 24 percent, while its peer group average has been 150 percent.

Summary

Lebenthal Taxable Municipal Bond is a very rate kind of bond fund. It was the first, and remains one of the few, portfolios to specialize in taxable municipal bonds. These are bonds whose money is used for things like shopping malls and stadiums. Manager Gammon has a buy-and-hold philosophy—something which is sorely missing by the vast majority of corporate, government, and tax-free bond fund managers. Management prefers small issues that are high-quality. Despite its name, this is the number one ranked "corporate" bond fund.

Profile

minimum initial investment $1,000	*IRA accounts available* . . . . yes
subsequent minimum investment . . $100	*IRA minimum investment* $1,000
available in all 50 states . . . . no	*date of inception* . . . . Dec. 1993
telephone exchanges . . . . yes	*dividend/income paid* . . . . monthly
number of other funds in family 2	*average credit quality* . . . . AA

New England Bond Income A

399 Boylston Street
Boston, MA 02116
800-225-7670

total return	★ ★ ★ ★
risk reduction	★
management	★ ★ ★
current income	★ ★ ★ ★ ★
expense control	★ ★ ★ ★ ★
symbol NEFRX	18 points
up-market performance	very good
down-market performance	good
predictability of returns	fair

Total Return   ★ ★ ★ ★

Over the past five years, New England Bond Income A has taken $10,000 and turned it into $15,078 ($12,890 over three years and $24,624 over the past ten years). This translates into an average annual return of 9 percent over the past five years, 9 percent over the past three years, and 9 percent for the decade. Over the past five years, this fund has outperformed 60 percent of all mutual funds; within its general category it has done better than 97 percent of its peers. Corporate bond funds have averaged 7 percent annually over these same five years.

During the past five years, a $10,000 initial investment grew to $12,620 after taxes, assuming a 39.6 percent income tax bracket (state and federal combined) and a capital gains rate of 28 percent. This means that investors in this fund were able to preserve 87 percent of their total returns. Compared to other fixed-income funds, this fund's tax savings are considered to be excellent.

Risk/Volatility   ★

Over the past five years, New England Bond Income A has been safer than 15 percent of all corporate bond funds. Over the past decade, the fund has had one negative year, while the Lehman Brothers Aggregate Bond Index has had one (off 3 percent in 1994); the Lehman Brothers Corporate Bond Index also fell once (off 4 percent in 1994). The fund has underperformed the Lehman Brothers Aggregate Bond Index four times and the Lehman Brothers Corporate Bond Index four times in the last ten years.

	last 5 years		last 10 years	
worst year	-4%	1994	-4%	1994
best year	21%	1995	21%	1995

In the past, New England Bond Income A has done better than 80 percent of its peer group in up markets and outperformed 55 percent of its competition in down markets. Consistency, or predictability, of returns for New England Bond Income A can be described as fair. This fund's risk-adjusted return is very good.

Management   ★ ★ ★
There are 121 fixed-income securities in this $230 million portfolio. The average corporate bond fund today is $265 million in size. Close to 98 percent of the funds holdings are in bonds. The average maturity of the bonds in this account is six years; the weighted coupon rate averages 7.7 percent. The portfolio's fixed-income holdings can be categorized as intermediate-term, medium-quality debt.

Catherine Bunting has managed this fund for the past ten years. There are twenty funds besides Bond Income within the New England family. Overall, the fund family's risk-adjusted performance can be described as good.

Current Income   ★ ★ ★ ★ ★
Over the past year, New England Bond Income A had a twelve-month yield of 6.5 percent. During this same twelve-month period, the typical corporate bond fund had a yield that averaged 5.7 percent.

Expenses   ★ ★ ★ ★ ★
New England Bond Income A's expense ratio is 1 percent; it has also averaged 1 percent annually over the past three calendar years. The average expense ratio for the 850 funds in this category is 1.0 percent. This fund's turnover rate over the past year has been 65 percent, while its peer group average has been 150 percent.

Summary
New England Bond Income A frequently includes a healthy does of high-yield bonds, sometimes at a 20 percent level versus 3 percent for its category average. Close to 40 percent of the portfolio is in BBB-rated issues, which translates into a very high current yield to investors. This fund is not for the conservative investor but does warrant consideration for all other bond investors.

Profile

minimum initial investment $2,500	*IRA accounts available* . . . . yes
subsequent minimum investment . . $100	*IRA minimum investment* $500
available in all 50 states. . . . . yes	*date of inception* . . . . Nov. 1973
telephone exchanges. . . . . yes	*dividend/income paid.* . . . . monthly
number of other funds in family 20	*average credit quality* . . . . A

Vanguard Long-Term Corporate Bond

Vanguard Financial Center
P.O. Box 2600
Valley Forge, PA 19482
800-662-7447

total return	★ ★ ★ ★
risk reduction	★ ★
management	★ ★ ★ ★
current income	★ ★ ★ ★ ★
expense control	★ ★ ★ ★ ★
symbol VWESX	20 points
up-market performance	poor
down-market performance	excellent
predictability of returns	poor

Total Return   ★ ★ ★ ★

Over the past five years, Vanguard Long-Term Corporate Bond has taken $10,000 and turned it into $15,351 ($12,915 over three years and $27,067 over the past ten years). This translates into an average annual return of 9 percent over the past five years, 9 percent over the past three years, and 10 percent for the decade. Over the past five years, this fund has outperformed 65 percent of all mutual funds; within its general category it has done better than 85 percent of its peers. Corporate bond funds have averaged 7 percent annually over these same five years.

During the past five years, a $10,000 initial investment grew to $12,900 after taxes, assuming a 39.6 percent income tax bracket (state and federal combined) and a capital gains rate of 28 percent. This means that investors in this fund were able to preserve 86 percent of their total returns. Compared to other fixed-income funds, this fund's tax savings are considered to be excellent.

Risk/Volatility   ★ ★

Over the past five years, Vanguard Long-Term Corporate Bond has been safer than 35 percent of all corporate bond funds. Over the past decade, the fund has had one negative year, while the Lehman Brothers Aggregate Bond Index has had one (off 3 percent in 1994); the Lehman Brothers Corporate Bond Index also fell once (off 4 percent in 1994). The fund has underperformed the Lehman Brothers Aggregate Bond Index three times and the Lehman Brothers Corporate Bond Index three times in the last ten years.

	last 5 years		last 10 years	
worst year	-5%	1994	-5%	1994
best year	26%	1995	26%	1995

In the past, Vanguard Long-Term Corporate Bond has done better than 20 percent of its peer group in up markets and outperformed 90 percent of its competition in down markets. Consistency, or predictability, of returns for Vanguard

Long-Term Corporate Bond can be described as poor. This fund's risk-adjusted return is very good.

Management   ★ ★ ★ ★

There are 146 fixed-income securities in this $4.1 billion portfolio. The average corporate bond fund today is $265 million in size. Close to 94 percent of the funds holdings are in bonds. The average maturity of the bonds in this account is nineteen years; the weighted coupon rate averages 7.3 percent. The portfolio's fixed-income holdings can be categorized as long-term, medium-quality debt.

Earl McEvoy has managed this fund for the past five years. There are sixty-eight funds besides Long-Term Corporate Bond within the Vanguard family. Overall, the fund family's risk-adjusted performance can be described as very good.

Current Income   ★ ★ ★ ★ ★

Over the past year, Vanguard Long-Term Corporate Bond had a twelve-month yield of 6.4 percent. During this same twelve-month period, the typical corporate bond fund had a yield that averaged 5.7 percent.

Expenses   ★ ★ ★ ★ ★

Vanguard Long-Term Corporate Bond's expense ratio is .3 percent; it has also averaged .3 percent annually over the past three calendar years. The average expense ratio for the 850 funds in this category is 1.0 percent. This fund's turnover rate over the past year has been 33 percent, while its peer group average has been 150 percent.

Summary

Vanguard Long-Term Corporate Bond shines when interest rates fall or remain level; the fund's long-term maturity is only of concern when rates are rising. The fund will appeal to those interested in current income. Expense control also has been great. There is nothing particularly exciting about this or most other quality bond funds, but this one does what most do not.

Profile

minimum initial investment $3,000	*IRA accounts available* . . . . yes
subsequent minimum investment . . $100	*IRA minimum investment* $1,000
available in all 50 states. . . . . yes	*date of inception* . . . . July 1973
telephone exchanges. . . . . yes	*dividend/income paid*. . . . . monthly
number of other funds in family 68	*average credit quality* . . . . A

Vanguard Preferred Stock
Vanguard Financial Center
P.O. Box 2600
Valley Forge, PA 19482
800-662-7447

total return	★ ★ ★ ★ ★
risk reduction	★ ★ ★ ★
management	★ ★ ★ ★ ★
current income	★ ★ ★
expense control	★ ★ ★ ★ ★
symbol VQIIX	22 points
up-market performance	poor
down-market performance	excellent
predictability of returns	good

Total Return   ★ ★ ★ ★ ★
Over the past five years, Vanguard Preferred Stock has taken $10,000 and turned it into $15,908 ($13,339 over three years and $28,241 over the past ten years). This translates into an average annual return of 10 percent over the past five years, 10 percent over the past three years, and 11 percent for the decade. Over the past five years, this fund has outperformed 65 percent of all mutual funds; within its general category it has done better than 95 percent of its peers. Corporate bond funds have averaged 7 percent annually over these same five years.

During the past five years, a $10,000 initial investment grew to $13,230 after taxes, assuming a 39.6 percent income tax bracket (state and federal combined) and a capital gains rate of 28 percent. This means that investors in this fund were able to preserve 87 percent of their total returns. Compared to other fixed-income funds, this fund's tax savings are considered to be excellent.

Risk/Volatility   ★ ★ ★ ★
Over the past five years, Vanguard Preferred Stock has been safer than 65 percent of all corporate bond funds. Over the past decade, the fund has had one negative year, while the Lehman Brothers Aggregate Bond Index has had one (off 3 percent in 1994); the Lehman Brothers Corporate Bond Index also fell once (off 4 percent in 1994). The fund has underperformed the Lehman Brothers Aggregate Bond Index three times and the Lehman Brothers Corporate Bond Index four times in the last ten years.

	last 5 years		last 10 years	
worst year	-8%	1994	-8%	1994
best year	26%	1995	26%	1995

In the past, Vanguard Preferred Stock has done better than 20 percent of its peer group in up markets and outperformed 100 percent of its competition in down markets. Consistency, or predictability, of returns for Vanguard Preferred Stock can be described as good. This fund's risk-adjusted return is excellent.

Management   ★ ★ ★ ★ ★

There are sixty-four fixed-income securities in this $380 million portfolio. The average corporate bond fund today is $265 million in size. Close to 100 percent of the funds holdings are in preferred stocks.

Earl McEvoy has managed this fund for the past seventeen years. There are sixty-eight funds besides Preferred Stock within the Vanguard family. Overall, the fund family's risk-adjusted performance can be described as very good.

Current Income   ★ ★ ★

Over the past year, Vanguard Preferred Stock had a twelve-month yield of 5.4 percent. During this same twelve-month period, the typical corporate bond fund had a yield that averaged 5.7 percent.

Expenses   ★ ★ ★ ★ ★

Vanguard Preferred Stock's expense ratio is .4 percent; it has also averaged .4 percent annually over the past three calendar years. The average expense ratio for the 850 funds in this category is 1.0 percent. This fund's turnover rate over the past year has been 39 percent, while its peer group average has been 150 percent.

Summary

Vanguard Preferred Stock has a unique objective: invest at least 75 percent of its assets in cumulative preferred stocks of U.S. companies that are rated at least BBB. The goal is to qualify for a little-known tax benefit that only helps corporate investors (the "70 percent intercorporate dividends-receiving deduction"). Almost the entire portfolio is in financial issues and utilities. Despite an objective that does not benefit the individual investor, this fund is highly recommended for a couple of reasons. First, it is one of only a small number of funds that specializes in preferred stocks and can add meaningful diversification to virtually any portfolio; second, returns, management, and expense minimization have been exceptional—risk reduction has also been quite good.

Profile

minimum initial investment $3,000	*IRA accounts available* . . . . yes
subsequent minimum investment . . $100	*IRA minimum investment* $1,000
available in all 50 states. . . . . yes	*date of inception*. . . . . Dec. 1975
telephone exchanges. . . . . yes	*dividend/income paid* . . . . quarterly
number of other funds in family 68	*average credit quality* . . . . A

Global Equity Funds

International funds, also known as foreign funds, invest only in stocks of foreign companies, while global funds invest in both foreign and U.S. stocks. For the purposes of this book, the universe of global equity funds shown encompasses both foreign (international) and world (global) portfolios.

The economic outlook of foreign countries is the major factor in mutual fund management's decision as to which nations and industries are to be favored. A secondary concern is the future anticipated value of the U.S. dollar relative to foreign currencies. A strong or weak dollar can detract or add to an international fund's overall performance. A strong dollar will lower a foreign portfolio's return; a weak dollar will enhance international performance. Trying to gauge the direction of any currency is as difficult as trying to figure out what the U.S. stock market will do tomorrow, next week, or the following year.

Investors who do not wish to be subjected to currency swings may wish to use a fund family that practices currency hedging for their foreign holdings. Currency hedging means that management is buying a kind of insurance policy that pays off in the event of a strong U.S. dollar. Basically, the foreign or international fund that is being hurt by the dollar is making a killing in currency futures contracts. When done properly, the gains in the futures contracts, the insurance policy, offset some, most, or all security losses attributable to a strong dollar. Some people may feel that buying currency contracts is risky business for the fund; it is not.

Like automobile insurance, currency hedging only pays off if there is an accident; that is, if the U.S. dollar increases in value against the currencies represented by the portfolio's securities. If the dollar remains level or decreases in value, so much the better; the foreign securities increase in value and the currency contracts become virtually worthless. The price of these contracts becomes a cost of doing business; as with car insurance, the protection is simply renewed. In the case of a currency contract, the contract expires and a new one is purchased, covering another period.

It is wise to consider investing abroad, since different economies experience prosperity and recession at different times. During the 1980s, foreign stocks were the number one performing investment, averaging a compound return of over 22 percent per year, compared to 18 percent for U.S. stocks and 5 percent for residential real estate. But during the past decade, U.S. stocks have outperformed foreign stocks (19.0 percent vs. 5.7 percent). Over the past fifteen years, U.S. stocks have had an average compound annual return of 18.5 percent versus 13.7 percent for foreign stocks (all periods ending 3/31/99).

To give you a broader perspective, take a look at how U.S. securities have fared against their foreign counterparts over each of the last twenty-six years.

Why Global Stocks and Bonds Deserve a Place in Every Investor's Portfolio

(The following table shows the total return for each investment category in each of the past twenty-seven years.)

Year	U.S. Stocks	U.S. Bonds	Non-U.S. Stocks	Non-U.S. Bonds
1972	+19.0	+5.7	+37.4	+ 4.4
1973	-14.6	-1.1	-14.2	+ 6.3
1974	-26.5	+4.4	-22.1	+ 5.3
1975	+37.2	+9.2	+37.0	+ 8.8
1976	+23.8	+16.8	+ 3.8	+10.5
1977	- 7.2	-0.7	+19.4	+38.9
1978	+ 6.6	-1.2	+34.3	+18.5
1979	+18.4	-1.2	+ 6.2	- 5.0
1980	+32.4	-4.0	+24.4	+13.7
1981	- 4.9	+1.9	- 1.0	- 4.6
1982	+22.5	+40.4	- 0.9	+11.9
1983	+22.6	+0.7	+24.6	+ 4.3
1984	+ 6.3	+15.5	+ 7.9	- 2.0
1985	+32.2	+31.0	+56.7	+37.2
1986	+18.5	+24.5	+67.9	+33.9
1987	+ 5.2	-2.7	+24.9	+36.1
1988	+16.8	+9.7	+28.6	+ 2.4
1989	+31.5	+18.1	+10.8	- 3.4
1990	- 3.2	+ 6.2	-14.9	+15.3
1991	+30.6	+19.3	+12.5	+16.2
1992	+ 7.7	+ 8.1	-12.2	+ 4.8
1993	+10.0	+18.2	+32.6	+15.1
1994	+ 1.3	- 7.8	+ 7.8	+ 6.0
1995	+37.4	+31.7	+11.2	+19.6
1996	+23.1	- 0.9	+6.1	+4.1
1997	+33.4	+15.9	+1.8	-4.3
1998	+28.6	+8.7	+20.0	+17.8
Number of years this category achieved the best results 10	4	8	5

Increasing your investment returns and reducing portfolio risk are two compelling reasons for investing worldwide. Global investing allows you to maximize your returns by investing in some of the world's best managed and most profitable companies. Japan, for example, is the world's leading producer of sophisticated electronics goods; Germany of heavy machinery; the United States of software, technology, and biotechnology; and Southeast Asia of commodity-manufactured goods.

By limiting a portfolio to U.S. stocks, an investor would have to ignore: ten of the world's ten largest real estate companies, nine of the world's ten largest construction and housing companies, eight of the world's ten largest electrical and electronics companies, eight of the world's ten largest insurance companies, and seven of the world's ten largest automobile companies.

World market dominance is constantly changing. Twenty years ago the United States represented 57 percent of the world's stock market capital, today it represents 44 percent of total world capitalization ($14 trillion for U.S. stocks vs. $18 trillion for foreign stocks). Only four times in the past ten years has the U.S. stock market been among the five best performers in the world (1991, 1992, 1995, and 1997). Performance has continued to shift: from 1970–1979 the S&P 500 was up 77 percent versus 162 percent for the EAFE, from 1980–1989 U.S. stocks were up 400 percent versus 678 percent for foreign equities, and from 1990–1997 the S&P 500 was up 242 percent versus 33 percent for the EAFE. The greatest potential for growth today lies in those countries that are industrializing, have the cheapest labor and the richest natural resources, and yet remain undervalued.

Diversification reduces investment risk: Recent studies have once again proven this most basic investment principle. A 1997 study showed that the least volatile investment portfolio over the past twenty years (1978–1997) would have been composed of 65 percent U.S. equities and 35 percent foreign equities. These results reflect the importance of balancing a portfolio between U.S. and foreign equities.

The newly industrialized countries are favored locations for the manufacture and assembly of consumer electronics products. Displaced from high-cost countries such as the United States and Japan, electronics factories in these developing countries significantly benefit from reduced labor costs. Today, in fact, Korea is the world's third-largest manufacturer of semiconductors.

The Pacific Region yields yet another country with strong economic growth: China. Opportunities to benefit from the industrialization of China come from firms listed on the Hong Kong Stock Exchange, in such basic areas as electricity, construction materials, public transportation, and fundamental telecommunications. Indeed, these low-tech and essential industries, once growth industries in the United States, are now the foundation of a natural growth progression occurring in the NICs of Southeast Asia.

Companies such as China Light and Power (Hong Kong), Siam Cement (Thailand), and Hyundai (Korea) offer much the same profit potential today as their northern European counterparts did one hundred years ago, their U.S. counterparts forty years ago, and their Japanese counterparts as recently as twenty years ago.

Investors have long been familiar with the names of many of Europe's major producers: Nestlé, Olivetti, Shell, Bayer, Volkswagen, and Perrier, to name just a few. Europe's impressive manufacturing capacity, diverse industrial base, quality labor pools, and many leading, multinational, blue-chip corporations can make it an environment for growth, accessible to you through foreign funds.

With economic deregulation and the elimination of internal trade barriers, many European companies are, for the first time in history, investing in and competing for exposure to the whole European market. Companies currently restricted to manufacturing and distributing within their national boundaries will soon be able to locate facilities anywhere in Europe, maximizing the efficient employment of labor, capital, and raw materials.

The global stock category is made up of 1,380 funds: 300 "World," 680 "Foreign," and 400 "European" and "Pacific." Total market capitalization of this entire category is $345 billion. These funds typically throw off a dividend of less than 1 percent and have an expense ratio of 1.9 percent. The price-earnings (p/e) ratio is 25, versus a p/e ratio of 35 for the typical stock in the S&P 500.

Over the past three years, global equity funds have had an average compound return of 6.7 percent per year. The annual return for the past five years has been 6.8 percent, 8.2 percent for the past ten years, and 12.0 percent for the last fifteen years. The standard deviation for global equity funds has been 19.6 percent over the past three years. This means that global equity funds have experienced about 15 percent less volatility than growth funds (all figures for periods ending 3/31/99).

International, or foreign, funds should be part of most equity portfolios. They can provide superior returns and reduce overall portfolio risk. As with any other fund category, this one should not be looked at in isolation.

Global Equity Funds

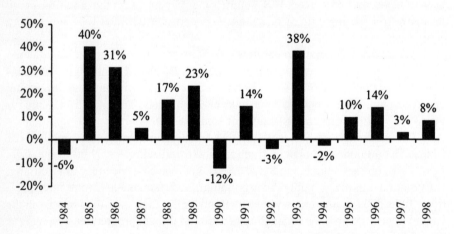

Bartlett Europe A
36 East Fourth Street
Cincinnati, OH 45202
800-800-3609

total return	★ ★ ★ ★ ★
risk reduction	★ ★
management	★ ★ ★
tax minimization	★ ★ ★ ★
expense control	★ ★
symbol BEPFX	16 points
up-market performance	very good
down-market performance	good
predictability of returns	good

Total Return   ★ ★ ★ ★ ★

Over the past five years, Bartlett Europe A has taken $10,000 and turned it into $25,533 ($19,452 over three years and $26,799 over the past ten years). This translates into an average annual return of 21 percent over the past five years, 25 percent over the past three years, and 10 percent for the decade. Over the past five years, this fund has outperformed 95 percent of all mutual funds; within its general category it has done better than 96 percent of its peers. Global equity funds have averaged 7 percent annually over these same five years.

Risk/Volatility   ★ ★

Over the past five years, Bartlett Europe A has been safer than 40 percent of all global equity funds. Over the past decade, the fund has had three negative years, while the S&P 500 has had one (off 3 percent in 1990); the EAFE fell twice (off 23 percent in 1990 and 12 percent in 1992). The fund has underperformed the S&P 500 seven times and the EAFE Index three times in the last ten years.

	last 5 years		last 10 years	
worst year	-4%	1994	-22%	1990
best year	42%	1998	42%	1998

In the past, Bartlett Europe A has done better than 75 percent of its peer group in up markets and outperformed 65 percent of its competition in down markets. Consistency, or predictability, of returns for Bartlett Europe A can be described as good. This fund's risk-adjusted return is excellent.

Management   ★ ★ ★

There are fifty-one stocks in this $58.9 million portfolio. The average global equity fund today is $265 million in size. Close to 95 percent of the fund's holdings are in stocks. The stocks in this portfolio have an average price-earnings (p/e) ratio of 28 and a median market capitalization of $23 billion. The portfolio's equity holdings can be categorized as large-cap and growth-oriented issues.

Neil Worsley and William Lovering have managed this fund for the past six years. There are two funds besides Europe within the Bartlett family. Overall, the fund family's risk-adjusted performance can be described as good.

Tax Minimization   ★ ★ ★ ★
During the past five years, a $10,000 initial investment grew to $21,080 after taxes, assuming a 39.6 percent income tax bracket (state and federal combined) and a capital gains rate of 28 percent. This means that investors in this fund were able to preserve 85 percent of their total returns. Compared to other equity funds, this fund's tax savings are considered to be good.

Expenses   ★ ★
Bartlett Europe A's expense ratio is 1.9 percent; it has also averaged 1.9 percent annually over the past three calendar years. The average expense ratio for the 1,350 funds in this category is 1.9 percent. This fund's turnover rate over the past year has been 123 percent, while its peer group average has been 85 percent.

Summary
Bartlett Europe is one of three recommended foreign funds that specializes in European stocks. This fund has better three- and five-year returns than its peers. This fund is part of a small family but not the only Bartlett offering you should consider. The fund is a fine choice for the global or foreign fund investor.

Profile

minimum initial investment $1,000	*IRA accounts available* . . . . yes
subsequent minimum investment . . $100	*IRA minimum investment* $1,000
available in all 50 states . . . . no	*date of inception* . . . . Aug. 1986
telephone exchanges. . . . . yes	*dividend/income paid* . . . . annually
number of other funds in family 2	*largest sector weighting* . . . . financials

Capital World Growth & Income
333 S. Hope Street
Los Angeles, CA 90071
800-421-4120

total return	★ ★ ★ ★ ★
risk reduction	★ ★ ★ ★ ★
management	★ ★ ★ ★ ★
tax minimization	★ ★ ★
expense control	★ ★ ★ ★
symbol CWGIX	22 points
up-market performance	fair
down-market performance	excellent
predictability of returns	excellent

Total Return   ★ ★ ★ ★ ★
Over the past five years, Capital World Growth & Income has taken $10,000 and turned it into $21,617 ($16,301 over three years). This translates into an average annual return of 17 percent over the past five years and 18 percent over the past three years. Over the past five years, this fund has outperformed 80 percent of all mutual funds; within its general category it has done better than 90 percent of its peers. Global equity funds have averaged 7 percent annually over these same five years.

Risk/Volatility   ★ ★ ★ ★ ★
Over the past five years, Capital World Growth & Income has been safer than 97 percent of all global equity funds. Over the past decade, the fund has not had a negative year, while the S&P 500 has had one (off 3 percent in 1990); the EAFE fell twice (off 23 percent in 1990 and 12 percent in 1992). The fund has underperformed the S&P 500 five times and the EAFE Index twice in the last ten years.

	last 5 years		since inception	
worst year	1%	1994	1%	1994
best year	22%	1996	22%	1996

In the past, Capital World Growth & Income has done better than 45 percent of its peer group in up markets and outperformed 90 percent of its competition in down markets. Consistency, or predictability, of returns for Capital World Growth & Income can be described as excellent. This fund's risk-adjusted return is excellent.

Management   ★ ★ ★ ★ ★
There are 289 stocks in this $9 billion portfolio. The average global equity fund today is $265 million in size. Close to 78 percent of the fund's holdings are in stocks. The stocks in this portfolio have an average price-earnings (p/e) ratio of 24 and a median market capitalization of $13 billion. The portfolio's equity holdings can be categorized as large-cap and a blend of growth and value stocks.

A team has managed this fund for the past six years. There are twenty-eight funds besides Capital World Growth & Income within the American Funds family.

Overall, the fund family's risk-adjusted performance can be described as very good.

Tax Minimization ★ ★ ★

During the past five years, a $10,000 initial investment grew to $18,400 after taxes, assuming a 39.6 percent income tax bracket (state and federal combined) and a capital gains rate of 28 percent. This means that investors in this fund were able to preserve 90 percent of their total returns. Compared to other equity funds, this fund's tax savings are considered to be very good.

Expenses ★ ★ ★ ★

Capital World Growth & Income's expense ratio is .8 percent; it has also averaged .8 percent annually over the past three calendar years. The average expense ratio for the 1,350 funds in this category is 1.9 percent. This fund's turnover rate over the past year has been 39 percent, while its peer group average has been 85 percent.

Summary

Capital World Growth & Income is part of the American Funds family; a number of other funds within the family appear in this and previous editions of the book. The beauty to this and other members of the family is that the longer the fund is held, the better it looks. The portfolio's stocks are primarily blue-chip, dividend-paying and come from developed nations. Like all other members of the American Funds group, a multiple-star management system is used which also rewards analysts. This fund is a great choice for any investor who wants to own domestic as well as foreign equities with just a dab of the emerging markets.

Profile

minimum initial investment $1,000	*IRA accounts available* . . . . yes
subsequent minimum investment . . . $50	*IRA minimum investment* $250
available in all 50 states. . . . . yes	*date of inception* . . . . March 1993
telephone exchanges. . . . . yes	*dividend/income paid* . . . . quarterly
number of other funds in family 28	*largest sector weighting* . . . . . . services

Idex JCC Global A

201 Highland Avenue
Largo, FL 34640
888-233-4339

total return	★ ★ ★ ★ ★
risk reduction	★ ★ ★ ★
management	★ ★ ★ ★
tax minimization	★ ★ ★ ★
expense control	★ ★ ★
symbol IGLBX	20 points
up-market performance	very good
down-market performance	fair
predictability of returns	very good

Total Return   ★ ★ ★ ★ ★

Over the past five years, Idex JCC Global A has taken $10,000 and turned it into $24,894 ($18,020 over three years). This translates into an average annual return of 20 percent over the past five years and 22 percent over the past three years. Over the past five years, this fund has outperformed 90 percent of all mutual funds; within its general category it has done better than 95 percent of its peers. Global equity funds have averaged 7 percent annually over these same five years.

Risk/Volatility   ★ ★ ★ ★

Over the past five years, Idex JCC Global A has been safer than 80 percent of all global equity funds. Over the past decade, the fund has not had a negative year, while the S&P 500 has had one (off 3 percent in 1990); the EAFE fell twice (off 23 percent in 1990 and 12 percent in 1992). The fund has underperformed the S&P 500 four times and the EAFE Index twice in the last ten years.

	last 5 years		since inception	
worst year	1%	1994	1%	1994
best year	27%	1996	27%	1996

In the past, Idex JCC Global A has done better than 80 percent of its peer group in up markets and outperformed 40 percent of its competition in down markets. Consistency, or predictability, of returns for Idex JCC Global A can be described as very good. This fund's risk-adjusted return is excellent.

Management   ★ ★ ★ ★

There are 176 stocks in this $400 million portfolio. The average global equity fund today is $265 million in size. Close to 93 percent of the fund's holdings are in stocks. The stocks in this portfolio have an average price-earnings (p/e) ratio of 37 and a median market capitalization of $20 billion. The portfolio's equity holdings can be categorized as large-cap and growth-oriented issues.

Helen Young Hayes has managed this fund for the past seven years. There are twelve funds besides JCC Global within the Idex family. Overall, the fund family's risk-adjusted performance can be described as very good.

Tax Minimization   ★ ★ ★ ★
During the past five years, a $10,000 initial investment grew to $21,400 after taxes, assuming a 39.6 percent income tax bracket (state and federal combined) and a capital gains rate of 28 percent. This means that investors in this fund were able to preserve 93 percent of their total returns. Compared to other equity funds, this fund's tax savings are considered to be excellent.

Expenses   ★ ★ ★
Idex JCC Global A's expense ratio is 1.8 percent; it has also averaged 1.8 percent annually over the past three calendar years. The average expense ratio for the 1,350 funds in this category is 1.9 percent. This fund's turnover rate over the past year has been 88 percent, while its peer group average has been 85 percent.

Summary
Idex JCC Global A has finished in the top performance quartile over each of the past four years. Management is fond of well-known telecommunication and information technology stocks as well as cable-related issues. Hayes uses fundamental bottom-up analysis, seeking out companies with growing earnings and increased product demand. Equities are sold when either they reach a predetermined price or the reasons for initial purchase has disappeared. Returns for this fund have been fantastic, particularly on a tax-adjusted basis.

Profile
minimum initial investment $500	*IRA accounts available* . . . . yes
subsequent minimum investment . . . $50	*IRA minimum investment* $50
available in all 50 states. . . . . yes	*date of inception* . . . . Oct. 1992
telephone exchanges. . . . . yes	*dividend/income paid* . . . . annually
number of other funds in family. 12	*largest sector weighting*. . . . . . services

Invesco European
P.O. Box 173706
Denver, CO 80217-3706
800-525-8085

total return	★ ★ ★ ★ ★
risk reduction	★
management	★ ★ ★
tax minimization	★ ★ ★
expense control	★ ★ ★ ★
symbol FEURX	16 points
up-market performance	poor
down-market performance	poor
predictability of returns	good

Total Return   ★ ★ ★ ★ ★
Over the past five years, Invesco European has taken $10,000 and turned it into
$22,122 ($17,760 over three years and $32,967 over the past ten years). This trans-
lates into an average annual return of 17 percent over the past five years, 21 percent over the past three years, and 13 percent for the decade. Over the past five
years, this fund has outperformed 90 percent of all mutual funds; within its general
category it has done better than 70 percent of its peers. Global equity funds have
averaged 7 percent annually over these same five years.

Risk/Volatility   ★
Over the past five years, Invesco European has been safer than 25 percent of all
global equity funds. Over the past decade, the fund has had two negative years,
while the S&P 500 has had one (off 3 percent in 1990); the EAFE fell twice (off
23 percent in 1990 and 12 percent in 1992). The fund has underperformed the S&P
500 six times and the EAFE Index three times in the last ten years.

	last 5 years		last 10 years	
worst year	-3%	1994	-8%	1992
best year	33%	1998	33%	1998

In the past, Invesco European has done better than 25 percent of its peer group
and outperformed 20 percent of its competition in down markets. Consistency, or
predictability, of returns for Invesco European can be described as good. This
fund's risk-adjusted return is excellent.

Management   ★ ★ ★
There are seventy-five stocks in this $650 million portfolio. The average global
equity fund today is $265 million in size. Close to 90 percent of the fund's hold-
ings are in stocks. The stocks in this portfolio have an average price-earnings (p/e)
ratio of 34 and a median market capitalization of $18 billion. The portfolio's equity
holdings can be categorized as large-cap and growth-oriented issues.

Steven Chamberlain has managed this fund for the past nine years. There are thirty-one funds besides European within the Invesco family. Overall, the fund family's risk-adjusted performance can be described as very good.

Tax Minimization   ★ ★ ★
During the past five years, a $10,000 initial investment grew to $19,390 after taxes, assuming a 39.6 percent income tax bracket (state and federal combined) and a capital gains rate of 28 percent. This means that investors in this fund were able to preserve 85 percent of their total returns. Compared to other equity funds, this fund's tax savings are considered to be good.

Expenses   ★ ★ ★ ★
Invesco European's expense ratio is 1.3 percent; it has also averaged 1.3 percent annually over the past three calendar years. The average expense ratio for the 1,350 funds in this category is 1.9 percent. This fund's turnover rate over the past year has been 102 percent, while its peer group average has been 85 percent.

Summary
Invesco European invests at least 80 percent of its assets in common stocks of companies located in Western Europe. Manager Chamberlin and his four analysts use a bottom-up approach, favoring those corporations that have earnings growth of at least 15 percent per annum. Stocks are sold when their p/e multiple exceeds its growth rate or when fundamentals deteriorate. There is no strong concentration in any one issue. This fund represents one of the very best European plays.

Profile
minimum initial investment $1,000	IRA accounts available . . . . yes
subsequent minimum investment . . . $50	IRA minimum investment $250
available in all 50 states. . . . . yes	date of inception. . . . . June 1986
telephone exchanges. . . . . yes	dividend/income paid . . . . annually
number of other funds in family 31	largest sector weighting . . . . . . services

Janus Worldwide
100 Fillmore Street, Suite 300
Denver, CO 80206-4923
800-525-8983

total return	★ ★ ★ ★ ★
risk reduction	★ ★ ★ ★ ★
management	★ ★ ★ ★ ★
tax minimization	★ ★ ★ ★ ★
expense control	★ ★ ★ ★
symbol JAWWX	24 points
up-market performance	excellent
down-market performance	fair
predictability of returns	very good

Total Return   ★ ★ ★ ★ ★
Over the past five years, Janus Worldwide has taken $10,000 and turned it into $26,077 ($18,419 over three years). This translates into an average annual return of 21 percent over the past five years and 23 percent over the past three years. Over the past five years, this fund has outperformed 90 percent of all mutual funds; within its general category it has done better than 97 percent of its peers. Global equity funds have averaged 7 percent annually over these same five years.

Risk/Volatility   ★ ★ ★ ★ ★
Over the past five years, Janus Worldwide has been safer than 85 percent of all global equity funds. Over the past decade, the fund has not had a negative year, while the S&P 500 has had one (off 3 percent in 1990); the EAFE fell twice (off 23 percent in 1990 and 12 percent in 1992). The fund has underperformed the S&P 500 three times and the EAFE Index twice in the last ten years.

	last 5 years		since inception	
worst year	4%	1994	4%	1994
best year	26%	1996	28%	1993

In the past, Janus Worldwide has done better than 90 percent of its peer group in up markets and outperformed 40 percent of its competition in down markets. Consistency, or predictability, of returns for Janus Worldwide can be described as very good. This fund's risk-adjusted return is excellent.

Management   ★ ★ ★ ★ ★
There are 151 stocks in this $180 billion portfolio. The average global equity fund today is $265 million in size. Close to 96 percent of the fund's holdings are in stocks. The stocks in this portfolio have an average price-earnings (p/e) ratio of 37 and a median market capitalization of $27 billion. The portfolio's equity holdings can be categorized as large-cap and growth-oriented issues.

Helen Young Hayes has managed this fund for the past seven years. There are fifteen funds besides Worldwide within the Janus family. Overall, the fund family's risk-adjusted performance can be described as excellent.

Tax Minimization ★★★★★

During the past five years, a $10,000 initial investment grew to $22,400 after taxes, assuming a 39.6 percent income tax bracket (state and federal combined) and a capital gains rate of 28 percent. This means that investors in this fund were able to preserve 93 percent of their total returns. Compared to other equity funds, this fund's tax savings are considered to be excellent.

Expenses ★★★★

Janus Worldwide's expense ratio is .9 percent; it has also averaged .9 percent annually over the past three calendar years. The average expense ratio for the 1,350 funds in this category is 1.9 percent. This fund's turnover rate over the past year has been 85 percent, while its peer group average has been 82 percent.

Summary

Janus Worldwide has ranked in the top performance quartile for each of the past four years. Roughly one-third of the portfolio is in U.S. equities with an emphasis on large-cap technology issues. Management's goal is to buy equities that are trading at a discount to their projected growth rate. With a near-perfect score of 24 out of a possible 25, this fund is the ideal choice for the global investor.

Profile

minimum initial investment $2,500	*IRA accounts available* . . . . yes
subsequent minimum investment . . $100	*IRA minimum investment* $500
available in all 50 states. . . . . yes	*date of inception.* . . . . May 1991
telephone exchanges. . . . . yes	*dividend/income paid* . . . . annually
number of other funds in family 15	*largest sector weighting.* . . . . . . services

New Perspective
333 South Hope Street
Los Angeles, CA 90071
800-421-4120

total return	★ ★ ★ ★ ★
risk reduction	★ ★ ★ ★ ★
management	★ ★ ★ ★ ★
tax minimization	★ ★ ★
expense control	★ ★ ★ ★
symbol ANWPX	22 points
up-market performance	excellent
down-market performance	excellent
predictability of returns	very good

Total Return ★ ★ ★ ★ ★

Over the past five years, New Perspective has taken $10,000 and turned it into $23,180 ($17,510 over three years and $43,773 over the past ten years). This translates into an average annual return of 18 percent over the past five years, 21 percent over the past three years, and 16 percent for the decade. Over the past five years, this fund has outperformed 85 percent of all mutual funds; within its general category it has done better than 95 percent of its peers. Global equity funds have averaged 7 percent annually over these same five years.

Risk/Volatility ★ ★ ★ ★ ★

Over the past five years, New Perspective has been safer than 90 percent of all global equity funds. Over the past decade, the fund has had one negative year, while the S&P 500 has had one (off 3 percent in 1990); the EAFE fell twice (off 23 percent in 1990 and 12 percent in 1992). The fund has underperformed the S&P 500 seven times and the EAFE Index twice in the last ten years.

	last 5 years		last 10 years	
worst year	3%	1994	-2%	1990
best year	29%	1998	29%	1998

In the past, New Perspective has done better than 90 percent of its peer group in up markets and outperformed 90 percent of its competition in down markets. Consistency, or predictability, of returns for New Perspective can be described as very good. This fund's risk-adjusted return is excellent.

Management ★ ★ ★ ★ ★

There are 233 stocks in this $22 billion portfolio. The average global equity fund today is $265 million in size. Close to 85 percent of the fund's holdings are in stocks. The stocks in this portfolio have an average price-earnings (p/e) ratio of 32 and a median market capitalization of $27 billion. The portfolio's equity holdings can be categorized as large-cap and growth-oriented issues.

A team has managed this fund for the past seventeen years. There are twenty-eight funds besides New Perspective within the American Funds family. Overall, the fund family's risk-adjusted performance can be described as very good.

Tax Minimization ★ ★ ★

During the past five years, a $10,000 initial investment grew to $19,770 after taxes, assuming a 39.6 percent income tax bracket (state and federal combined) and a capital gains rate of 28 percent. This means that investors in this fund were able to preserve 92 percent of their total returns. Compared to other equity funds, this fund's tax savings are considered to be excellent.

Expenses ★ ★ ★ ★

New Perspective's expense ratio is .8 percent; it has also averaged .8 percent annually over the past three calendar years. The average expense ratio for the 1,350 funds in this category is 1.9 percent. This fund's turnover rate over the past year has been 30 percent, while its peer group average has been 85 percent.

Summary

New Perspective is the best global equity fund. Its near-perfect score of 24 out of 25 possible points not only makes it a shining star among its peers, it is also one of the few funds in the entire universe to earn such a score. Other members of the American Funds group appear in this and previous editions of the book. This is truly an exceptional offering and represents the kind of quality seasoned investors have come to expect from the folks at Capital Guardian Trust (the money management division of American Funds).

Profile

minimum initial investment $250	*IRA accounts available* . . . . yes
subsequent minimum investment . . . $50	*IRA minimum investment* $250
available in all 50 states. . . . . yes	*date of inception* . . . . March 1973
telephone exchanges. . . . . yes	*dividend/income paid.* . . . . semiannually
number of other funds in family 28	*largest sector weighting* . . . . . . services

Pioneer Europe A
60 State Street
Boston, MA 02109-1820
800-225-6292

total return	★ ★ ★ ★ ★
risk reduction	★ ★
management	★ ★ ★ ★
tax minimization	★ ★ ★ ★
expense control	★ ★ ★ ★
symbol PEURX	19 points
up-market performance	excellent
down-market performance	excellent
predictability of returns	very good

Total Return   ★ ★ ★ ★ ★
Over the past five years, Pioneer Europe A has taken $10,000 and turned it into $22,559 ($16,636 over three years). This translates into an average annual return of 18 percent over the past five years and 18 percent over the past three years. Over the past five years, this fund has outperformed 95 percent of all mutual funds; within its general category it has done better than 85 percent of its peers. Global equity funds have averaged 7 percent annually over these same five years.

Risk/Volatility   ★ ★
Over the past five years, Pioneer Europe A has been safer than 45 percent of all global equity funds. Over the past decade, the fund has had one negative year, while the S&P 500 has had one (off 3 percent in 1990); the EAFE fell twice (off 23 percent in 1990 and 12 percent in 1992). The fund has underperformed the S&P 500 four times and the EAFE Index twice in the last ten years.

	last 5 years		since inception	
worst year	6%	1994	-3%	1992
best year	27%	1996	27%	1996

In the past, Pioneer Europe A has done better than 100 percent of its peer group in up markets and outperformed 100 percent of its competition in down markets. Consistency, or predictability, of returns for Pioneer Europe A can be described as very good. This fund's risk-adjusted return is excellent.

Management   ★ ★ ★ ★
There are ninety-seven stocks in this $310 million portfolio. The average global equity fund today is $265 million in size. Close to 96 percent of the fund's holdings are in stocks. The stocks in this portfolio have an average price-earnings (p/e) ratio of 22 and a median market capitalization of $6 billion. The portfolio's equity holdings can be categorized as large-cap and growth-oriented issues.

Patrick Smith has managed this fund for the past five years. There are twenty funds besides Europe within the Pioneer family. Overall, the fund family's risk-adjusted performance can be described as very good.

Tax Minimization ★ ★ ★ ★
During the past five years, a $10,000 initial investment grew to $21,020 after taxes, assuming a 39.6 percent income tax bracket (state and federal combined) and a capital gains rate of 28 percent. This means that investors in this fund were able to preserve 88 percent of their total returns. Compared to other equity funds, this fund's tax savings are considered to be very good.

Expenses ★ ★ ★ ★
Pioneer Europe A's expense ratio is 1.5 percent; it has averaged 1.8 percent annually over the past three calendar years. The average expense ratio for the 1,350 funds in this category is 1.9 percent. This fund's turnover rate over the past year has been 39 percent, while its peer group average has been 85 percent.

Summary
Pioneer Europe A has a bias toward small to mid-cap issues, despite its current weighting of large-cap stocks. Manager Smith maintains an eye toward value and sometimes hedges the fund's holdings with forward contracts. Equity selection is driven by fundamentals with a bottom-up approach. Stocks that are trading at the low end of a valuation scale are constantly being sought out. Total return is where this fund really shines. This portfolio is recommended for anyone needing some European diversification.

Profile
minimum initial investment . . . . . $1,000   *IRA accounts available* . . . . yes
subsequent minimum investment . . . $50   *IRA minimum investment* $1,000
available in all 50 states. . . . . yes   *date of inception* . . . . April 1991
telephone exchanges. . . . . yes   *dividend/income paid* . . . . annually
number of other funds in family 20   *largest sector weighting* . . . . . . services

Vanguard European Stock Index
Vanguard Financial Center
P.O. Box 2600
Valley Forge, PA 19482
800-662-7447

total return	★ ★ ★ ★ ★
risk reduction	★ ★ ★ ★ ★
management	★ ★ ★ ★ ★
tax minimization	★ ★ ★ ★ ★
expense control	★ ★ ★ ★ ★
symbol VEURX	25 points
up-market performance	fair
down-market performance	good
predictability of returns	very good

Total Return   ★ ★ ★ ★ ★
Over the past five years, Vanguard European Stock Index has taken $10,000 and turned it into $24,176 ($18,315 over three years). This translates into an average annual return of 19 percent over the past five years and 22 percent over the past three years. Over the past five years, this fund has outperformed 95 percent of all mutual funds; within its general category it has done better than 95 percent of its peers. Global equity funds have averaged 7 percent annually over these same five years.

Risk/Volatility   ★ ★ ★ ★ ★
Over the past five years, Vanguard European Stock Index has been safer than 85 percent of all global equity funds. Over the past decade, the fund has had one negative year, while the S&P 500 has had one (off 3 percent in 1990); the EAFE fell twice (off 23 percent in 1990 and 12 percent in 1992). The fund has underperformed the S&P 500 five times and the EAFE Index twice in the last ten years.

	last 5 years		since inception	
worst year	2%	1994	-3%	1992
best year	29%	1998	29%	1993

In the past, Vanguard European Stock Index has done better than 40 percent of its peer group in up markets and outperformed 65 percent of its competition in down markets. Consistency, or predictability, of returns for Vanguard European Stock Index can be described as very good. This fund's risk-adjusted return is excellent.

Management   ★ ★ ★ ★ ★
There are 585 stocks in this $4.6 billion portfolio. The average global equity fund today is $265 million in size. Close to 97 percent of the fund's holdings are in stocks. The stocks in this portfolio have an average price-earnings (p/e) ratio of 27 and a median market capitalization of $26 billion. The portfolio's equity holdings can be categorized as large-cap and growth-oriented issues.

George Sauter has managed this fund for the past nine years. There are sixty-eight funds besides European Stock Index within the Vanguard family. Overall, the fund family's risk-adjusted performance can be described as very good.

Tax Minimization   ★ ★ ★ ★ ★

During the past five years, a $10,000 initial investment grew to $22,170 after taxes, assuming a 39.6 percent income tax bracket (state and federal combined) and a capital gains rate of 28 percent. This means that investors in this fund were able to preserve 92 percent of their total returns. Compared to other equity funds, this fund's tax savings are considered to be excellent.

Expenses   ★ ★ ★ ★ ★

Vanguard European Stock Index's expense ratio is .3 percent; it has also averaged .3 percent annually over the past three calendar years. The average expense ratio for the 1,350 funds in this category is 1.9 percent. This fund's turnover rate over the past year has been 7 percent, while its peer group average has been 85 percent.

Summary

Vanguard European Stock Index rates a perfect score: 25 out of 25 possible points. This makes it the number one global equity pick as well as one of only a handful of funds in any category to receive such a high point rating. Management's goal is to match the price and yield performance of the MSCI Europe Index; roughly 80 percent of the portfolio is represented by this index's stocks. Issues from the U.K., Germany, and France dominate the portfolio. Management is passive but, much more often than not, is able to easily beat out its active counterparts.

Profile

minimum initial investment $3,000	*IRA accounts available* . . . . yes
subsequent minimum investment . . $100	*IRA minimum investment* $1,000
available in all 50 states. . . . . yes	*date of inception.* . . . . June 1990
telephone exchanges . . . . no	*dividend/income paid* . . . . annually
number of other funds in family. 68	*largest sector weighting* . . . . financials

Government Bond Funds

These funds invest in direct and indirect U.S. government obligations. Government bond funds are made up of one or more of the following: T-bills, T-notes, T-bonds, GNMAs, and FNMAs. Treasury bills, notes, and bonds make up the entire marketable debt of the U.S. government. Such instruments are exempt from state income taxes.

Although GNMAs are considered an indirect obligation of the government, they are still backed by the full faith and credit of the United States. FNMAs are not issued by the government but are considered virtually identical in safety to GNMAs. FNMAs and GNMAs are both subject to state and local income taxes. All of the securities in a government bond fund are subject to federal income taxes.

The average maturity of securities found in government bond funds varies broadly, depending upon the type of fund, as well as on management's perception of risk and the future direction of interest rates. A more thorough discussion of interest rates and the volatility of bond fund prices can be found in the introductory pages of the corporate bond section.

Over the past fifteen years (1984–1998), government bonds have returned an average compound return of 12.8 percent versus 12.2 for long-term corporate bonds and 10.5 percent for mortgage-backed securities such as GNMAs and FNMAs. Government bonds were an even better investment than GNMAs, FNMAs, or corporate bonds since their interest is exempt from state income taxes plus there is no chance of default or a reduction in quality rating. A $10,000 investment in U.S. government bonds grew to $60,530 over the past fifteen years; a similar initial investment in corporate bonds grew to $56,360. For the fifteen years ending 3/31/99, government bond *funds* have underperformed corporate bond *funds*, returning 8.8 percent, compared to 9.5 percent for corporate bond funds.

Looking at a longer time frame, government bonds have only slightly outperformed inflation. A dollar invested in governments in 1949 grew to $17.50 by the end of 1998. This translates into an average compound return of 5.9 percent per year. Over the past fifty years, the worst year for government bonds was 1967, when a loss of 9 percent was suffered. The best year so far has been 1982, when government bonds posted a gain of 40 percent. All of these figures are based on total return (current yield plus or minus any appreciation or loss of principal).

Over the past half century, there have been forty-six five-year periods (1949–1953, 1950–1954, etc.). On a pretax basis, government bonds have outperformed inflation during twenty-five of the forty-six five-year periods. Over the past fifty years, there have been forty-one ten-year periods (1949–1958, 1950–1959, etc.). On a pretax basis, government bonds have outperformed inflation during only twenty of the forty-one ten-year periods. Over the past half century, there have been thirty-one twenty-year periods (1949–1968, 1950–1969, etc.). On a pretax basis, government bonds have outperformed inflation during only thirteen of these thirty-one periods. All twelve of those twenty-year periods were the most recent (1967–1986, 1968–1987, etc.).

Six hundred funds make up the government bonds category. Total market capitalization of this category is $130 billion.

Over the past three and five years, government funds have had an average compound annual return of 6.5 and 6.4 percent, respectively. For the decade, these funds have averaged 7.9 percent a year; over the last fifteen years, 8.8 percent a year. The standard deviation for government bond funds has been 3.4 percent over the past three years (all figures for periods ending 3/31/99). This means that these funds have been less volatile than any other category except money market funds.

Government bond funds are the perfect choice for the conservative investor who wants to avoid any possibility of defaults. These securities should be avoided by even conservative investors who are in a high tax bracket or unable to shelter such an investment in a retirement plan or annuity. Such investors should first look at the advantages of municipal bond funds.

The prospective investor should always remember that government and corporate bonds are generally not a good investment once inflation and taxes are factored in. The investor who appreciates the cumulative effects of even low levels of inflation should probably avoid government and corporate bonds except as part of a retirement plan.

Government Bond Funds

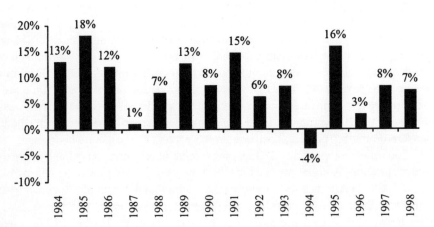

Franklin U.S. Government Securities A

777 Mariners Island Boulevard
San Mateo, CA 94403-7777
800-342-5236

total return	★ ★ ★ ★
risk reduction	★ ★
management	★ ★ ★ ★
current income	★ ★ ★ ★ ★
expense control	★ ★ ★ ★ ★
symbol FKUSX	20 points
up-market performance	excellent
down-market performance	poor
predictability of returns	excellent

Total Return   ★ ★ ★ ★

Over the past five years, Franklin U.S. Government Securities A has taken $10,000 and turned it into $14,356 ($12,364 over three years and $22,568 over the past ten years). This translates into an average annual return of 8 percent over the past five years, 7 percent over the past three years, and 8 percent for the decade. Over the past five years, this fund has outperformed 55 percent of all mutual funds; within its general category it has done better than 85 percent of its peers. Government bond funds have averaged 6 percent annually over these same five years.

During the past five years, a $10,000 initial investment grew to $11,970 after taxes, assuming a 39.6 percent income tax bracket (state and federal combined) and a capital gains rate of 28 percent. This means that investors in this fund were able to preserve 86 percent of their total returns. Compared to other fixed-income funds, this fund's tax savings are considered to be excellent.

Risk/Volatility   ★ ★

Over the past five years, Franklin U.S. Government Securities A has been safer than 90 percent of all government bond funds. Over the past decade, the fund has had one negative year, while the Lehman Brothers Aggregate Bond Index had one (off 3 percent in 1994). The fund has underperformed the Lehman Brothers Aggregate Bond Index six times and the Lehman Brothers Government Bond Index six times in the last ten years.

	last 5 years		last 10 years	
worst year	-3%	1994	-3%	1994
best year	17%	1995	17%	1995

In the past, Franklin U.S. Government Securities A has done better than 90 percent of its peer group in up markets and outperformed 20 percent of its competition in down markets. Consistency, or predictability, of returns for Franklin U.S. Government Securities A can be described as excellent. This fund's risk-adjusted return is excellent.

Management   ★ ★ ★ ★

There are 21,986 fixed-income securities in this $8.6 billion portfolio. The average government bond fund today is $214 million in size. Close to 98 percent of the funds holdings are in bonds. The average maturity of the bonds in this account is twenty-four years; the weighted coupon rate averages 7.4 percent. The portfolio's fixed-income holdings can be categorized as short-term, high-quality debt.

A team has managed this fund for the past ten years. There are eighty funds besides U.S. Government Securities within the Franklin-Templeton family. Overall, the fund family's risk-adjusted performance can be described as very good.

Current Income   ★ ★ ★ ★ ★

Over the past year, Franklin U.S. Government Securities A had a twelve-month yield of 6.5 percent. During this same twelve-month period, the typical government bond fund had a yield that averaged 5.5 percent.

Expenses   ★ ★ ★ ★ ★

Franklin U.S. Government Securities A's expense ratio is .7 percent; it has averaged .6 percent annually over the past three calendar years. The average expense ratio for the 600 funds in this category is 1.1 percent. This fund's turnover rate over the past year has been 26 percent, while its peer group average has been 180 percent.

Summary

Franklin U.S. Government Securities A is a consistent winner; the fund's risk-adjusted returns have been very good over the past three, five, and ten years. The portfolio has the vast majority of its assets in GNMAs, mortgage-backed debt instruments that pay more than government securities but are similar in quality. These securities are particularly attractive when rates have leveled off or are rising or falling slightly. This is a solid offering that has not disappointed or surprised investors since its 1970 inception. For what it does, this fund is a real winner.

Profile

minimum initial investment $1,000	*IRA accounts available* . . . . yes
subsequent minimum investment . . . $50	*IRA minimum investment* $250
available in all 50 states. . . . . yes	*date of inception*. . . . . May 1970
telephone exchanges. . . . . yes	*dividend/income paid*. . . . . monthly
number of other funds in family. 80	*average credit quality* . . . . AAA

Principal Government Securities Income A

P.O. Box 10423
Des Moines, IA 50306
800-451-5447

total return	★ ★ ★ ★
risk reduction	★ ★
management	★ ★ ★ ★
current income	★ ★ ★ ★
expense control	★ ★ ★ ★ ★
symbol PRGVX	19 points
up-market performance	very good
down-market performance	fair
predictability of returns	good

Total Return   ★ ★ ★ ★

Over the past five years, Principal Government Securities Income A has taken $10,000 and turned it into $14,537 ($12,496 over three years and $23,522 over the past ten years). This translates into an average annual return of 8 percent over the past five years, 8 percent over the past three years, and 9 percent for the decade. Over the past five years, this fund has outperformed 50 percent of all mutual funds; within its general category it has done better than 85 percent of its peers. Government bond funds have averaged 6 percent annually over these same five years.

During the past five years, a $10,000 initial investment grew to $12,260 after taxes, assuming a 39.6 percent income tax bracket (state and federal combined) and a capital gains rate of 28 percent. This means that investors in this fund were able to preserve 89 percent of their total returns. Compared to other fixed-income funds, this fund's tax savings are considered to be excellent.

Risk/Volatility   ★ ★

Over the past five years, Principal Government Securities Income A has been safer than 30 percent of all government bond funds. Over the past decade, the fund has had one negative year, while the Lehman Brothers Aggregate Bond Index had one (off 3 percent in 1994). The fund has underperformed the Lehman Brothers Aggregate Bond Index four times and the Lehman Brothers Government Bond Index four times in the last ten years.

	last 5 years		last 10 years	
worst year	-5%	1994	-5%	1994
best year	19%	1995	19%	1995

In the past, Principal Government Securities Income A has done better than 85 percent of its peer group in up markets and outperformed 35 percent of its competition in down markets. Consistency, or predictability, of returns for Principal Government Securities Income A can be described as good. This fund's risk-adjusted return is excellent.

Management   ★ ★ ★ ★

There are six fixed-income securities in this $250 million portfolio. The average government bond fund today is $214 million in size. Close to 99 percent of the funds holdings are in bonds. The average maturity of the bonds in this account is six years; the weighted coupon rate averages 6.7 percent. The portfolio's fixed-income holdings can be categorized as short-term, high-quality debt.

Martin Schafer has managed this fund for the past fourteen years. There are seventeen funds besides Government Securities Income within the Principal family. Overall, the fund family's risk-adjusted performance can be described as very good.

Current Income   ★ ★ ★ ★

Over the past year, Principal Government Securities Income A had a twelve-month yield of 6.1 percent. During this same twelve-month period, the typical government bond fund had a yield that averaged 5.5 percent.

Expenses   ★ ★ ★ ★ ★

Principal Government Securities Income A's expense ratio is .9 percent; it has averaged .8 percent annually over the past three calendar years. The average expense ratio for the 600 funds in this category is 1.1 percent. This fund's turnover rate over the past year has been 17 percent, while its peer group average has been 180 percent.

Summary

Principal Government Securities Income A concentrates on long-term GNMAs. The strategy has paid off, making this one of the very best funds among its peers. Management keeps overhead costs comparatively low, resulting in some very good returns and a hefty stream of current income.

Profile

minimum initial investment $1,000	*IRA accounts available* . . . . yes
subsequent minimum investment . . $100	*IRA minimum investment* $500
available in all 50 states. . . . . yes	*date of inception*. . . . . May 1985
telephone exchanges. . . . . yes	*dividend/income paid*. . . . . monthly
number of other funds in family 17	*average credit quality* . . . . AAA

Vanguard GNMA

Vanguard Financial Center
P.O. Box 2600
Valley Forge, PA 19482
800-662-7447

total return	★ ★ ★ ★
risk reduction	★ ★ ★ ★ ★
management	★ ★ ★ ★ ★
current income	★ ★ ★ ★ ★
expense control	★ ★ ★ ★ ★
symbol VFIIX	24 points
up-market performance	excellent
down-market performance	poor
predictability of returns	very good

Total Return   ★ ★ ★ ★

Over the past five years, Vanguard GNMA has taken $10,000 and turned it into $14,734 ($12,517 over three years and $23,826 over the past ten years). This translates into an average annual return of 8 percent over the past five years, 8 percent over the past three years, and 9 percent for the decade. Over the past five years, this fund has outperformed 55 percent of all mutual funds; within its general category it has done better than 98 percent of its peers. Government bond funds have averaged 6 percent annually over these same five years.

During the past five years, a $10,000 initial investment grew to $12,520 after taxes, assuming a 39.6 percent income tax bracket (state and federal combined) and a capital gains rate of 28 percent. This means that investors in this fund were able to preserve 88 percent of their total returns. Compared to other fixed-income funds, this fund's tax savings are considered to be excellent.

Risk/Volatility   ★ ★ ★ ★ ★

Over the past five years, Vanguard GNMA has been safer than 95 percent of all government bond funds. Over the past decade, the fund has had one negative year, while the Lehman Brothers Aggregate Bond Index had one (off 3 percent in 1994). The fund has underperformed the Lehman Brothers Aggregate Bond Index five times and the Lehman Brothers Government Bond Index five times in the last ten years.

	last 5 years		last 10 years	
worst year	-1%	1994	-1%	1994
best year	17%	1995	17%	1995

In the past, Vanguard GNMA has done better than 100 percent of its peer group in up markets and outperformed 10 percent of its competition in down markets. Consistency, or predictability, of returns for Vanguard GNMA can be described as very good. This fund's risk-adjusted return is excellent.

Management   ★ ★ ★ ★ ★

There are 162 fixed-income securities in this $12 billion portfolio. The average government bond fund today is $214 million in size. Close to 99 percent of the funds holdings are in bonds. The average maturity of the bonds in this account is six years; the weighted coupon rate averages 7.1 percent. The portfolio's fixed-income holdings can be categorized as intermediate-term, high-quality debt.

Paul Kaplan has managed this fund for the past five years. There are sixty-eight funds besides GNMA within the Vanguard family. Overall, the fund family's risk-adjusted performance can be described as very good.

Current Income   ★ ★ ★ ★ ★

Over the past year, Vanguard GNMA had a twelve-month yield of 6.6 percent. During this same twelve-month period, the typical government bond fund had a yield that averaged 5.5 percent.

Expenses   ★ ★ ★ ★ ★

Vanguard GNMA's expense ratio is .3 percent; it has also averaged .3 percent annually over the past three calendar years. The average expense ratio for the 600 funds in this category is 1.1 percent. This fund's turnover rate over the past year has been 3 percent, while its peer group average has been 180 percent.

Summary

Vanguard GNMA ranks number one as the best overall government securities fund. There is no secret to Vanguard's successes in a number of categories. Management keeps transactions and expenses to a minimum. There is nothing fancy about this offering, it just keeps delivering. This fund is highly recommended.

Profile

minimum initial investment $3,000	IRA accounts available . . . . yes
subsequent minimum investment . . $100	IRA minimum investment $1,000
available in all 50 states. . . . . yes	date of inception. . . . . June 1980
telephone exchanges. . . . . yes	dividend/income paid. . . . . monthly
number of other funds in family 68	average credit quality . . . . AAA

Vanguard Intermediate-Term U. S. Treasury

Vanguard Financial Center
P.O. Box 2600
Valley Forge, PA 19482
800-662-7447

total return	★ ★ ★ ★
risk reduction	★
management	★ ★ ★
current income	★ ★ ★ ★
expense control	★ ★ ★ ★ ★
symbol VFITX	17 points
up-market performance	fair
down-market performance	very good
predictability of returns	fair

Total Return   ★ ★ ★ ★

Over the past five years, Vanguard Intermediate-Term U.S. Treasury has taken $10,000 and turned it into $14,410 ($12,399 over three years). This translates into an average annual return of 8 percent over the past five years and 7 percent over the past three years. Over the past five years, this fund has outperformed 55 percent of all mutual funds; within its general category it has done better than 95 percent of its peers. Government bond funds have averaged 6 percent annually over these same five years.

During the past five years, a $10,000 initial investment grew to $12,400 after taxes, assuming a 39.6 percent income tax bracket (state and federal combined) and a capital gains rate of 28 percent. This means that investors in this fund were able to preserve 88 percent of their total returns. Compared to other fixed-income funds, this fund's tax savings are considered to be excellent.

Risk/Volatility   ★

Over the past five years, Vanguard Intermediate-Term U.S. Treasury has been safer than 25 percent of all government bond funds. Over the past decade, the fund has had one negative year, while the Lehman Brothers Aggregate Bond Index had one (off 3 percent in 1994). The fund has underperformed the Lehman Brothers Aggregate Bond Index three times and the Lehman Brothers Government Bond Index three times in the last ten years.

	last 5 years		since inception	
worst year	-4%	1994	-4%	1994
best year	20%	1995	20%	1995

In the past, Vanguard Intermediate-Term U.S. Treasury has done better than 35 percent of its peer group in up markets and outperformed 80 percent of its competition in down markets. Consistency, or predictability, of returns for Vanguard Intermediate-Term U.S. Treasury can be described as fair. This fund's risk-adjusted return is very good.

Management   ★ ★ ★

There are twenty-eight fixed-income securities in this $1.8 billion portfolio. The average government bond fund today is $214 million in size. Close to 96 percent of the funds holdings are in bonds. The average maturity of the bonds in this account is seven years; the weighted coupon rate averages 7.9 percent. The portfolio's fixed-income holdings can be categorized as intermediate-term, high-quality debt.

Ian MacKinnon and Robert Auwaerter have managed this fund for the past eight years. There are sixty-eight funds besides Intermediate-Term U.S. Treasury within the Vanguard family. Overall, the fund family's risk-adjusted performance can be described as very good.

Current Income   ★ ★ ★ ★

Over the past year, Vanguard Intermediate-Term U.S. Treasury had a twelve-month yield of 5.8 percent. During this same twelve-month period, the typical government bond fund had a yield that averaged 5.5 percent.

Expenses   ★ ★ ★ ★ ★

Vanguard Intermediate-Term U.S. Treasury's expense ratio is .3 percent; it has also averaged .3 percent annually over the past three calendar years. The average expense ratio for the 600 funds in this category is 1.1 percent. This fund's turnover rate over the past year has been 30 percent, while its peer group average has been 180 percent.

Summary

Vanguard Intermediate-Term U.S. Treasury avoids the problems that are sometimes associated with mortgage-backed bonds by emphasizing direct U.S. obligations that cannot be "called away" or paid down. This philosophy is different than the better-rated Vanguard GNMA fund, but this offering does have its place. The fund is recommended more for the purist.

Profile

minimum initial investment $3,000	*IRA accounts available* . . . . yes
subsequent minimum investment . . $100	*IRA minimum investment* $1,000
available in all 50 states . . . . yes	*date of inception* . . . . Oct. 1991
telephone exchanges . . . . yes	*dividend/income paid* . . . . monthly
number of other funds in family 68	*average credit quality* . . . . AAA

Vanguard Long-Term U.S. Treasury

Vanguard Financial Center
P.O. Box 2600
Valley Forge, PA 19482
800-662-7447

total return	★ ★ ★ ★ ★
risk reduction	★ ★
management	★ ★ ★ ★ ★
current income	★ ★ ★ ★
expense control	★ ★ ★ ★ ★
symbol VUSTX	21 points
up-market performance	poor
down-market performance	very good
predictability of returns	poor

Total Return   ★ ★ ★ ★ ★

Over the past five years, Vanguard Long-Term U.S. Treasury has taken $10,000 and turned it into $15,613 ($13,083 over three years and $27,775 over the past ten years). This translates into an average annual return of 9 percent over the past five years, 9 percent over the past three years, and 10 percent for the decade. Over the past five years, this fund has outperformed 65 percent of all mutual funds; within its general category it has done better than 80 percent of its peers. Government bond funds have averaged 6 percent annually over these same five years.

During the past five years, a $10,000 initial investment grew to $12,920 after taxes, assuming a 39.6 percent income tax bracket (state and federal combined) and a capital gains rate of 28 percent. This means that investors in this fund were able to preserve 84 percent of their total returns. Compared to other fixed-income funds, this fund's tax savings are considered to be excellent.

Risk/Volatility   ★ ★

Over the past five years, Vanguard Long-Term U.S. Treasury has been safer than 35 percent of all government bond funds. Over the past decade, the fund has had two negative years, while the Lehman Brothers Aggregate Bond Index had one (off 3 percent in 1994). The fund has underperformed the Lehman Brothers Aggregate Bond Index three times and the Lehman Brothers Government Bond Index nine times in the last ten years.

	last 5 years		last 10 years	
worst year	-5%	1994	-5%	1994
best year	26%	1995	26%	1995

In the past, Vanguard Long-Term U.S. Treasury has done better than 25 percent of its peer group in up markets and outperformed 80 percent of its competition in down markets. Consistency, or predictability, of returns for Vanguard

Long-Term U.S. Treasury can be described as poor. This fund's risk-adjusted return is very good.

Management   ★ ★ ★ ★ ★
There are sixteen fixed-income securities in this $1.4 billion portfolio. The average government bond fund today is $214 million in size. Close to 99 percent of the funds holdings are in bonds. The average maturity of the bonds in this account is twenty-one years; the weighted coupon rate averages 7.6 percent. The portfolio's fixed-income holdings can be categorized as long-term, high-quality debt.

Ian MacKinnon and Robert Auwaerter have managed this fund for the past nine years. There are sixty-eight funds besides Long-Term U.S. Treasury within the Vanguard family. Overall, the fund family's risk-adjusted performance can be described as very good.

Current Income   ★ ★ ★ ★
Over the past year, Vanguard Long-Term U.S. Treasury had a twelve-month yield of 5.8 percent. During this same twelve-month period, the typical government bond fund had a yield that averaged 5.5 percent.

Expenses   ★ ★ ★ ★ ★
Vanguard Long-Term U.S. Treasury's expense ratio is .3 percent; it has also averaged .3 percent annually over the past three calendar years. The average expense ratio for the 600 funds in this category is 1.1 percent. This fund's turnover rate over the past year has been 18 percent, while its peer group average has been 180 percent.

Summary
Vanguard Long-Term U.S. Treasury is just one of a large number of Vanguard offerings to appear in this book. Like other members of the family, this fund keeps costs to a bare minimum; total return figures and management are also quite impressive. As the name suggests, this fund mostly invests in long-term securities backed by the U.S. government. For shareholders, such securities are exempt from state and any local income tax. For conservative fund investors who want to maximize current income, this and Vanguard's GNMA portfolio are both highly recommended.

Profile

minimum initial investment $3,000	*IRA accounts available* . . . . yes
subsequent minimum investment . . $100	*IRA minimum investment* $1,000
available in all 50 states. . . . . yes	*date of inception.* . . . . May 1986
telephone exchanges. . . . . yes	*dividend/income paid.* . . . . monthly
number of other funds in family 68	*average credit quality* . . . . AAA

Growth Funds

These funds generally seek capital appreciation, with current income as a distant secondary concern. Growth funds typically invest in U.S. common stocks, while avoiding speculative issues and aggressive trading techniques. The goal of most of these funds is long-term growth. The approaches used to attain this appreciation can vary significantly among growth funds.

Over the past fifteen years, U.S. stocks have outperformed both corporate and government bonds. From 1984 through 1998, common stocks have averaged 17.9 percent compounded per year, compared to 12.2 percent for corporate bonds and 12.8 for government bonds. A $10,000 investment in stocks, as measured by the S&P 500, grew to $118,290 over the past fifteen years; a similar initial investment in corporate bonds grew to $56,360.

Looking at a longer time frame, common stocks have also fared quite well. A dollar invested in stocks in 1949 grew to $578 by the end of 1998. This translates into an average compound return of 13.6 percent per year. Over the past fifty years, the worst year for common stocks was 1974, when a loss of 26 percent was suffered. One year later, these same stocks posted a gain of 37 percent. The best year so far has been 1954, when growth stocks posted a gain of 53 percent.

Since the end of the 1930s, common stocks have outperformed bonds in every single decade. If President George Washington had invested $1 in common stocks with an average return of 12 percent, his investment would be worth over $336 billion today. If George had been a bit lucky and averaged 14 percent on his stock portfolio, his portfolio would be large enough to pay our national debt four times over!

To give you an idea as to the likelihood of making money in common stocks, look at the table below. It covers more than 120 years and shows the odds of making money (a positive return) over each of several different time periods.

Standard & Poor's Composite 500 Stock Index
Various periods, 1871–1997 (dividends not included)

Length of Period	Total Number of Periods	Number of Periods in which Stock Prices			Percentage Opportunity for Profit (not including dividends)
		Rose	Declined	Unchanged	
1 year	127	81	45	1	64%
5 years	123	97	25	1	79%
10 years	118	106	12	0	90%
15 years	113	104	9	0	92%
20 years	108	105	3	0	97%
25 years	103	102	1	0	99%
30 years	98	98	0	0	100%

Eighteen hundred funds make up the growth category. Total market capitalization of this category is $1 trillion. The standard deviation for this group is 23.0 percent; beta (stock market-related risk) is 1.0, the same as the overall market, as measured by the S&P 500. The typical portfolio of a growth fund is divided up as follows: 90 percent U.S. stocks, 3 percent foreign stocks, and the balance in money market instruments. Turnover rate is 94 percent per year. The yield on growth funds averages about 0.3 percent annually. Fund expenses for this group average 1.5 percent per year.

Over the past three years, growth funds have had an average compound return of 19.8 percent per year; the annual return for the past five years has been 19.5 percent. For the past decade, growth funds have averaged 16.0 percent annually and 15.5 percent per year for the past fifteen years (all periods ending 3/31/99).

Growth Funds

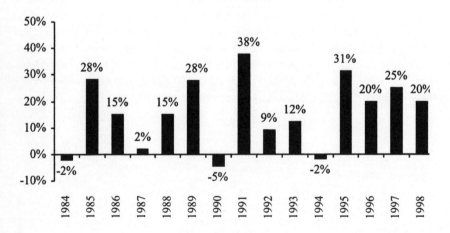

Enterprise Growth A
3343 Peachtree Road, Suite 450
Atlanta, GA 30326
800-432-4320

total return	★ ★ ★ ★ ★
risk reduction	★ ★ ★
management	★ ★ ★ ★ ★
tax minimization	★ ★ ★ ★ ★
expense control	★ ★ ★ ★
symbol ENGRX	22 points
up-market performance	very good
down-market performance	fair
predictability of returns	good

Total Return   ★ ★ ★ ★ ★
Over the past five years, Enterprise Growth A has taken $10,000 and turned it into $34,846 ($22,693 over three years and $64,386 over the past ten years). This translates into an average annual return of 28 percent over the past five years, 31 percent over the past three years, and 20 percent for the decade. Over the past five years, this fund has outperformed 99 percent of all mutual funds; within its general category it has done better than 95 percent of its peers. Growth funds have averaged 20 percent annually over these same five years.

Risk/Volatility   ★ ★ ★
Over the past five years, Enterprise Growth A has been safer than 65 percent of all growth funds. Over the past decade, the fund has had two negative years, while the S&P 500 has had one (off 3 percent in 1990). The fund has underperformed the S&P 500 four times in the last ten years.

	last 5 years		last 10 years	
worst year	-1%	1994	-3%	1990
best year	40%	1995	42%	1991

In the past, Enterprise Growth A has done better than 80 percent of its peer group in up markets and outperformed 35 percent of its competition in down markets. Consistency, or predictability, of returns for Enterprise Growth A can be described as good. This fund's risk-adjusted return is excellent.

Management   ★ ★ ★ ★ ★
There are thirty-three stocks in this $900 million portfolio. The average growth fund today is $560 million in size. Close to 96 percent of the fund's holdings are in stocks. The stocks in this portfolio have an average price-earnings (p/e) ratio of 43 and a median market capitalization of $82 billion. The portfolio's equity holdings can be categorized as large-cap and growth-oriented issues.

Ronald Canakaris has managed this fund for the past nineteen years. There are eleven funds besides Growth within the Enterprise family. Overall, the fund family's risk-adjusted performance can be described as excellent.

Tax Minimization   ★ ★ ★ ★ ★
During the past five years, a $10,000 initial investment grew to $28,270 after taxes, assuming a 39.6 percent income tax bracket (state and federal combined) and a capital gains rate of 28 percent. This means that investors in this fund were able to preserve 89 percent of their total returns. Compared to other equity funds, this fund's tax savings are considered to be very good.

Expenses   ★ ★ ★ ★
Enterprise Growth A's expense ratio is 1.4 percent; it has averaged 1.5 percent annually over the past three calendar years. The average expense ratio for the 1,800 funds in this category is 1.5 percent. This fund's turnover rate over the past year has been 22 percent, while its peer group average has been 95 percent.

Summary
Enterprise Growth A has ranked in the top performance quartile for five of the past six years. Management believes that the best choices are determined by the present worth of a company's future income stream. The portfolio is concentrated in just a few dozen large-cap stocks, many of which are household names that derive a moderate amount of their revenue from overseas sales. Manager Canakaris has no difficulty in going into cash heavily when warranted. This fund is a very good choice for any equity investor.

Profile
minimum initial investment $1,000	*IRA accounts available* . . . . yes
subsequent minimum investment . . . $50	*IRA minimum investment* $250
available in all 50 states. . . . . yes	*date of inception.* . . . . May 1968
telephone exchanges. . . . . yes	*dividend/income paid* . . . . annually
number of other funds in family 11	*largest sector weighting* . . . . health

Harbor Capital Appreciation
One SeaGate
Toledo, OH 43666
800-422-1050

total return	★ ★ ★ ★ ★
risk reduction	★ ★
management	★ ★ ★ ★ ★
tax minimization	★ ★ ★ ★
expense control	★ ★ ★ ★ ★
symbol HACAX	21 points
up-market performance	excellent
down-market performance	poor
predictability of returns	fair

Total Return   ★ ★ ★ ★ ★
Over the past five years, Harbor Capital Appreciation has taken $10,000 and turned it into $35,433 ($23,110 over three years and $75,415 over the past ten years). This translates into an average annual return of 29 percent over the past five years, 32 percent over the past three years, and 22 percent for the decade. Over the past five years, this fund has outperformed 98 percent of all mutual funds; within its general category it has done better than 90 percent of its peers. Growth funds have averaged 20 percent annually over these same five years.

Risk/Volatility   ★ ★
Over the past five years, Harbor Capital Appreciation has been safer than 35 percent of all growth funds. Over the past decade, the fund has had one negative year, while the S&P 500 has had one (off 3 percent in 1990). The fund has underperformed the S&P 500 three times in the last ten years.

	last 5 years		last 10 years	
worst year	3%	1994	-2%	1990
best year	38%	1995	55%	1991

In the past, Harbor Capital Appreciation has done better than 90 percent of its peer group in up markets and outperformed 25 percent of its competition in down markets. Consistency, or predictability, of returns for Harbor Capital Appreciation can be described as fair. This fund's risk-adjusted return is fair.

Management   ★ ★ ★ ★ ★
There are fifty-five stocks in this $5.6 billion portfolio. The average growth fund today is $560 million in size. Close to 96 percent of the fund's holdings are in stocks. The stocks in this portfolio have an average price-earnings (p/e) ratio of 43 and a median market capitalization of $61 billion. The portfolio's equity holdings can be categorized as large-cap and growth-oriented issues.

Spiros Segalas has managed this fund for the past nine years. There are seven funds besides Capital Appreciation within the Harbor family. Overall, the fund family's risk-adjusted performance can be described as very good.

Tax Minimization   ★ ★ ★ ★
During the past five years, a $10,000 initial investment grew to $26,840 after taxes, assuming a 39.6 percent income tax bracket (state and federal combined) and a capital gains rate of 28 percent. This means that investors in this fund were able to preserve 87 percent of their total returns. Compared to other equity funds, this fund's tax savings are considered to be very good.

Expenses   ★ ★ ★ ★ ★
Harbor Capital Appreciation's expense ratio is .7 percent; it has also averaged .7 percent annually over the past three calendar years. The average expense ratio for the 1,800 funds in this category is 1.5 percent. This fund's turnover rate over the past year has been 70 percent, while its peer group average has been 95 percent.

Summary
Harbor Capital Appreciation seeks out common and convertible securities of well-established companies that have above-average growth prospects. Manager Spiros frequently visits prospective companies and favors the "top line"—excellent sales growth, high levels of unit growth, very good returns on equity and assets as well as a strong balance sheet. This fund receives excellent marks in the areas of total return, management, and expense minimization.

Profile

minimum initial investment $2,000	*IRA accounts available* . . . . yes
subsequent minimum investment . . $500	*IRA minimum investment* $500
available in all 50 states. . . . . yes	*date of inception.* . . . . Dec. 1987
telephone exchanges. . . . . yes	*dividend/income paid* . . . . annually
number of other funds in family. 7	*largest sector weighting* . . . technology

Janus Mercury
100 Fillmore Street, Suite 300
Denver, CO 80206-4923
800-525-8983

total return	★ ★ ★ ★ ★
risk reduction	★ ★
management	★ ★ ★ ★ ★
tax minimization	★ ★ ★ ★
expense control	★ ★ ★ ★
symbol JAMRX	20 points
up-market performance	excellent
down-market performance	excellent
predictability of returns	fair

Total Return   ★ ★ ★ ★ ★
Over the past five years, Janus Mercury has taken $10,000 and turned it into
$37,617 ($23,857 over three years). This translates into an average annual return
of 30 percent over the past five years and 34 percent over the past three years. Over
the past five years, this fund has outperformed 98 percent of all mutual funds;
within its general category it has done better than 90 percent of its peers. Growth
funds have averaged 20 percent annually over these same five years.

Risk/Volatility   ★ ★
Over the past five years, Janus Mercury has been safer than 35 percent of all
growth funds. Over the past decade, the fund has not had a negative year, while the
S&P 500 has had one (off 3 percent in 1990). The fund has underperformed the
S&P 500 three times in the last ten years.

	last 5 years		since inception	
worst year	16%	1994	16%	1994
best year	58%	1998	58%	1998

In the past, Janus Mercury has done better than 100 percent of its peer group
in up markets and outperformed 90 percent of its competition in down markets.
Consistency, or predictability, of returns for Janus Mercury can be described as
fair. This fund's risk-adjusted return is excellent.

Management   ★ ★ ★ ★ ★
There are sixty-five stocks in this $3.8 billion portfolio. The average growth fund
today is $560 million in size. Close to 94 percent of the fund's holdings are in
stocks. The stocks in this portfolio have an average price-earnings (p/e) ratio of 46
and a median market capitalization of $27 billion. The portfolio's equity holdings
can be categorized as large-cap and growth-oriented issues.

Warren Lammert has managed this fund for the past six years. There are fifteen funds besides Mercury within the Janus family. Overall, the fund family's
risk-adjusted performance can be described as excellent.

Tax Minimization   ★ ★ ★ ★

During the past five years, a $10,000 initial investment grew to $25,110 after taxes, assuming a 39.6 percent income tax bracket (state and federal combined) and a capital gains rate of 28 percent. This means that investors in this fund were able to preserve 78 percent of their total returns. Compared to other equity funds, this fund's tax savings are considered to be fair.

Expenses   ★ ★ ★ ★

Janus Mercury's expense ratio is 1 percent; it has also averaged 1 percent annually over the past three calendar years. The average expense ratio for the 1,800 funds in this category is 1.5 percent. This fund's turnover rate over the past year has been 105 percent, while its peer group average has been 95 percent.

Summary

Janus Mercury is categorized as an "aggressive growth" fund by some sources and a "growth" fund by others; the fund is a very good choice for either camp. Close to a fifth of the portfolio's assets are in internet stocks; management also favors technology and cable issues. Decisions are not based on the size of the company. Manager Lammert has no bias toward any size cap. Equities are targeted based on very detailed fundamentals that emphasize long-term earnings potential. At times, foreign stocks may make up a moderate portion of the portfolio. Total return figures and management are tops.

Profile

minimum initial investment $2,500	*IRA accounts available* . . . . yes
subsequent minimum investment . . $100	*IRA minimum investment* $500
available in all 50 states. . . . . yes	*date of inception*. . . . . May 1993
telephone exchanges. . . . . yes	*dividend/income paid* . . . . annually
number of other funds in family 15	*largest sector weighting* . . . . . . services

Legg Mason Value Trust—Primary Class

111 South Calvert Street
Baltimore, MD 21203-1476
800-577-8589

total return	★ ★ ★ ★ ★
risk reduction	★
management	★ ★ ★ ★ ★
tax minimization	★ ★ ★ ★ ★
expense control	★ ★ ★ ★
symbol LMVTX	20 points
up-market performance	excellent
down-market performance	poor
predictability of returns	fair

Total Return ★ ★ ★ ★ ★

Over the past five years, Legg Mason Value Trust—Primary Class has taken $10,000 and turned it into $48,527 ($31,115 over three years and $73,587 over the past ten years). This translates into an average annual return of 37 percent over the past five years, 46 percent over the past three years, and 22 percent for the decade. Over the past five years, this fund has outperformed 99 percent of all mutual funds; within its general category it has done better than 99 percent of its peers. Growth funds have averaged 20 percent annually over these same five years.

Risk/Volatility ★

Over the past five years, Legg Mason Value Trust—Primary Class has been safer than 25 percent of all growth funds. Over the past decade, the fund has had one negative year, while the S&P 500 has had one (off 3 percent in 1990). The fund has underperformed the S&P 500 two times in the last ten years.

	last 5 years		last 10 years	
worst year	1%	1994	-17%	1990
best year	48%	1998	48%	1998

In the past, Legg Mason Value Trust—Primary Class has done better than 100 percent of its peer group in up markets and outperformed 20 percent of its competition in down markets. Consistency, or predictability, of returns for Legg Mason Value Trust—Primary Class can be described as fair. This fund's risk-adjusted return is excellent.

Management ★ ★ ★ ★ ★

There are forty-eight stocks in this $10.1 billion portfolio. The average growth fund today is $560 million in size. Close to 92 percent of the fund's holdings are in stocks. The stocks in this portfolio have an average price-earnings (p/e) ratio of 33 and a median market capitalization of $50 billion. The portfolio's equity holdings can be categorized as large-cap and value-oriented issues.

William Miller III has managed this fund for the past seventeen years. There are fifteen funds besides Value Trust—Primary Class within the Legg Mason family. Overall, the fund family's risk-adjusted performance can be described as very good.

Tax Minimization   ★ ★ ★ ★ ★

During the past five years, a $10,000 initial investment grew to $32,290 after taxes, assuming a 39.6 percent income tax bracket (state and federal combined) and a capital gains rate of 28 percent. This means that investors in this fund were able to preserve 81 percent of their total returns. Compared to other equity funds, this fund's tax savings are considered to be good.

Expenses   ★ ★ ★ ★

Legg Mason Value Trust—Primary Class's expense ratio is 1.7 percent; it has averaged 1.8 percent annually over the past three calendar years. The average expense ratio for the 1,800 funds in this category is 1.5 percent. This fund's turnover rate over the past year has been 13 percent, while its peer group average has been 95 percent.

Summary

Legg Mason Value Trust—Primary Class has ranked in the top quartile of performance for each of the past five years. Management is value-driven and uses a bottom-up approach to equity selection. Manager Miller seeks out companies selling at a significant discount to the value of their underlying businesses. Positions are held until values are realized by the marketplace. Purchases are made for the long term; the portfolio has no interest in trying to gauge short-term market directions. This is quite a volatile fund but its performance has been superb, rewarding patient investors.

Profile

minimum initial investment $1,000	*IRA accounts available* . . . . yes
subsequent minimum investment . . $100	*IRA minimum investment* $1,000
available in all 50 states . . . . no	*date of inception* . . . . April 1982
telephone exchanges. . . . . yes	*dividend/income paid* . . . . quarterly
number of other funds in family 15	*largest sector weighting* . . . technology

Merger
100 Summit Lake Drive
Valhalla, NY 10595
800-343-8959

total return	★
risk reduction	★ ★ ★ ★ ★
management	★ ★
tax minimization	★ ★
expense control	★ ★
symbol MERFX	12 points
up-market performance	poor
down-market performance	excellent
predictability of returns	excellent

Total Return   ★
Over the past five years, Merger has taken $10,000 and turned it into $16,215 ($12,897 over three years and $24,647 over the past ten years). This translates into an average annual return of 10 percent over the past five years, 9 percent over the past three years, and 9 percent for the decade. Over the past five years, this fund has outperformed 65 percent of all mutual funds; within its general category it has done better than 20 percent of its peers. Growth funds have averaged 20 percent annually over these same five years.

Risk/Volatility   ★ ★ ★ ★ ★
Over the past five years, Merger has been safer than 99 percent of all growth funds. Over the past decade, the fund has not had a negative year, while the S&P 500 has had one (off 3 percent in 1990). The fund has underperformed the S&P 500 six times in the last ten years.

	last 5 years		last 10 years	
worst year	5%	1998	1%	1990
best year	14%	1995	18%	1993

In the past, Merger has done better than 20 percent of its peer group in up markets and outperformed 90 percent of its competition in down markets. Consistency, or predictability, of returns for Merger can be described as excellent. This fund's risk-adjusted return is excellent.

Management   ★ ★
There are forty-three stocks in this $340 million portfolio. The average growth fund today is $560 million in size. Close to 95 percent of the fund's holdings are in stocks. The stocks in this portfolio have an average price-earnings (p/e) ratio of 36 and a median market capitalization of $9 billion. The portfolio's equity holdings can be categorized as mid-cap and value-oriented issues.

Frederick Green and Bonnie Smith have managed this fund for the past ten years. There are no other funds besides Merger within the Merger family. Overall, the fund family's risk-adjusted performance can be described as excellent.

Tax Minimization ★★
During the past five years, a $10,000 initial investment grew to $13,930 after taxes, assuming a 39.6 percent income tax bracket (state and federal combined) and a capital gains rate of 28 percent. This means that investors in this fund were able to preserve 88 percent of their total returns. Compared to other equity funds, this fund's tax savings are considered to be very good.

Expenses ★★
Merger's expense ratio is 1.3 percent; it has averaged 1.4 percent annually over the past three calendar years. The average expense ratio for the 1,800 funds in this category is 1.5 percent. This fund's turnover rate over the past year has been 355 percent, while its peer group average has been 95 percent.

Summary
Merger, as its name implies, seeks capital appreciation by buying companies in mergers. At least two-thirds of the portfolio's assets are invested in companies that are the object of a publicly announced acquisition. When the merger involves stock-for-stock, management will often short the stock of the acquiring corporation in order to reduce any market risk. For investors of this fund, the risk is that the announced merger does not go through. This fund is not recommended for anyone looking for high appreciation but it is strongly recommended for those interested in being in stocks with a minimal amount of risk.

Profile

minimum initial investment $2,000	IRA accounts available . . . . yes
subsequent minimum investment $1	IRA minimum investment $2,000
available in all 50 states. . . . . yes	date of inception . . . . Jan. 1989
telephone exchanges . . . . no	dividend/income paid . . . . annually
number of other funds in family. 0	largest sector weighting . . . . financials

Spectra

1 World Trade Center, Suite 9333
New York, NY 10048
800-992-3863

total return	★ ★ ★ ★ ★
risk reduction	★
management	★ ★
tax minimization	★ ★ ★
expense control	★
symbol SPECX	12 points
up-market performance	excellent
down-market performance	excellent
predictability of returns	fair

Total Return   ★ ★ ★ ★ ★

Over the past five years, Spectra has taken $10,000 and turned it into $40,349 ($24,007 over three years and $106,015 over the past ten years). This translates into an average annual return of 32 percent over the past five years, 34 percent over the past three years, and 27 percent for the decade. Over the past five years, this fund has outperformed 99 percent of all mutual funds; within its general category it has done better than 99 percent of its peers. Growth funds have averaged 20 percent annually over these same five years.

Risk/Volatility   ★

Over the past five years, Spectra has been safer than 10 percent of all growth funds. Over the past decade, the fund has not had a negative year, while the S&P 500 has had one (off 3 percent in 1990). The fund has underperformed the S&P 500 three times in the last ten years.

	last 5 years		last 10 years	
worst year	4%	1994	3%	1990
best year	48%	1998	57%	1991

In the past, Spectra has done better than 100 percent of its peer group in up markets and outperformed 100 percent of its competition in down markets. Consistency, or predictability, of returns for Spectra can be described as fair. This fund's risk-adjusted return is excellent.

Management   ★ ★

There are sixty-six stocks in this $320 million portfolio. The average growth fund today is $560 million in size. Close to 100 percent of the fund's holdings are in stocks. The stocks in this portfolio have an average price-earnings (p/e) ratio of 47 and a median market capitalization of $41 billion. The portfolio's equity holdings can be categorized as large-cap and growth-oriented issues.

David Alger and David Hyun have managed this fund for the past thirteen years. There are eight funds besides Spectra within the Alger family. Overall, the fund family's risk-adjusted performance can be described as very good.

Tax Minimization   ★ ★ ★
During the past five years, a $10,000 initial investment grew to $23,290 after taxes, assuming a 39.6 percent income tax bracket (state and federal combined) and a capital gains rate of 28 percent. This means that investors in this fund were able to preserve 69 percent of their total returns. Compared to other equity funds, this fund's tax savings are considered to be poor.

Expenses   ★
Spectra's expense ratio is 2.1 percent; it has averaged 2.3 percent annually over the past three calendar years. The average expense ratio for the 1,800 funds in this category is 1.5 percent. This fund's turnover rate over the past year has been 134 percent, while its peer group average has been 95 percent.

Summary
Spectra, like other equity funds managed by David Alger, is not for the faint of heart. This aggressive portfolio has never disappointed the patient investor who is looking for maximum returns. Alger and co-manager Hyun, along with a group of over twenty analysts, look at over 1,400 candidates, trying to find candidates that have high unit volume growth and life-cycle changes. The fund has no size restriction when it comes to equity selection. Management has the freedom to invest all of its assets in micro-caps, mid-caps or large-caps. Due to its tax policy, this fund is best suited for qualified retirement accounts.

Profile

minimum initial investment $1,000	IRA accounts available . . . . yes
subsequent minimum investment . . $100	IRA minimum investment $250
available in all 50 states. . . . . yes	date of inception . . . . July 1969
telephone exchanges. . . . . yes	dividend/income paid . . . . annually
number of other funds in family. 8	largest sector weighting . . . technology

Vanguard Growth Index
Vanguard Financial Center
P.O. Box 2600
Valley Forge, PA 19482
800-662-7447

total return	★ ★ ★ ★ ★
risk reduction	★ ★ ★ ★ ★
management	★ ★ ★ ★ ★
tax minimization	★ ★ ★ ★ ★
expense control	★ ★ ★ ★ ★
symbol VIGRX	25 points
up-market performance	very good
down-market performance	excellent
predictability of returns	good

Total Return
★ ★ ★ ★ ★

Over the past five years, Vanguard Growth Index has taken $10,000 and turned it into $38,125 ($24,593 over three years). This translates into an average annual return of 31 percent over the past five years and 35 percent over the past three years. Over the past five years, this fund has outperformed 99 percent of all mutual funds; within its general category it has done better than 98 percent of its peers. Growth funds have averaged 20 percent annually over these same five years.

Risk/Volatility
★ ★ ★ ★ ★

Over the past five years, Vanguard Growth Index has been safer than 95 percent of all growth funds. Over the past decade, the fund has not had a negative year, while the S&P 500 has had one (off 3 percent in 1990). The fund has underperformed the S&P 500 once in the last ten years.

	last 5 years		since inception	
worst year	3%	1994	2%	1993
best year	42%	1998	42%	1998

In the past, Vanguard Growth Index has done better than 70 percent of its peer group in up markets and outperformed 90 percent of its competition in down markets. Consistency, or predictability, of returns for Vanguard Growth Index can be described as good. This fund's risk-adjusted return is excellent.

Management
★ ★ ★ ★ ★

There are 155 stocks in this $8.4 billion portfolio. The average growth fund today is $560 million in size. Close to 99 percent of the fund's holdings are in stocks. The stocks in this portfolio have an average price-earnings (p/e) ratio of 41 and a median market capitalization of $120 billion. The portfolio's equity holdings can be categorized as large-cap and growth-oriented issues.

George Sauter has managed this fund for the past seven years. There are sixty-eight funds besides Growth Index within the Vanguard family. Overall, the fund family's risk-adjusted performance can be described as very good.

Tax Minimization ★ ★ ★ ★ ★

During the past five years, a $10,000 initial investment grew to $30,790 after taxes, assuming a 39.6 percent income tax bracket (state and federal combined) and a capital gains rate of 28 percent. This means that investors in this fund were able to preserve 90 percent of their total returns. Compared to other equity funds, this fund's tax savings are considered to be excellent.

Expenses ★ ★ ★ ★ ★

Vanguard Growth Index's expense ratio is .2 percent; it has also averaged .2 percent annually over the past three calendar years. The average expense ratio for the 1,800 funds in this category is 1.5 percent. This fund's turnover rate over the past year has been 29 percent, while its peer group average has been 95 percent.

Summary

Vanguard Growth Index has exceptional risk-adjusted returns since its 1992 inception. Unlike the more popular Vanguard 500 Index fund, this fund invests its assets so that performance and risk mimic the S&P/Barra Growth Index. This index is mostly comprised of very large growth companies and does not include any value plays (which make up the balance of the S&P 500). The market has favored large-cap growth stocks for each of the past several years and there is no strong sign that this trend is going to wane anytime soon.

Profile

minimum initial investment $3,000	*IRA accounts available* . . . . yes
subsequent minimum investment . . $100	*IRA minimum investment* $1,000
available in all 50 states. . . . . yes	*date of inception* . . . . Nov. 1992
telephone exchanges. . . . . yes	*dividend/income paid* . . . . quarterly
number of other funds in family 68	*largest sector weighting* . . . technology

Vanguard U.S. Growth
Vanguard Financial Center
P.O. Box 2600
Valley Forge, PA 19482
800-662-7447

total return	★ ★ ★ ★
risk reduction	★ ★ ★ ★ ★
management	★ ★ ★ ★ ★
tax minimization	★ ★ ★ ★
expense control	★ ★ ★ ★ ★
symbol VWUSX	23 points
up-market performance	good
down-market performance	very good
predictability of returns	very good

Total Return   ★ ★ ★ ★
Over the past five years, Vanguard U.S. Growth has taken $10,000 and turned it into $34,132 ($21,582 over three years and $65,626 over the past ten years). This translates into an average annual return of 26 percent over the past five years, 29 percent over the past three years, and 21 percent for the decade. Over the past five years, this fund has outperformed 99 percent of all mutual funds; within its general category it has done better than 95 percent of its peers. Growth funds have averaged 20 percent annually over these same five years.

Risk/Volatility   ★ ★ ★ ★ ★
Over the past five years, Vanguard U.S. Growth has been safer than 95 percent of all growth funds. Over the past decade, the fund has had one negative year, while the S&P 500 has had one (off 3 percent in 1990). The fund has underperformed the S&P 500 three times in the last ten years.

	last 5 years		last 10 years	
worst year	4%	1994	-1%	1993
best year	40%	1998	47%	1991

In the past, Vanguard U.S. Growth has done better than 60 percent of its peer group in up markets and outperformed 80 percent of its competition in down markets. Consistency, or predictability, of returns for Vanguard U.S. Growth can be described as very good. This fund's risk-adjusted return is excellent.

Management   ★ ★ ★ ★ ★
There are seventy-seven stocks in this $14.6 billion portfolio. The average growth fund today is $560 million in size. Close to 95 percent of the fund's holdings are in stocks. The stocks in this portfolio have an average price-earnings (p/e) ratio of 42 and a median market capitalization of $108 billion. The portfolio's equity holdings can be categorized as large-cap and growth-oriented issues.

David Fowler and J. Parker Hall have managed this fund for the past twelve years. There are sixty-eight funds besides U.S. Growth within the Vanguard family. Overall, the fund family's risk-adjusted performance can be described as very good.

Tax Minimization   ★ ★ ★ ★
During the past five years, a $10,000 initial investment grew to $28,070 after taxes, assuming a 39.6 percent income tax bracket (state and federal combined) and a capital gains rate of 28 percent. This means that investors in this fund were able to preserve 88 percent of their total returns. Compared to other equity funds, this fund's tax savings are considered to be very good.

Expenses   ★ ★ ★ ★ ★
Vanguard U.S. Growth's expense ratio is .4 percent; it has also averaged .4 percent annually over the past three calendar years. The average expense ratio for the 1,800 funds in this category is 1.5 percent. This fund's turnover rate over the past year has been 48 percent, while its peer group average has been 95 percent.

Summary
Vanguard U.S. Growth frequently appears in the top performance quartile. Performance has been very good because management has concentrated on roughly 50 stocks that represent some of the most-recognized companies in the U.S. The universe of stocks management draws from numbers roughly 200 candidates. Selection is based on valuation, market position, and below-average sensitivity to changing economic conditions. This is one of the top-rated growth funds in the book and is highly recommended.

Profile
minimum initial investment $3,000	*IRA accounts available* . . . . yes
subsequent minimum investment . . $100	*IRA minimum investment* $1,000
available in all 50 states. . . . . yes	*date of inception* . . . . Jan. 1959
telephone exchanges. . . . . yes	*dividend/income paid* . . . . annually
number of other funds in family 68	*largest sector weighting* . . . technology

White Oak Growth Stock
P.O. Box 419441
Kansas City, MO 64141-6441
888-462-5386

total return	★ ★ ★ ★ ★
risk reduction	★
management	★ ★ ★ ★
tax minimization	★ ★ ★ ★ ★
expense control	★ ★ ★ ★ ★
symbol WOGSX	20 points
up-market performance	excellent
down-market performance	poor
predictability of returns	poor

Total Return   ★ ★ ★ ★ ★
Over the past five years, White Oak Growth Stock has taken $10,000 and turned it into $42,499 ($25,044 over three years). This translates into an average annual return of 34 percent over the past five years and 36 percent over the past three years. Over the past five years, this fund has outperformed 99 percent of all mutual funds; within its general category it has done better than 99 percent of its peers. Growth funds have averaged 20 percent annually over these same five years.

Risk/Volatility   ★
Over the past five years, White Oak Growth Stock has been safer than 15 percent of all growth funds. Over the past decade, the fund has had one negative year, while the S&P 500 has had one (off 3 percent in 1990). The fund has underperformed the S&P 500 two times in the last ten years.

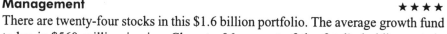

	last 5 years		since inception	
worst year	6%	1994	-0.3%	1993
best year	40%	1998	53%	1995

In the past, White Oak Growth Stock has done better than 100 percent of its peer group in up markets and outperformed 20 percent of its competition in down markets. Consistency, or predictability, of returns for White Oak Growth Stock can be described as poor. This fund's risk-adjusted return is fair.

Management   ★ ★ ★ ★
There are twenty-four stocks in this $1.6 billion portfolio. The average growth fund today is $560 million in size. Close to 96 percent of the fund's holdings are in stocks. The stocks in this portfolio have an average price-earnings (p/e) ratio of 43 and a median market capitalization of $53 billion. The portfolio's equity holdings can be categorized as large-cap and growth-oriented issues.

A team has managed this fund for the past seven years. There is one fund besides Growth Stock within the Oak Associates family. Overall, the fund family's risk-adjusted performance can be described as good.

Tax Minimization   ★ ★ ★ ★ ★
During the past five years, a $10,000 initial investment grew to $35,170 after taxes, assuming a 39.6 percent income tax bracket (state and federal combined) and a capital gains rate of 28 percent. This means that investors in this fund were able to preserve 94 percent of their total returns. Compared to other equity funds, this fund's tax savings are considered to be excellent.

Expenses   ★ ★ ★ ★ ★
White Oak Growth Stock's expense ratio is 1 percent; it has also averaged 1 percent annually over the past three calendar years. The average expense ratio for the 1,800 funds in this category is 1.5 percent. This fund's turnover rate over the past year has been 6 percent, while its peer group average has been 95 percent.

Summary
White Oak Growth Stock almost always ends in the top performance quartile. Manager Oelschlager invests mostly in mid- and large-cap undervalued companies. The portfolio is comprised of only a couple of dozen stocks and turnover is infrequent. The fund generally stays fully invested and management does not attempt to time the market or look for cyclicals. The fund receives top marks for performance, expense control, and tax control.

Profile

minimum initial investment $2,000	*IRA accounts available* . . . . yes
subsequent minimum investment . . . $50	*IRA minimum investment* $2,000
available in all 50 states. . . . . yes	*date of inception* . . . . Aug. 1992
telephone exchanges. . . . . yes	*dividend/income paid* . . . . quarterly
number of other funds in family 1	*largest sector weighting* . . . technology

Growth and Income Funds

These funds attempt to produce both capital appreciation and current income, with priority given to appreciation potential in the stocks purchased. Growth and income fund portfolios include seasoned, well-established firms that pay relatively high cash dividends. The goal of these funds is to provide long-term growth without excessive volatility in share price. Portfolio composition is almost always exclusively U.S. stocks, with an emphasis on financial, industrial cyclical, service, health, technology, and energy common stocks.

Over the past fifty years (ending 12/31/98), common stocks have outperformed inflation, on average, 70 percent of the time over one-year periods, 87 percent of the time over five-year periods, 83 percent over ten-year periods, 89 percent of the time over fifteen-year periods and 100 percent of the time over any given twenty-year period of time. Over the same period, high-quality, long-term corporate bonds have outperformed inflation, on average, 62 percent of the time over one-year periods, 63 percent of the time over five-year periods, 56 percent of the time over ten-year periods, 72 percent of the time over fifteen-year periods, and 61 percent over any given twenty-year period of time.

As you can see by the table below, crossing a 1,000 point barrier has become easier and easier for the Dow Jones Industrial Average (DJIA). As of March 12, 1997 (the most recent changes in the composition of the Dow), the thirty stocks that comprise the DJIA were/are: AlliedSignal, Alcoa, American Express, AT&T, Boeing, Caterpillar, Chevron, Coca-Cola, Walt Disney, DuPont, Eastman Kodak, Exxon, GE, GM, Goodyear, Hewlett-Packard, IBM, International Paper, Johnson & Johnson, McDonald's, Merck, 3M, J.P. Morgan, Philip Morris, Procter & Gamble, Sears, Travelers Group, Union Carbide, United Technology, and WalMart.

Dow Milestones

Level of the Dow and Date Reached   **Description**

Level of the Dow and Date Reached	Description
100 (1/12/06)	Not until 10 years after the DJIA is created does it hit 100.
1,000 (11/14/72)	Flirts with the 1,000 mark many times during the previous 6 yrs.
2,000 (1/8/87)	Four years of a bull market.
3,000 (4/17/91)	Rally after Gulf War.
5,000 (11/21/95)	Nine months earlier the Dow breaks 3,000.
6,000 (10/14/96)	Inflationary concerns are subdued.
7,000 (2/13/97)	The second quickest 1,000 point gain for the Dow.
8,000 (7/16/97)	Market recovers after 9.8% March and April drop.

9,000 (4/6/98)	Six months later the market is down 14.3%
10,000 (3/29/99)	Market drops almost 1% the very next day.
11,000 (4/99)	The quickest 1,000 point gain ever for the Dow.

Eight hundred funds make up the growth and income category. Another category, "equity-income" funds, has been combined with growth and income. Thus, for this section, there were a total of 1,050 possible candidates. Total market capitalization of these two categories combined is over $950 billion.

Over the past three and five years, growth and income funds have had an average compound return of 20.6 percent per year and 20.4 percent during the last five years (vs. 16.9 and 17.4 percent for equity-income funds). These funds have averaged 14.9 percent annually over the last ten years and 14.4 percent annually for the past fifteen years (vs. 13.7 and 14.1 percent for equity-income). The standard deviation for growth and income funds has been 19.1 percent over the past three years (compared to 15.7 for equity-income and 16.6 percent for growth funds). This means that growth and income funds have had slightly higher volatility as "world stock" funds but have been about 18 percent less predictable than pure equity-income funds.

Growth & Income Funds

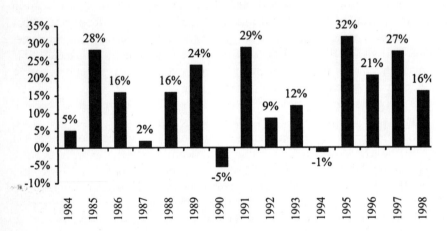

Domini Social Equity
11 West 57th Street, 7th Floor
New York, NY 10010-2001
800-762-6814

total return	★ ★ ★ ★ ★
risk reduction	★ ★ ★ ★
management	★ ★ ★ ★ ★
tax minimization	★ ★ ★ ★ ★
expense control	★ ★ ★ ★ ★
symbol DSEFX	24 points
up-market performance	good
down-market performance	very good
predictability of returns	fair

Total Return   ★ ★ ★ ★ ★
Over the past five years, Domini Social Equity has taken $10,000 and turned it into $32,329 ($22,066 over three years). This translates into an average annual return of 26 percent over the past five years and 30 percent over the past three years. Over the past five years, this fund has outperformed 98 percent of all mutual funds; within its general category it has done better than 95 percent of its peers. Growth and income funds have averaged 20 percent annually over these same five years.

Risk/Volatility   ★ ★ ★ ★
Over the past five years, Domini Social Equity has been safer than 80 percent of all growth and income funds. Over the past decade, the fund has had one negative year, while the S&P 500 has had one (off 3 percent in 1990). The fund has under-performed the S&P 500 four times in the last ten years.

	last 5 years		since inception	
worst year	-0.4%	1994	-0.4%	1994
best year	36%	1997	36%	1997

In the past, Domini Social Equity has done better than 60 percent of its peer group in up markets and outperformed 70 percent of its competition in down markets. Consistency, or predictability, of returns for Domini Social Equity can be described as fair. This fund's risk-adjusted return is excellent.

Management   ★ ★ ★ ★ ★
There are 400 stocks in this $820 million portfolio. The average growth and income fund today is $945 million in size. Close to 100 percent of the fund's holdings are in stocks. The stocks in this portfolio have an average price-earnings (p/e) ratio of 35 and a median market capitalization of $66 billion. The portfolio's equity holdings can be categorized as large-cap and a blend of growth and value stocks.

John O'Toole has managed this fund for the past eight years. There are no other funds besides Social Equity within the Domini family. Overall, the fund family's risk-adjusted performance can be described as excellent.

Tax Minimization   ★ ★ ★ ★ ★

During the past five years, a $10,000 initial investment grew to $27,170 after taxes, assuming a 39.6 percent income tax bracket (state and federal combined) and a capital gains rate of 28 percent. This means that investors in this fund were able to preserve 92 percent of their total returns. Compared to other equity funds, this fund's tax savings are considered to be excellent.

Expenses   ★ ★ ★ ★ ★

Domini Social Equity's expense ratio is 1.2 percent; it has averaged 1 percent annually over the past three calendar years. The average expense ratio for the 1,000 funds in this category is 1.3 percent. This fund's turnover rate over the past year has been 5 percent, while its peer group average has been 65 percent.

Summary

Domini Social Equity tries to mimic the performance of a 400-stock index which has characteristics that are similar to the S&P 500. The fund will not invest in corporations involved in alcohol, gambling, tobacco, nuclear power, or arms. Management will invest in the stocks of companies that are concerned with employee and community relations. This is the only socially-conscious fund in the book and is highly recommended with its near-perfect score of 24 out of 25 possible points.

Profile

minimum initial investment $1,000

subsequent minimum investment . . . $50

available in all 50 states. . . . . yes

telephone exchanges . . . . no

number of other funds in family 0

IRA accounts available . . . . yes

IRA minimum investment $250

date of inception. . . . . June 1991

dividend/income paid. . . . semiannually

largest sector weighting . . . technology

Dreyfus Disciplined Stock
One Exchange Place
Boston, MA 02109
800-373-9387

total return	★ ★ ★ ★
risk reduction	★ ★
management	★ ★ ★ ★
tax minimization	★ ★ ★ ★ ★
expense control	★ ★ ★ ★
symbol DDSTX	19 points
up-market performance	very good
down-market performance	fair
predictability of returns	fair

Total Return   ★ ★ ★ ★
Over the past five years, Dreyfus Disciplined Stock has taken $10,000 and turned it into $30,153 ($20,329 over three years and $58,644 over the past ten years). This translates into an average annual return of 25 percent over the past five years, 27 percent over the past three years, and 19 percent for the decade. Over the past five years, this fund has outperformed 96 percent of all mutual funds; within its general category it has done better than 85 percent of its peers. Growth and income funds have averaged 20 percent annually over these same five years.

Risk/Volatility   ★ ★
Over the past five years, Dreyfus Disciplined Stock has been safer than 45 percent of all growth and income funds. Over the past decade, the fund has had one nega- tive year, while the S&P 500 has had one (off 3 percent in 1990). The fund has underperformed the S&P 500 five times in the last ten years.

	last 5 years		last 10 years	
worst year	-1%	1994	-1%	1994
best year	37%	1995	37%	1995

In the past, Dreyfus Disciplined Stock has done better than 80 percent of its peer group in up markets and outperformed 45 percent of its competition in down markets. Consistency, or predictability, of returns for Dreyfus Disciplined Stock can be described as fair. This fund's risk-adjusted return is fair.

Management   ★ ★ ★ ★
There are 185 stocks in this $3 billion portfolio. The average growth and income fund today is $945 million in size. Close to 100 percent of the fund's holdings are in stocks. The stocks in this portfolio have an average price-earnings (p/e) ratio of 32 and a median market capitalization of $61 billion. The portfolio's equity hold- ings can be categorized as large-cap and a blend of growth and value stocks.

Bert Mullins has managed this fund for the past twelve years. There are sixty-three funds besides Disciplined Stock within the Dreyfus family. Overall, the fund family's risk-adjusted performance can be described as good.

Tax Minimization   ★ ★ ★ ★ ★

During the past five years, a $10,000 initial investment grew to $24,630 after taxes, assuming a 39.6 percent income tax bracket (state and federal combined) and a capital gains rate of 28 percent. This means that investors in this fund were able to preserve 87 percent of their total returns. Compared to other equity funds, this fund's tax savings are considered to be very good.

Expenses   ★ ★ ★ ★

Dreyfus Disciplined Stock's expense ratio is 1 percent; it has averaged .9 percent annually over the past three calendar years. The average expense ratio for the 1,000 funds in this category is 1.3 percent. This fund's turnover rate over the past year has been 54 percent, while its peer group average has been 65 percent.

Summary

Dreyfus Disciplined Stock tries to beat the S&P 500 by using a highly disciplined approach to stock selection. A computerized model analyzes over 2,000 equities that are screened via fifteen relative-value and momentum programs. Screening criteria is adjusted every two weeks in order to keep the model current. Potential candidates are then evaluated based on recent developments. This fund scores very well in almost every category.

Profile

minimum initial investment . . . . . $2,500   *IRA accounts available* . . . . yes
subsequent minimum investment . . $100   *IRA minimum investment* $750
available in all 50 states. . . . . yes   *date of inception.* . . . . Dec. 1987
telephone exchanges. . . . . yes   *dividend/income paid* . . . . quarterly
number of other funds in family 63   *largest sector weighting* . . . technology

Fidelity
82 Devonshire Street
Boston, MA 02109
800-544-8888

total return	★ ★ ★ ★
risk reduction	★ ★ ★ ★
management	★ ★ ★ ★
tax minimization	★ ★ ★ ★
expense control	★ ★ ★ ★
symbol FFIDX	20 points
up-market performance	excellent
down-market performance	fair
predictability of returns	good

Total Return
Over the past five years, Fidelity has taken $10,000 and turned it into $30,640 ($20,751 over three years and $54,922 over the past ten years). This translates into an average annual return of 25 percent over the past five years, 28 percent over the past three years, and 19 percent for the decade. Over the past five years, this fund has outperformed 96 percent of all mutual funds; within its general category it has done better than 85 percent of its peers. Growth and income funds have averaged 20 percent annually over these same five years.

Risk/Volatility   ★ ★ ★ ★
Over the past five years, Fidelity has been safer than 80 percent of all growth and income funds. Over the past decade, the fund has had one negative year, while the S&P 500 has had one (off 3 percent in 1990). The fund has underperformed the S&P 500 six times in the last ten years.

	last 5 years		last 10 years	
worst year	3%	1994	-5%	1990
best year	33%	1995	33%	1995

In the past, Fidelity has done better than 90 percent of its peer group in up markets and outperformed 35 percent of its competition in down markets. Consistency, or predictability, of returns for Fidelity can be described as good. This fund's risk-adjusted return is very good.

Management
There are 160 stocks in this $12.4 billion portfolio. The average growth and income fund today is $945 million in size. Close to 90 percent of the fund's holdings are in stocks. The stocks in this portfolio have an average price-earnings (p/e) ratio of 35 and a median market capitalization of $52 billion. The portfolio's equity holdings can be categorized as large-cap and a blend of growth and value stocks.

Beth Terrana has managed this fund for the past six years. There are seventy-eight funds besides Fidelity within the Fidelity family. Overall, the fund family's risk-adjusted performance can be described as very good.

Tax Minimization   ★ ★ ★ ★

During the past five years, a $10,000 initial investment grew to $23,310 after taxes, assuming a 39.6 percent income tax bracket (state and federal combined) and a capital gains rate of 28 percent. This means that investors in this fund were able to preserve 83 percent of their total returns. Compared to other equity funds, this fund's tax savings are considered to be good.

Expenses   ★ ★ ★ ★

Fidelity's expense ratio is .6 percent; it has also averaged .6 percent annually over the past three calendar years. The average expense ratio for the 1,000 funds in this category is 1.3 percent. This fund's turnover rate over the past year has been 65 percent, while its peer group average has been 65 percent.

Summary

Fidelity looks for turnaround situations and restructurings when selecting stocks. Manager Terrana believes that it is difficult for companies to improve earnings through unit growth alone. Positions are sold when such stocks enter an earnings momentum phase. The fund is comprised of both growth and value issues. The portfolio scores well in every category and is recommended.

Profile

minimum initial investment $2,500	*IRA accounts available* . . . . yes
subsequent minimum investment . . $250	*IRA minimum investment* $500
available in all 50 states. . . . . yes	*date of inception* . . . . April 1930
telephone exchanges. . . . . yes	*dividend/income paid* . . . . quarterly
number of other funds in family. 78	*largest sector weighting*. . . . . . services

Gateway

400 TechneCener Drive, Suite 200
Milford, OH 45150
800-354-6339

total return	★
risk reduction	★ ★ ★ ★ ★
management	★ ★ ★
tax minimization	★
expense control	★ ★ ★ ★
symbol GATEX	14 points
up-market performance	poor
down-market performance	excellent
predictability of returns	excellent

Total Return   ★
Over the past five years, Gateway has taken $10,000 and turned it into $17,412 ($14,227 over three years and $28,858 over the past ten years). This translates into an average annual return of 12 percent over the past five years, 12 percent over the past three years, and 11 percent for the decade. Over the past five years, this fund has outperformed 60 percent of all mutual funds; within its general category it has done better than 15 percent of its peers. Growth and income funds have averaged 20 percent annually over these same five years.

Risk/Volatility   ★ ★ ★ ★ ★
Over the past five years, Gateway has been safer than 99 percent of all growth and income funds. Over the past decade, the fund has not had a negative year, while the S&P 500 has had one (off 3 percent in 1990). The fund has underperformed the S&P 500 eight times in the last ten years.

	last 5 years		last 10 years	
worst year	6%	1994	5%	1992
best year	12%	1997	19%	1989

In the past, Gateway has done better than 20 percent of its peer group in up markets and outperformed 100 percent of its competition in down markets. Consistency, or predictability, of returns for Gateway can be described as excellent. This fund's risk-adjusted return is excellent.

Management
There are 101 stocks in this $570 million portfolio. The average growth and income fund today is $945 million in size. Close to 92 percent of the fund's holdings are in stocks. The stocks in this portfolio have an average price-earnings (p/e) ratio of 36 and a median market capitalization of $136 billion. The portfolio's equity holdings can be categorized as large-cap and a blend of growth and value stocks.

J. Patrick Rogers has managed this fund for the past five years. There are two funds besides Gateway within the Gateway family. Overall, the fund family's risk-adjusted performance can be described as fair.

Tax Minimization ★

During the past five years, a $10,000 initial investment grew to $15,150 after taxes, assuming a 39.6 percent income tax bracket (state and federal combined) and a capital gains rate of 28 percent. This means that investors in this fund were able to preserve 93 percent of their total returns. Compared to other equity funds, this fund's tax savings are considered to be excellent.

Expenses ★ ★ ★ ★

Gateway's expense ratio is 1 percent; it has averaged 1.1 percent annually over the past three calendar years. The average expense ratio for the 1,000 funds in this category is 1.3 percent. This fund's turnover rate over the past year has been 12 percent, while its peer group average has been 65 percent.

Summary

Gateway is the ideal choice for the conservative equity investor. Returns are great, but risk reduction is the best. Management buys stocks comprising the S&P 100, in the same proportion as the index and then sells covered call options on the entire portfolio. Such sales bring in a lot of money for the shareholders but upside potential is obviously limited. Risk is further reduced when the fund buys puts, particularly during market declines. Even though this is an equity fund, manager Roger likens it to a "portfolio index" that has 60 percent of its assets in T-Bills and 40 percent in large-cap stocks.

Profile

minimum initial investment $1,000	*IRA accounts available* . . . . yes
subsequent minimum investment . . $100	*IRA minimum investment* $500
available in all 50 states. . . . . yes	*date of inception.* . . . . Dec. 1977
telephone exchanges. . . . . yes	*dividend/income paid* . . . . quarterly
number of other funds in family 2	*largest sector weighting* . . . technology

Pioneer A

60 State Street
Boston, MA 02109-1820
800-225-6292

total return	★ ★ ★ ★
risk reduction	★ ★ ★ ★ ★
management	★ ★ ★ ★ ★
tax minimization	★ ★ ★ ★
expense control	★ ★ ★ ★ ★
symbol PIODX	23 points
up-market performance	very good
down-market performance	very good
predictability of returns	good

Total Return   ★ ★ ★ ★

Over the past five years, Pioneer A has taken $10,000 and turned it into $28,153 ($20,644 over three years and $45,425 over the past ten years). This translates into an average annual return of 23 percent over the past five years, 27 percent over the past three years, and 16 percent for the decade. Over the past five years, this fund has outperformed 95 percent of all mutual funds; within its general category it has done better than 75 percent of its peers. Growth and income funds have averaged 20 percent annually over these same five years.

Risk/Volatility   ★ ★ ★ ★ ★

Over the past five years, Pioneer A has been safer than 90 percent of all growth and income funds. Over the past decade, the fund has had two negative years, while the S&P 500 has had one (off 3 percent in 1990). The fund has underperformed the S&P 500 six times in the last ten years.

	last 5 years		last 10 years	
worst year	-1%	1994	-11%	1990
best year	38%	1997	38%	1997

In the past, Pioneer A has done better than 75 percent of its peer group in up markets and outperformed 80 percent of its competition in down markets. Consistency, or predictability, of returns for Pioneer A can be described as good. This fund's risk-adjusted return is excellent.

Management   ★ ★ ★ ★ ★

There are 140 stocks in this $5.6 billion portfolio. The average growth and income fund today is $945 million in size. Close to 99 percent of the fund's holdings are in stocks. The stocks in this portfolio have an average price-earnings (p/e) ratio of 30 and a median market capitalization of $38 billion. The portfolio's equity holdings can be categorized as large-cap and value-oriented issues.

John Carey has managed this fund for the past thirteen years. There are twenty funds besides Pioneer A within the Pioneer family. Overall, the fund family's risk-adjusted performance can be described as very good.

Tax Minimization   ★ ★ ★ ★

During the past five years, a $10,000 initial investment grew to $23,160 after taxes, assuming a 39.6 percent income tax bracket (state and federal combined) and a capital gains rate of 28 percent. This means that investors in this fund were able to preserve 86 percent of their total returns. Compared to other equity funds, this fund's tax savings are considered to be very good.

Expenses   ★ ★ ★ ★ ★

Pioneer A's expense ratio is 1 percent; it has also averaged 1 percent annually over the past three calendar years. The average expense ratio for the 1,000 funds in this category is 1.3 percent. This fund's turnover rate over the past year has been 17 percent, while its peer group average has been 65 percent.

Summary

Pioneer A invests in both domestic and foreign undervalued stocks of companies that consistently pay dividends. Manager Carey waits until he can "buy on weakness." Stocks are sold when their prices reflect the securities' intrinsic value. Although normally fully invested, Carey sometimes may put massive amounts of the portfolio in cash. This fund ranks as one of the very best growth and income portfolios.

Profile

minimum initial investment $50	*IRA accounts available* .... yes
subsequent minimum investment ... $50	*IRA minimum investment* $50
available in all 50 states. .... yes	*date of inception* .... Feb. 1928
telephone exchanges. .... yes	*dividend/income paid* .... annually
number of other funds in family. 20	*largest sector weighting* .... financials

Schwab 1000 Investors

10 Montgomery Street
San Francisco, CA 94104
800-435-4000

total return	★ ★ ★ ★
risk reduction	★ ★ ★
management	★ ★ ★ ★
tax minimization	★ ★ ★ ★ ★
expense control	★ ★ ★ ★ ★
symbol SNXFX	21 points
up-market performance	very good
down-market performance	good
predictability of returns	good

Total Return   ★ ★ ★ ★

Over the past five years, Schwab 1000 Investors has taken $10,000 and turned it into $30,262 ($20,181 over three years). This translates into an average annual return of 25 percent over the past five years and 26 percent over the past three years. Over the past five years, this fund has outperformed 95 percent of all mutual funds; within its general category it has done better than 80 percent of its peers. Growth and income funds have averaged 20 percent annually over these same five years.

Risk/Volatility   ★ ★ ★

Over the past five years, Schwab 1000 Investors has been safer than 55 percent of all growth and income funds. Over the past decade, the fund has had one negative year, while the S&P 500 has had one (off 3 percent in 1990). The fund has under-performed the S&P 500 six times in the last ten years.

	last 5 years		since inception	
worst year	-0.1%	1994	-0.1%	1994
best year	37%	1995	37%	1995

In the past, Schwab 1000 Investors has done better than 85 percent of its peer group in up markets and outperformed 50 percent of its competition in down markets. Consistency, or predictability, of returns for Schwab 1000 Investors can be described as good. This fund's risk-adjusted return is good.

Management   ★ ★ ★ ★

There are 948 stocks in this $4.2 billion portfolio. The average growth and income fund today is $945 million in size. Close to 100 percent of the fund's holdings are in stocks. The stocks in this portfolio have an average price-earnings (p/e) ratio of 33 and a median market capitalization of $50 billion. The portfolio's equity hold-ings can be categorized as large-cap and a blend of growth and value stocks.

Geraldine Hom has managed this fund for the past five years. There are twenty funds besides 1000 Investors within the Schwab family. Overall, the fund family's risk-adjusted performance can be described as good.

Tax Minimization   ★ ★ ★ ★ ★

During the past five years, a $10,000 initial investment grew to $25,930 after taxes, assuming a 39.6 percent income tax bracket (state and federal combined) and a capital gains rate of 28 percent. This means that investors in this fund were able to preserve 93 percent of their total returns. Compared to other equity funds, this fund's tax savings are considered to be excellent.

Expenses   ★ ★ ★ ★ ★

Schwab 1000 Investors' expense ratio is .5 percent; it has also averaged .5 percent annually over the past three calendar years. The average expense ratio for the 1,000 funds in this category is 1.3 percent. This fund's turnover rate over the past year has been 2 percent, while its peer group average has been 65 percent.

Summary

Schwab 1000 Investors has ranked in the top performance half of its peer group for each of the past four years, a surprisingly somewhat uncommon accomplishment. Risk-adjusted returns since the fund's 1991 inception have been superior. The goal of the fund is to achieve returns that are somewhere between those of the S&P 500 and the Wilshire 5000. This fund is a smart alternative for the investor who wants a broader base than the traditional domestic equity-indexed portfolio.

Profile

minimum initial investment $1,000	*IRA accounts available* . . . . yes
subsequent minimum investment . . $100	*IRA minimum investment* $500
available in all 50 states. . . . . yes	*date of inception* . . . . April 1991
telephone exchanges. . . . . yes	*dividend/income paid* . . . . annually
number of other funds in family 20	*largest sector weighting* . . . . . . services

Smith Breeden U.S. Equity Market Plus
100 Europa Drive, Suite 200
Chapel Hill, NC 27514
800-221-3138

total return	★ ★ ★ ★ ★
risk reduction	★ ★ ★
management	★ ★ ★
tax minimization	★ ★ ★
expense control	★ ★
symbol SBEPX	16 points
up-market performance	very good
down-market performance	good
predictability of returns	good

Total Return ★ ★ ★ ★ ★
Over the past five years, Smith Breeden U.S. Equity Market Plus has taken $10,000 and turned it into $32,138 ($20,727 over three years). This translates into an average annual return of 26 percent over the past five years and 28 percent over the past three years. Over the past five years, this fund has outperformed 97 percent of all mutual funds; within its general category it has done better than 95 percent of its peers. Growth and income funds have averaged 20 percent annually over these same five years.

Risk/Volatility ★ ★ ★
Over the past five years, Smith Breeden U.S. Equity Market Plus has been safer than 60 percent of all growth and income funds. Over the past decade, the fund has not had a negative year, while the S&P 500 has had one (off 3 percent in 1990). The fund has underperformed the S&P 500 three times in the last ten years.

	last 5 years		since inception	
worst year	2%	1994	2%	1994
best year	37%	1995	37%	1995

In the past, Smith Breeden U.S. Equity Market Plus has done better than 80 percent of its peer group in up markets and outperformed 55 percent of its competition in down markets. Consistency, or predictability, of returns for Smith Breeden U.S. Equity Market Plus can be described as good. This fund's risk-adjusted return is very good.

Management ★ ★ ★
There are no stocks in this $200 million portfolio. The average growth and income fund today is $945 million in size. Close to 77 percent of the fund's holdings are in high-quality bonds and the balance is in cash. Virtually all of the bonds are GNMAs and FNMAs with an average coupon rate of 6.5 percent.

John Sprow has managed this fund for the past seven years. There are three funds besides U.S. Equity Market Plus within the Smith Breeden family. Overall, the fund family's risk-adjusted performance can be described as very good.

Tax Minimization ★ ★ ★

During the past five years, a $10,000 initial investment grew to $21,640 after taxes, assuming a 39.6 percent income tax bracket (state and federal combined) and a capital gains rate of 28 percent. This means that investors in this fund were able to preserve 75 percent of their total returns. Compared to other equity funds, this fund's tax savings are considered to be fair.

Expenses ★ ★

Smith Breeden U.S. Equity Market Plus's expense ratio is .9 percent; it has also averaged .9 percent annually over the past three calendar years. The average expense ratio for the 1,000 funds in this category is 1.3 percent. This fund's turnover rate over the past year has been 420 percent, while its peer group average has been 65 percent.

Summary

Smith Breeden U.S. Equity Market Plus is a rather unique growth and income fund because it does not directly invest in stocks. Instead it invests in equity swap and futures contracts based on the S&P 500. In order to reduce risk and increase current income, management purchases mortgage-backed securities. Due to the high leverage involved in futures, only about 5 percent of the portfolio is in these contracts while the rest is in fixed-income such as T-Bills and high-quality agency issues. Since its inception, performance has always been in the top one or two quartiles.

Profile

minimum initial investment $1,000	*IRA accounts available* . . . . yes
subsequent minimum investment . . . $50	*IRA minimum investment* $250
available in all 50 states. . . . . yes	*date of inception*. . . . . June 1992
telephone exchanges. . . . . yes	*dividend/income paid* . . . . quarterly
number of other funds in family. 3	*largest sector weighting* . . . . bonds

Vanguard 500 Index
Vanguard Financial Center
P.O. Box 2600
Valley Forge, PA 19482
800-662-7447

total return	★ ★ ★ ★ ★
risk reduction	★ ★ ★ ★
management	★ ★ ★ ★ ★
tax minimization	★ ★ ★ ★
expense control	★ ★ ★ ★ ★
symbol VFINX	23 points
up-market performance	excellent
down-market performance	good
predictability of returns	good

Total Return   ★ ★ ★ ★ ★
Over the past five years, Vanguard 500 Index has taken $10,000 and turned it into
$31,960 ($20,976 over three years and $56,044 over the past ten years). This trans-
lates into an average annual return of 26 percent over the past five years, 28 percent over the past three years, and 19 percent for the decade. Over the past five
years, this fund has outperformed 98 percent of all mutual funds; within its general
category it has done better than 95 percent of its peers. Growth and income funds
have averaged 20 percent annually over these same five years.

Risk/Volatility   ★ ★ ★ ★
Over the past five years, Vanguard 500 Index has been safer than 75 percent of all
growth and income funds. Over the past decade, the fund has had one negative
year, while the S&P 500 has had one (off 3 percent in 1990). The fund has underperformed the S&P 500 nine times in the last ten years.

	last 5 years		last 10 years	
worst year	1%	1994	-3%	1990
best year	37%	1995	37%	1995

In the past, Vanguard 500 Index has done better than 90 percent of its peer
group in up markets and outperformed 65 percent of its competition in down markets. Consistency, or predictability, of returns for Vanguard 500 Index can be
described as good. This fund's risk-adjusted return is very good.

Management   ★ ★ ★ ★ ★
There are 507 stocks in this $79 billion portfolio. The average growth and income
fund today is $945 million in size. Close to 99 percent of the fund's holdings are
in stocks. The stocks in this portfolio have an average price-earnings (p/e) ratio of
35 and a median market capitalization of $66 billion. The portfolio's equity hold-
ings can be categorized as large-cap and a blend of growth and value stocks.

George Sauter has managed this fund for the past twelve years. There are sixty-eight funds besides 500 Index within the Vanguard family. Overall, the fund family's risk-adjusted performance can be described as very good.

Tax Minimization   ★ ★ ★ ★
During the past five years, a $10,000 initial investment grew to $26,750 after taxes, assuming a 39.6 percent income tax bracket (state and federal combined) and a capital gains rate of 28 percent. This means that investors in this fund were able to preserve 91 percent of their total returns. Compared to other equity funds, this fund's tax savings are considered to be excellent.

Expenses   ★ ★ ★ ★ ★
Vanguard 500 Index's expense ratio is .2 percent; it has also averaged .2 percent annually over the past three calendar years. The average expense ratio for the 1,000 funds in this category is 1.3 percent. This fund's turnover rate over the past year has been 6 percent, while its peer group average has been 65 percent.

Summary
Vanguard 500 Index continues to outpace and outclass its competition with a simple formula of cost-cutting and index duplication. This fund ties for first place as the best growth and income portfolio. The performance correlation between this fund and the S&P 500 is always expected to be at least 0.95 or greater. This fund is the perfect choice for investors who are tired of the ongoing broken promises made by other funds. It is highly recommended. It is the second most popular equity fund in the U.S. and may take over the number one slot within a couple of years.

Profile

minimum initial investment $3,000	*IRA accounts available* . . . . yes
subsequent minimum investment . . $100	*IRA minimum investment* $1,000
available in all 50 states. . . . . yes	*date of inception* . . . . Aug. 1976
telephone exchanges. . . . . yes	*dividend/income paid* . . . . quarterly
number of other funds in family 68	*largest sector weighting* . . . technology

Vanguard Growth & Income

Vanguard Financial Center
P.O. Box 2600
Valley Forge, PA 19482
800-662-7447

total return	★ ★ ★ ★
risk reduction	★ ★
management	★ ★ ★ ★
tax minimization	★ ★ ★
expense control	★ ★ ★ ★ ★
symbol VQNPX	18 points
up-market performance	poor
down-market performance	fair
predictability of returns	fair

Total Return ★ ★ ★ ★

Over the past five years, Vanguard Growth & Income has taken $10,000 and turned it into $30,481 ($20,426 over three years and $55,621 over the past ten years). This translates into an average annual return of 25 percent over the past five years, 27 percent over the past three years, and 19 percent for the decade. Over the past five years, this fund has outperformed 97 percent of all mutual funds; within its general category it has done better than 96 percent of its peers. Growth and income funds have averaged 20 percent annually over these same five years.

Risk/Volatility ★ ★

Over the past five years, Vanguard Growth & Income has been safer than 25 percent of all growth and income funds. Over the past decade, the fund has had two negative years, while the S&P 500 has had one (off 3 percent in 1990). The fund has underperformed the S&P 500 five times in the last ten years.

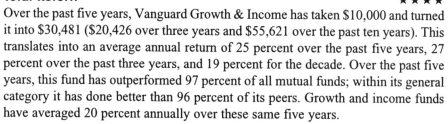

	last 5 years		last 10 years	
worst year	-1%	1994	-2%	1990
best year	36%	1995	36%	1995

In the past, Vanguard Growth & Income has done better than 25 percent of its peer group in up markets and outperformed 35 percent of its competition in down markets. Consistency, or predictability, of returns for Vanguard Growth & Income can be described as fair. This fund's risk-adjusted return is good.

Management ★ ★ ★ ★

There are 255 stocks in this $5.6 billion portfolio. The average growth and income fund today is $945 million in size. Close to 98 percent of the fund's holdings are in stocks. The stocks in this portfolio have an average price-earnings (p/e) ratio of 31 and a median market capitalization of $44 billion. The portfolio's equity holdings can be categorized as large-cap and value-oriented issues.

John Nagorniak has managed this fund for the past thirteen years. There are sixty-eight funds besides Growth & Income within the Vanguard family. Overall, the fund family's risk-adjusted performance can be described as very good.

Tax Minimization   ★ ★ ★

During the past five years, a $10,000 initial investment grew to $21,520 after taxes, assuming a 39.6 percent income tax bracket (state and federal combined) and a capital gains rate of 28 percent. This means that investors in this fund were able to preserve 77 percent of their total returns. Compared to other equity funds, this fund's tax savings are considered to be fair.

Expenses   ★ ★ ★ ★ ★

Vanguard Growth & Income's expense ratio is .4 percent; it has also averaged .4 percent annually over the past three calendar years. The average expense ratio for the 1,000 funds in this category is 1.3 percent. This fund's turnover rate over the past year has been 47 percent, while its peer group average has been 65 percent.

Summary

Vanguard Growth & Income seeks to outperform the S&P 500 by investing in stocks inside as well as outside the index. Manager Nagorniak analyzes a stock's dividend yield, p/e ratio, beta, return on equity as well as its price-to-earnings ratio. A computer-driven model based on thirty different criteria is also utilized.

Profile

minimum initial investment $3,000	*IRA accounts available* . . . . yes
subsequent minimum investment . . $100	*IRA minimum investment* $1,000
available in all 50 states. . . . . yes	*date of inception.* . . . . Dec. 1986
telephone exchanges . . . . no	*dividend/income paid.* . . . . semiannually
number of other funds in family 68	*largest sector weighting* . . . . financials

Victory Diversified Stock A

P.O. Box 8527
Boston, MA 02266
800-539-3863

total return	★ ★ ★ ★
risk reduction	★ ★ ★
management	★ ★ ★ ★
tax minimization	★ ★ ★
expense control	★ ★ ★
symbol SRVEX	17 points
up-market performance	very good
down-market performance	very good
predictability of returns	good

Total Return   ★ ★ ★ ★

Over the past five years, Victory Diversified Stock A has taken $10,000 and turned it into $30,008 ($19,275 over three years). This translates into an average annual return of 25 percent over the past five years and 24 percent over the past three years. Over the past five years, this fund has outperformed 96 percent of all mutual funds; within its general category it has done better than 85 percent of its peers. Growth and income funds have averaged 20 percent annually over these same five years.

Risk/Volatility   ★ ★ ★

Over the past five years, Victory Diversified Stock A has been safer than 50 percent of all growth and income funds. Over the past decade, the fund has not had a negative year, while the S&P 500 has had one (off 3 percent in 1990). The fund has underperformed the S&P 500 four times in the last ten years.

	last 5 years		last 10 years	
worst year	4%	1994	1%	1990
best year	35%	1995	35%	1995

In the past, Victory Diversified Stock A has done better than 80 percent of its peer group in up markets and outperformed 90 percent of its competition in down markets. Consistency, or predictability, of returns for Victory Diversified Stock A can be described as good. This fund's risk-adjusted return is fair.

Management   ★ ★ ★ ★

There are eighty-eight stocks in this $960 million portfolio. The average growth and income fund today is $945 million in size. Close to 97 percent of the fund's holdings are in stocks. The stocks in this portfolio have an average price-earnings (p/e) ratio of 34 and a median market capitalization of $19 billion. The portfolio's equity holdings can be categorized as large-cap and value-oriented issues.

Lawrence Babin has managed this fund for the past ten years. There are twenty-five funds besides Diversified Stock within the Victory family. Overall, the fund family's risk-adjusted performance can be described as good.

Tax Minimization   ★ ★ ★

During the past five years, a $10,000 initial investment grew to $21,940 after taxes, assuming a 39.6 percent income tax bracket (state and federal combined) and a capital gains rate of 28 percent. This means that investors in this fund were able to preserve 79 percent of their total returns. Compared to other equity funds, this fund's tax savings are considered to be good.

Expenses   ★ ★ ★

Victory Diversified Stock A's expense ratio is 1 percent; it has also averaged 1 percent annually over the past three calendar years. The average expense ratio for the 1,000 funds in this category is 1.3 percent. This fund's turnover rate over the past year has been 84 percent, while its peer group average has been 63 percent.

Summary

Victory Diversified Stock A invests in both common stock and convertible securities that can be converted into common stock. A value and growth approach is used when selecting issues. Once a stock's price shows up in the bottom half of management's "equity universe" and its sector weighting is marked down, it becomes a candidate for sale. This fund does not excel in any one given category but scores well across the board.

Profile

minimum initial investment $500	IRA accounts available . . . . yes
subsequent minimum investment . . . $25	IRA minimum investment $100
available in all 50 states. . . . . yes	date of inception . . . . Oct. 1989
telephone exchanges. . . . . yes	dividend/income paid . . . . quarterly
number of other funds in family 65	largest sector weighting . . . technology

Washington Mutual Investors

1101 Vermont Avenue N.W.
Washington, DC 20005
800-421-4120

total return	★ ★ ★ ★
risk reduction	★ ★ ★ ★ ★
management	★ ★ ★ ★ ★
tax minimization	★ ★ ★ ★
expense control	★ ★ ★ ★ ★
symbol AWSHX	23 points
up-market performance	fair
down-market performance	excellent
predictability of returns	very good

Total Return   ★ ★ ★ ★

Over the past five years, Washington Mutual Investors has taken $10,000 and turned it into $28,637 ($18,423 over three years and $47,904 over the past ten years). This translates into an average annual return of 23 percent over the past five years, 23 percent over the past three years, and 17 percent for the decade. Over the past five years, this fund has outperformed 96 percent of all mutual funds; within its general category it has done better than 95 percent of its peers. Growth and income funds have averaged 20 percent annually over these same five years.

Risk/Volatility   ★ ★ ★ ★ ★

Over the past five years, Washington Mutual Investors has been safer than 85 percent of all growth and income funds. Over the past decade, the fund has had one negative year, while the S&P 500 has had one (off 3 percent in 1990). The fund has underperformed the S&P 500 seven times in the last ten years.

	last 5 years		last 10 years	
worst year	0.5%	1994	-4%	1990
best year	41%	1995	41%	1995

In the past, Washington Mutual Investors has done better than 35 percent of its peer group in up markets and outperformed 90 percent of its competition in down markets. Consistency, or predictability, of returns for Washington Mutual Investors can be described as very good. This fund's risk-adjusted return is very good.

Management   ★ ★ ★ ★ ★

There are 160 stocks in this $51.7 billion portfolio. The average growth and income fund today is $945 million in size. Close to 96 percent of the fund's holdings are in stocks. The stocks in this portfolio have an average price-earnings (p/e) ratio of 29 and a median market capitalization of $26 billion. The portfolio's equity holdings can be categorized as large-cap and value-oriented issues.

A team has managed this fund for the past ten years. There are twenty-eight funds besides Washington Mutual Investors within the American Funds family. Overall, the fund family's risk-adjusted performance can be described as very good.

Tax Minimization ★ ★ ★ ★

During the past five years, a $10,000 initial investment grew to $22,750 after taxes, assuming a 39.6 percent income tax bracket (state and federal combined) and a capital gains rate of 28 percent. This means that investors in this fund were able to preserve 84 percent of their total returns. Compared to other equity funds, this fund's tax savings are considered to be good.

Expenses ★ ★ ★ ★ ★

Washington Mutual Investors' expense ratio is .6 percent; it has also averaged .6 percent annually over the past three calendar years. The average expense ratio for the 1,000 funds in this category is 1.3 percent. This fund's turnover rate over the past year has been 18 percent, while its peer group average has been 65 percent.

Summary

Washington Mutual can only invest in stocks that meet the criteria of the District of Columbia's "Legal List" of investments deemed appropriate for trusts. The list is comprised of roughly 300 candidates, all of which are selected based on the company's underlying financial strength and ethical integrity. The management team at Washington Mutual typically selects approximately 200 stocks from the list with an eye toward maintaining these positions indefinitely if possible. This is simply one of the very best growth and income funds and like other members of the American Funds family is highly recommended. Knowledgeable fund investors will be particularly attracted to this fund family.

Profile

minimum initial investment $250	*IRA accounts available* . . . . yes
subsequent minimum investment . . . $50	*IRA minimum investment* $250
available in all 50 states. . . . . yes	*date of inception* . . . . July 1952
telephone exchanges. . . . . yes	*dividend/income paid* . . . . quarterly
number of other funds in family 28	*largest sector weighting* . . . . financials

High-Yield Funds

Sometimes referred to as "junk bond" funds, high-yield funds invest in corporate bonds rated lower than BBB or BAA. The world of bonds is divided into two general categories: "investment grade" and "high-yield." Investment grade, sometimes referred to as "bank quality," means that the bond issue has been rated AAA, AA, A, or BAA (or BBB if the rating service is Standard and Poor's instead of Moody's). Certain institutions and fiduciaries are forbidden to invest their clients' monies in anything less than investment grade. Everything less than bank quality is considered junk.

Yet the world of bonds is not black and white. There are several categories of high-yield bonds. Junk bond funds contain issues that range from BB to C; a rating less than single-C means that the bond is in default, and payment of interest and/or principal is in arrears. High-yield bond funds perform best during good economic times. Such issues should be avoided by traditional investors during recessionary periods, since the underlying corporations may have difficulty making interest and principal payments when business slows down. However, these bonds, like common stocks, can perform very well during the second half of a recession.

Although junk bonds may exhibit greater volatility than their investment-grade peers, they are safer when it comes to *interest rate risk*. Since junk issues have higher-yielding coupons and often shorter maturities than quality corporate bond funds, they fluctuate less in value when interest rates change. Thus, during expansionary periods in the economy when interest rates are rising, high-yield funds will generally drop less in value than high-quality corporate or government bond funds. Conversely, when interest rates are falling, government and corporate bonds will appreciate more in value than junk funds. High-yield bonds resemble equities at least as much as they do traditional bonds when it comes to economic cycles and certain important technical factors. Studies show that only 19 percent of the average junk fund's total return is explained by the up or down movement of the Lehman Brothers Government/Corporate Bond Index. To give an idea of how low this number is, 94 percent of a typical *high-quality* corporate bond fund's performance is explainable by movement in the same index. Indeed, even international bond funds have a higher correlation coefficient than junk, with 25 percent of their performance explained by the Lehman index.

The table below covers different periods ending 3/31/99 and compares the total return of six well known bond indexes: First Boston High Yield Index (bonds rated BBB or lower), the Lehman Aggregate Bond Index (securities from the Lehman Government/Corporate, Mortgage-Backed Securities, and Asset-Backed

Indexes), the Lehman Corporate Bond Index, the Lehman Government Bond Index (all publicly traded domestic debt of the U.S. Government), the Lehman Municipal Bond Index, and the Salomon Brothers Non–U.S. World Government Bond Index.

Performance of Various Bond Indices Through 3/31/99

index	1 year	3 years	5 years	10 years	15 years
high-yield	-0.8%	8.2%	8.8%	11.7%	n/a
aggregate	6.5%	7.8%	7.8%	9.1%	10.2%
corporate	6.1%	8.0%	8.3%	9.6%	11.0%
government	6.7%	7.7%	7.5%	8.9%	9.9%
municipal	6.2%	7.4%	7.6%	8.3%	9.4%
foreign	11.6%	4.4%	6.8%	8.9%	n/a

The high end of the junk bond market, those debentures rated BA and BB, have been able to withstand the general beating the junk bond market incurred during the late 1980s and early 1990s. Moderate and conservative investors who want high-yield bonds as part of their portfolio should focus on funds that have a high percentage of their assets in higher-rated bonds, BB or better.

According to Salomon Brothers, the people who are responsible for the Lehman Brothers corporate, government, and municipal bond indices used in this book, junk bond defaults averaged only 0.8 percent from 1980 to 1984. This rate almost tripled from 1985 to 1989 as defaults averaged 2.2 percent per year. Then, in 1990, defaults surged to 4.6 percent. Analysis based on historical data did not predict this huge increase in defaults. Bear in mind that BB-rated junk bonds can be expected to perform closer to high-quality bonds than will lower-rated junk. During 1990, for example, BB-rated bonds declined only slightly in price and actually delivered positive returns, whereas bonds rated CCC declined over 30 percent. During the mid-1990s, the default risk for the entire category had fallen to about 1.5 percent per year (well under 1 percent in the case of high-yield bond funds). By the end of the 1999s, the rate had fallen even more.

Over the past three and five years, high-yield corporate bond funds have had an average compound total return of 8.1 and 8.2 percent, respectively. The *annual* return for the past ten years has been 9.5 percent, and 10.2 percent for the last fifteen years (all figures as of 3/31/99). The standard deviation for high-yield bond funds has been 7.6 percent over the past three years. This means that these funds have been less volatile than any equity fund or world bond funds (9.2 percent standard deviation), but more than twice the variance of municipal bonds (3.0 percent standard deviation) and corporate bonds (3.5 percent standard deviation). Three hundred corporate bond funds make up the high-yield category. Total market capitalization of this category is $120 billion.

The majority of investors believe that the track record of high-yield bonds has been mixed, particularly in recent years. There was a crash in this market in 1990, but the overall track record has been quite good. These bond funds were up 13.4 percent in 1987, the year of the stock market crash. As the junk bond scare started in 1989, the fund category was still able to show a 12.9 percent return for the calendar year. The following year the group showed a negative return of just over one half percent.

Then, in 1991, high-yield bond funds suffered an almost unprecedented loss, ending the year with a 9.8 percent loss. The loss was caused by regulatory agencies putting pressure on the insurance industry, formerly the largest owner of this investment category. This, together with the demise of Drexel Burnham, the largest issuer of junk bonds, caused high-yield bonds to suffer their biggest loss in recent memory. And yet the very next two years were quite good, up 17.6 percent in 1992 and 18.9 percent in 1993. The following year, 1994, these funds fell 3.5 percent, followed by a gain of 13.8 percent in 1996, 12.9 percent in 1997, a loss of less than 0.5 percent in 1998, and a 2.7 percent gain for the first quarter of 1999.

For stock investors, high-yield bonds can potentially smooth out performance during down markets while providing long-term volatility reduction. Because these debt instruments have historically delivered returns approaching that of the stock market, equity (stock) investors may find them a useful way to obtain diversification. Part of the beauty of high-yield bonds is that only about 50 percent of their movement (return) is correlated (related to) fluctuations in the stock market.

High-Yield Bond Funds

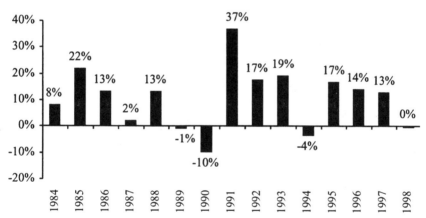

Fidelity Advisor High-Yield Fund T

82 Devonshire Street
Boston, MA 02109
800-522-7297

total return	★ ★ ★ ★
risk reduction	★ ★
management	★ ★ ★ ★
current income	★ ★ ★
expense control	★ ★ ★ ★
symbol FAHYX	17 points
up-market performance	excellent
down-market performance	poor
predictability of returns	good

Total Return   ★ ★ ★ ★

Over the past five years, Fidelity Advisor High-Yield Fund T has taken $10,000 and turned it into $16,223 ($13,310 over three years and $35,012 over the past ten years). This translates into an average annual return of 10 percent over the past five years, 10 percent over the past three years, and 13 percent for the decade. Over the past five years, this fund has outperformed 60 percent of all mutual funds; within its general category it has done better than 85 percent of its peers. High-yield bond funds have averaged 8 percent annually over these same five years.

During the past five years, a $10,000 initial investment grew to $12,760 after taxes, assuming a 39.6 percent income tax bracket (state and federal combined) and a capital gains rate of 28 percent. This means that investors in this fund were able to preserve 84 percent of their total returns. Compared to other fixed-income funds, this fund's tax savings are considered to be very good.

Risk/Volatility   ★ ★

Over the past five years, Fidelity Advisor High-Yield Fund T has been safer than 35 percent of all high-yield bond funds. Over the past decade, the fund has had two negative years, while the Lehman Brothers Aggregate Bond Index has had one (off 3 percent in 1994); the First Boston High-Yield Bond Index fell twice (off 6 percent in 1990 and 1 percent in 1994). The fund has underperformed the Lehman Brothers Aggregate Bond Index three times and the First Boston High-Yield Bond Index three times in the last ten years.

	last 5 years		last 10 years	
worst year	-2%	1994	-2%	1994
best year	19%	1995	35%	1991

In the past, Fidelity Advisor High-Yield Fund T has done better than 100 percent of its peer group in up markets and outperformed 25 percent of its competition in down markets. Consistency, or predictability, of returns for Fidelity Advisor High-Yield Fund T can be described as good. This fund's risk-adjusted return is fair.

Management   ★★★★

There are 250 fixed-income securities in this $2.6 billion portfolio. The average high-yield bond fund today is $386 million in size. Close to 76 percent of the fund's holdings are in bonds. The average maturity of the bonds in this account is eight years; the weighted coupon rate averages 7.6 percent. The portfolio's fixed-income holdings can be categorized as intermediate-term, low-quality debt.

Margaret Eagle has managed this fund for the past twelve years. There are twenty-seven funds besides High-Yield Fund T within the Fidelity Advisor family. Overall, the fund family's risk-adjusted performance can be described as very good.

Current Income   ★★★

Over the past year, Fidelity Advisor High-Yield Fund T had a twelve-month yield of 9.2 percent. During this same twelve-month period, the typical high-yield bond fund had a yield that averaged 9.2 percent.

Expenses   ★★★★

Fidelity Advisor High-Yield Fund T's expense ratio is 1.1 percent; it has also averaged 1.1 percent annually over the past three calendar years. The average expense ratio for the 300 funds in this category is 1.3 percent. This fund's turnover rate over the past year has been 75 percent, while its peer group average has been 125 percent.

Summary

Fidelity Advisor High-Yield is one of those few funds that look better-and-better the longer you own its. Its 10-year risk-adjusted returns are excellent. Management is very confident about its large research department's ability to find attractive less-liquid smaller issues. Manager Eagle is widely viewed as a star within the much-respected Fidelity Advisor group.

Profile

minimum initial investment $2,500	*IRA accounts available* . . . . yes
subsequent minimum investment . . $250	*IRA minimum investment* $500
available in all 50 states. . . . . yes	*date of inception* . . . . Jan. 1987
telephone exchanges. . . . . yes	*dividend/income paid.* . . . . monthly
number of other funds in family 27	*average credit quality* . . . . B

Franklin's AGE High Income A

777 Mariners Island Boulevard
San Mateo, CA 94403-777
800-342-5236

total return	★ ★ ★ ★
risk reduction	★ ★ ★ ★
management	★ ★ ★ ★ ★
current income	★ ★ ★ ★
expense control	★ ★ ★ ★ ★
symbol AGEFX	22 points
up-market performance	good
down-market performance	very good
predictability of returns	very good

Total Return   ★ ★ ★ ★

Over the past five years, Franklin's AGE High Income A has taken $10,000 and turned it into $15,966 ($12,954 over three years and $25,446 over the past ten years). This translates into an average annual return of 10 percent over the past five years, 9 percent over the past three years, and 10 percent for the decade. Over the past five years, this fund has outperformed 60 percent of all mutual funds; within its general category it has done better than 85 percent of its peers. High-yield bond funds have averaged 8 percent annually over these same five years.

During the past five years, a $10,000 initial investment grew to $12,610 after taxes, assuming a 39.6 percent income tax bracket (state and federal combined) and a capital gains rate of 28 percent. This means that investors in this fund were able to preserve 83 percent of their total returns. Compared to other fixed-income funds, this fund's tax savings are considered to be very good.

Risk/Volatility   ★ ★ ★ ★

Over the past five years, Franklin's AGE High Income A has been safer than 80 percent of all high-yield bond funds. Over the past decade, the fund has had three negative years, while the Lehman Brothers Aggregate Bond Index has had one (off 3 percent in 1994); the First Boston High-Yield Bond Index fell twice (off 6 percent in 1990 and 1 percent in 1994). The fund has underperformed the Lehman Brothers Aggregate Bond Index three times and the First Boston High-Yield Bond Index six times in the last ten years.

	last 5 years		last 10 years	
worst year	-2%	1994	-14%	1990
best year	19%	1995	48%	1991

In the past, Franklin's AGE High Income A has done better than 65 percent of its peer group in up markets and outperformed 75 percent of its competition in down markets. Consistency, or predictability, of returns for Franklin's AGE High Income A can be described as very good. This fund's risk-adjusted return is fair.

Management   ★ ★ ★ ★ ★

There are 250 fixed-income securities in this $3.2 billion portfolio. The average high-yield bond fund today is $386 million in size. Close to 94 percent of the fund's holdings are in bonds. The average maturity of the bonds in this account is nine years; the weighted coupon rate averages 8.1 percent. The portfolio's fixed-income holdings can be categorized as intermediate-term, low-quality debt.

Christopher Molumphy and R. Martin Wiskemann have managed this fund for the past eighteen years. There are eighty funds besides AGE High Income within the Franklin-Templeton family. Overall, the fund family's risk-adjusted performance can be described as very good.

Current Income   ★ ★ ★ ★

Over the past year, Franklin's AGE High Income A had a twelve-month yield of 9.6 percent. During this same twelve-month period, the typical high-yield bond fund had a yield that averaged 9.2 percent.

Expenses   ★ ★ ★ ★ ★

Franklin's AGE High Income A's expense ratio is .7 percent; it has also averaged .7 percent annually over the past three calendar years. The average expense ratio for the 300 funds in this category is 1.3 percent. This fund's turnover rate over the past year has been 30 percent, while its peer group average has been 125 percent.

Summary

Franklin's AGE High Income A typically keeps a bond for 3–5 years and usually limits any industry weighting to 10 percent of assets. The fund's co-managers Molumphy and Wiskemann keep a low profile by keeping things simple. The results have been quite impressive. This is the second-best ranked high-yield corporate bond fund and is highly recommended.

Profile

minimum initial investment $1,000	IRA accounts available . . . . yes
subsequent minimum investment . . . $50	IRA minimum investment $250
available in all 50 states. . . . . yes	date of inception. . . . . Dec. 1969
telephone exchanges. . . . . yes	dividend/income paid. . . . . monthly
number of other funds in family 80	average credit quality . . . . B

Invesco High-Yield
P.O. Box 173706
Denver, CO 80217-3706
800-525-8085

total return	★★★★
risk reduction	★★
management	★★★
current income	★★★
expense control	★★
symbol FHYPX	14 points
up-market performance	very good
down-market performance	fair
predictability of returns	good

Total Return   ★★★★

Over the past five years, Invesco High-Yield has taken $10,000 and turned it into $16,378 ($13,773 over three years and $25,216 over the past ten years). This translates into an average annual return of 10 percent over the past five years, 11 percent over the past three years, and 10 percent for the decade. Over the past five years, this fund has outperformed 60 percent of all mutual funds; within its general category it has done better than 80 percent of its peers. High-yield bond funds have averaged 8 percent annually over these same five years.

During the past five years, a $10,000 initial investment grew to $12,100 after taxes, assuming a 39.6 percent income tax bracket (state and federal combined) and a capital gains rate of 28 percent. This means that investors in this fund were able to preserve 81 percent of their total returns. Compared to other fixed-income funds, this fund's tax savings are considered to be very good.

Risk/Volatility   ★★

Over the past five years, Invesco High-Yield has been safer than 30 percent of all high-yield bond funds. Over the past decade, the fund has had two negative years, while the Lehman Brothers Aggregate Bond Index has had one (off 3 percent in 1994); the First Boston High-Yield Bond Index fell twice (off 6 percent in 1990 and 1 percent in 1994). The fund has underperformed the Lehman Brothers Aggregate Bond Index five times and the First Boston High-Yield Bond Index five times in the last ten years.

	last 5 years		last 10 years	
worst year	-5%	1994	-5%	1994
best year	18%	1995	24%	1991

In the past, Invesco High-Yield has done better than 80 percent of its peer group in up markets and outperformed 45 percent of its competition in down markets. Consistency, or predictability, of returns for Invesco High-Yield can be described as good. This fund's risk-adjusted return is very good.

Management ★ ★ ★

There are 100 fixed-income securities in this $930 million portfolio. The average high-yield bond fund today is $386 million in size. Close to 96 percent of the fund's holdings are in bonds. The average maturity of the bonds in this account is seven years; the weighted coupon rate averages 6.9 percent. The portfolio's fixed-income holdings can be categorized as intermediate-term, low-quality debt.

Jerry Paul has managed this fund for the past five years. There are thirty-one funds besides High-Yield within the Invesco family. Overall, the fund family's risk-adjusted performance can be described as very good.

Current Income ★ ★ ★

Over the past year, Invesco High-Yield had a twelve-month yield of 9.3 percent. During this same twelve-month period, the typical high-yield bond fund had a yield that averaged 9.2 percent.

Expenses ★ ★

Invesco High-Yield's expense ratio is .9 percent; it has averaged 1 percent annually over the past three calendar years. The average expense ratio for the 300 funds in this category is 1.3 percent. This fund's turnover rate over the past year has been 280 percent, while its peer group average has been 125 percent.

Summary

Invesco High-Yield is consistent across the board. There is no one area where this fund excels and no area where it is a real disappointment. The fund distinguishes itself from its peer group by owning about twice as many bonds as its category average. Despite its modest overall rating, this is still a very attractive candidate for the junk bond investor.

Profile

minimum initial investment $1,000	*IRA accounts available* . . . . yes
subsequent minimum investment . . . $50	*IRA minimum investment* $250
available in all 50 states. . . . . yes	*date of inception* . . . . March 1984
telephone exchanges. . . . . yes	*dividend/income paid.* . . . . monthly
number of other funds in family 31	*average credit quality* . . . . B

Legg Mason High-Yield Portfolio Primary Shares
111 South Calvert Street
Baltimore, MD 21203-1476
800-577-8589

total return	★ ★ ★ ★ ★
risk reduction	★ ★ ★ ★
management	★ ★ ★ ★
current income	★ ★
expense control	★ ★ ★
symbol LMHYX	18 points
up-market performance	excellent
down-market performance	poor
predictability of returns	very good

Total Return   ★ ★ ★ ★ ★

Over the past five years, Legg Mason High-Yield Portfolio Primary Shares has taken $10,000 and turned it into $16,911 ($14,000 over three years). This translates into an average annual return of 11 percent over the past five years and 12 percent over the past three years. Over the past five years this fund has outperformed 60 percent of all mutual funds; within its general category it has done better than 80 percent of its peers. High-yield bond funds have averaged 8 percent annually over these same five years.

During the past five years, a $10,000 initial investment grew to $14,200 after taxes, assuming a 39.6 percent income tax bracket (state and federal combined) and a capital gains rate of 28 percent. This means that investors in this fund were able to preserve 92 percent of their total returns. Compared to other fixed-income funds, this fund's tax savings are considered to be excellent.

Risk/Volatility   ★ ★ ★ ★

Over the past five years, Legg Mason High-Yield Portfolio Primary Shares has been safer than 70 percent of all high-yield bond funds. Over the past decade, the fund has had one negative year, while the Lehman Brothers Aggregate Bond Index has had one (off 3 percent in 1994); the First Boston High-Yield Bond Index fell twice (off 6 percent in 1990 and 1 percent in 1994). The fund has underperformed the Lehman Brothers Aggregate Bond Index twice and the First Boston High-Yield Bond Index once in the last ten years.

	last 5 years		since inception	
worst year	-2%	1998	-2%	1998
best year	18%	1995	18%	1995

In the past, Legg Mason High-Yield Portfolio Primary Shares has done better than 100 percent of its peer group in up markets and outperformed 25 percent of its competition in down markets. Consistency, or predictability, of returns for Legg Mason High-Yield Portfolio Primary Shares can be described as very good. This fund's risk-adjusted return is excellent.

Management   ★ ★ ★ ★

There are 115 fixed-income securities in this $500 million portfolio. The average high-yield bond fund today is $386 million in size. Close to 70 percent of the fund's holdings are in bonds. The average maturity of the bonds in this account is seven years; the weighted coupon rate averages 9.3 percent. The portfolio's fixed-income holdings can be categorized as intermediate-term, low-quality debt.

A team has managed this fund for the past five years. There are fifteen funds besides High-Yield Portfolio within the Legg Mason family. Overall, the fund family's risk-adjusted performance can be described as very good.

Current Income   ★ ★

Over the past year, Legg Mason High-Yield Portfolio Primary Shares had a twelve-month yield of 7.5 percent. During this same twelve-month period, the typical high-yield bond fund had a yield that averaged 9.2 percent.

Expenses   ★ ★ ★

Legg Mason High-Yield Portfolio Primary Shares' expense ratio is 1.3 percent; it has also averaged 1.3 percent annually over the past three calendar years. The average expense ratio for the 300 funds in this category is 1.3 percent. This fund's turnover rate over the past year has been 116 percent, while its peer group average has been 125 percent.

Summary

Legg Mason High-Yield Portfolio Primary Shares rates as one of the very top-performing bond funds. Risk-adjusted returns over the past five years have been outstanding. Close to one-third of the fund's assets are in stocks, management favors telecommunications issues. Despite such an unconventional weighting in stocks, the fund's risk level has been quite low. This fund would be a very good choice for the investor who wants to minimize the number of funds he owns.

Profile

minimum initial investment $1,000	IRA accounts available . . . . yes
subsequent minimum investment . . $100	IRA minimum investment $1,000
available in all 50 states . . . . no	date of inception . . . . Feb. 1994
telephone exchanges. . . . . yes	dividend/income paid. . . . . monthly
number of other funds in family 15	average credit quality . . . . B

MainStay High-Yield Corporate Bond B

260 Cherry Hill Road
Parsippany, NJ 07054
800-624-6782

total return	★ ★ ★ ★
risk reduction	★ ★ ★ ★ ★
management	★ ★ ★ ★
current income	★ ★ ★
expense control	★ ★
symbol MKHCX	18 points
up-market performance	excellent
down-market performance	fair
predictability of returns	very good

Total Return   ★ ★ ★ ★

Over the past five years, MainStay High-Yield Corporate Bond B has taken $10,000 and turned it into $16,171 ($13,075 over three years and $27,912 over the past ten years). This translates into an average annual return of 10 percent over the past five years, 9 percent over the past three years, and 11 percent for the decade. Over the past five years, this fund has outperformed 65 percent of all mutual funds; within its general category it has done better than 95 percent of its peers. High-yield bond funds have averaged 8 percent annually over these same five years.

During the past five years, a $10,000 initial investment grew to $13,060 after taxes, assuming a 39.6 percent income tax bracket (state and federal combined) and a capital gains rate of 28 percent. This means that investors in this fund were able to preserve 83 percent of their total returns. Compared to other fixed-income funds, this fund's tax savings are considered to be very good.

Risk/Volatility   ★ ★ ★ ★ ★

Over the past five years, MainStay High-Yield Corporate Bond B has been safer than 95 percent of all high-yield bond funds. Over the past decade, the fund has had two negative years, while the Lehman Brothers Aggregate Bond Index has had one (off 3 percent in 1994); the First Boston High-Yield Bond Index fell twice (off 6 percent in 1990 and 1 percent in 1994). The fund has underperformed the Lehman Brothers Aggregate Bond Index three times and the First Boston High-Yield Bond Index four times in the last ten years.

	last 5 years		last 10 years	
worst year	1%	1998	-8%	1990
best year	20%	1995	32%	1991

In the past, MainStay High-Yield Corporate Bond B has done better than 90 percent of its peer group in up markets and outperformed 45 percent of its competition in down markets. Consistency, or predictability, of returns for MainStay High-Yield Corporate Bond B can be described as very good. This fund's risk-adjusted return is fair.

Management   ★ ★ ★ ★

There are 263 fixed-income securities in this $3.3 billion portfolio. The average high-yield bond fund today is $386 million in size. Close to 78 percent of the fund's holdings are in bonds. The average maturity of the bonds in this account is nine years; the weighted coupon rate averages 7.7 percent. The portfolio's fixed-income holdings can be categorized as intermediate-term, low-quality debt.

Dennis Laplaige and Steven Tananbaum have managed this fund for the past nine years. There are twenty funds besides High-Yield Corporate Bond within the MainStay family. Overall, the fund family's risk-adjusted performance can be described as very good.

Current Income   ★ ★ ★

Over the past year, MainStay High-Yield Corporate Bond B had a twelve-month yield of 9.0 percent. During this same twelve-month period, the typical high-yield bond fund had a yield that averaged 9.2 percent.

Expenses   ★ ★

MainStay High-Yield Corporate Bond B's expense ratio is 1.6 percent; it has also averaged 1.6 percent annually over the past three calendar years. The average expense ratio for the 300 funds in this category is 1.3 percent. This fund's turnover rate over the past year has been 128 percent, while its peer group average has been 125 percent.

Summary

MainStay High-Yield Corporate Bond B has turned in exceptional risk-adjusted returns over the past five and ten years. Conservative managers Laplaige and Tananbaum favor larger bond issues from established companies that have rising cash flows. Roughly one-quarter of the portfolio's assets are in less-liquid smaller domestic and foreign markets. Despite these holdings, this fund remains as one of the safest within its category.

Profile

minimum initial investment $500	IRA accounts available . . . . yes
subsequent minimum investment . . . $50	IRA minimum investment $500
available in all 50 states. . . . . yes	date of inception. . . . . May 1986
telephone exchanges. . . . . yes	dividend/income paid. . . . . monthly
number of other funds in family 20	average credit quality . . . . B

Northeast Investors
50 Congress Street
Boston, MA 02109-4096
800-225-6704

total return	★ ★ ★ ★
risk reduction	★ ★ ★ ★
management	★ ★ ★ ★ ★
current income	★ ★ ★
expense control	★ ★ ★ ★ ★
symbol NTHEX	21 points
up-market performance	excellent
down-market performance	poor
predictability of returns	very good

Total Return   ★ ★ ★ ★

Over the past five years, Northeast Investors has taken $10,000 and turned it into $16,341 ($13,372 over three years and $27,761 over the past ten years). This translates into an average annual return of 10 percent over the past five years, 10 percent over the past three years, and 11 percent for the decade. Over the past five years, this fund has outperformed 65 percent of all mutual funds; within its general category it has done better than 97 percent of its peers. High-yield bond funds have averaged 8 percent annually over these same five years.

During the past five years, a $10,000 initial investment grew to $13,620 after taxes, assuming a 39.6 percent income tax bracket (state and federal combined) and a capital gains rate of 28 percent. This means that investors in this fund were able to preserve 83 percent of their total returns. Compared to other fixed-income funds, this fund's tax savings are considered to be very good.

Risk/Volatility   ★ ★ ★ ★

Over the past five years, Northeast Investors has been safer than 65 percent of all high-yield bond funds. Over the past decade, the fund has had two negative years, while the Lehman Brothers Aggregate Bond Index has had one (off 3 percent in 1994); the First Boston High-Yield Bond Index fell twice (off 6 percent in 1990 and 1 percent in 1994). The fund has underperformed the Lehman Brothers Aggregate Bond Index four times and the First Boston High-Yield Bond Index five times in the last ten years.

	last 5 years		last 10 years	
worst year	-0.3%	1998	-9%	1990
best year	20%	1996	26%	1991

In the past, Northeast Investors has done better than 90 percent of its peer group in up markets and outperformed 20 percent of its competition in down markets. Consistency, or predictability, of returns for Northeast Investors can be described as very good. This fund's risk-adjusted return is excellent.

Management   ★ ★ ★ ★ ★
There are 139 fixed-income securities in this $2.3 billion portfolio. The average high-yield bond fund today is $386 million in size. Close to 87 percent of the fund's holdings are in bonds. The average maturity of the bonds in this account is eight years; the weighted coupon rate averages 10.1 percent. The portfolio's fixed-income holdings can be categorized as intermediate-term, low-quality debt.

Ernest Monrad and Bruce Monrad have managed this fund for the past twenty-three years. There is one other fund besides Investors within the Northeast family. Overall, the fund family's risk-adjusted performance can be described as very good.

Current Income   ★ ★ ★
Over the past year, Northeast Investors had a twelve-month yield of 9.1 percent. During this same twelve-month period, the typical high-yield bond fund had a yield that averaged 9.2 percent.

Expenses   ★ ★ ★ ★ ★
Northeast Investors' expense ratio is .6 percent; it has also averaged .6 percent annually over the past three calendar years. The average expense ratio for the 300 funds in this category is 1.3 percent. This fund's turnover rate over the past year has been 64 percent, while its peer group average has been 125 percent.

Summary
Northeast Investors has had outstanding risk-adjusted returns over the past five and ten years. Over half of the fund's assets are in single B-rated bonds. Management is not afraid to stray into common stocks or debt from emerging markets. The leveraging of assets has also worked out well. This fund scores very high across the board. The managers are considered to be excellent and cost control has been extremely effective.

Profile
minimum initial investment . . . . . $1,000   IRA accounts available . . . . yes
subsequent minimum investment . . . $50   IRA minimum investment $500
available in all 50 states. . . . . yes   date of inception . . . . Aug. 1950
telephone exchanges. . . . . yes   dividend/income paid . . . . quarterly
number of other funds in family 1   average credit quality . . . . B

Seligman High-Yield Bond A
100 Park Avenue
New York, NY 10017
800-221-2783

total return	★ ★ ★ ★
risk reduction	★ ★ ★ ★
management	★ ★ ★ ★ ★
current income	★ ★ ★ ★ ★
expense control	★ ★ ★ ★ ★
symbol SHYBX	23 points
up-market performance	fair
down-market performance	good
predictability of returns	very good

Total Return ★ ★ ★ ★

Over the past five years, Seligman High-Yield Bond A has taken $10,000 and turned it into $16,512 ($12,968 over three years and $29,014 over the past ten years). This translates into an average annual return of 11 percent over the past five years, 9 percent over the past three years, and 11 percent for the decade. Over the past five years, this fund has outperformed 65 percent of all mutual funds; within its general category it has done better than 96 percent of its peers. High-yield bond funds have averaged 8 percent annually over these same five years.

During the past five years, a $10,000 initial investment grew to $13,390 after taxes, assuming a 39.6 percent income tax bracket (state and federal combined) and a capital gains rate of 28 percent. This means that investors in this fund were able to preserve 83 percent of their total returns. Compared to other fixed-income funds, this fund's tax savings are considered to be very good.

Risk/Volatility ★ ★ ★ ★

Over the past five years, Seligman High-Yield Bond A has been safer than 80 percent of all high-yield bond funds. Over the past decade, the fund has had one negative year, while the Lehman Brothers Aggregate Bond Index has had one (off 3 percent in 1994); the First Boston High-Yield Bond Index fell twice (off 6 percent in 1990 and 1 percent in 1994). The fund has underperformed the Lehman Brothers Aggregate Bond Index three times and the First Boston High-Yield Bond Index twice in the last ten years.

	last 5 years		last 10 years	
worst year	1%	1994	-7%	1990
best year	21%	1995	31%	1991

In the past, Seligman High-Yield Bond A has done better than 45 percent of its peer group in up markets and outperformed 65 percent of its competition in down markets. Consistency, or predictability, of returns for Seligman High-Yield Bond A can be described as very good. This fund's risk-adjusted return is fair.

Management   ★ ★ ★ ★ ★

There are 145 fixed-income securities in this $1.1 billion portfolio. The average high-yield bond fund today is $386 million in size. Close to 88 percent of the fund's holdings are in bonds. The average maturity of the bonds in this account is eight years; the weighted coupon rate averages 10 percent. The portfolio's fixed-income holdings can be categorized as intermediate-term, low-quality debt.

Daniel Charleston has managed this fund for the past ten years. There are thirty funds besides High-Yield Bond A within the Seligman family. Overall, the fund family's risk-adjusted performance can be described as good.

Current Income   ★ ★ ★ ★ ★

Over the past year, Seligman High-Yield Bond A had a twelve-month yield of 10.0 percent. During this same twelve-month period, the typical high-yield bond fund had a yield that averaged 9.2 percent.

Expenses   ★ ★ ★ ★ ★

Seligman High-Yield Bond A's expense ratio is 1.1 percent; it has also averaged 1.1 percent annually over the past three calendar years. The average expense ratio for the 300 funds in this category is 1.3 percent. This fund's turnover rate over the past year has been 62 percent, while its peer group average has been 125 percent.

Summary

Seligman High-Yield Bond A rates as one of the very best bond funds. Risk-adjusted returns for the past five and ten years have been tops. Manager Charleston is regarded as one of the best in the industry. He has been able to successfully navigate the fund through some domestic and global events that proved troublesome for many of his peers. It is hard to find anything of fault with the number one rated high-yield bond fund. This portfolio is highly recommended.

Profile

minimum initial investment $1,000	*IRA accounts available* . . . . yes
subsequent minimum investment . . $100	*IRA minimum investment* $1,000
available in all 50 states. . . . . yes	*date of inception* . . . . March 1985
telephone exchanges. . . . . yes	*dividend/income paid*. . . . . monthly
number of other funds in family 33	*average credit quality* . . . . B

Vanguard High-Yield Corporate
Vanguard Financial Center
P.O. Box 2600
Valley Forge, PA 19482
800-662-7447

total return	★ ★ ★ ★
risk reduction	★ ★ ★ ★ ★
management	★ ★ ★ ★ ★
current income	★ ★
expense control	★ ★ ★ ★ ★
symbol VWEHX	21 points
up-market performance	fair
down-market performance	excellent
predictability of returns	excellent

Total Return   ★ ★ ★ ★
Over the past five years, Vanguard High-Yield Corporate has taken $10,000 and turned it into $15,945 ($13,126 over three years and $25,377 over the past ten years). This translates into an average annual return of 10 percent over the past five years, 9 percent over the past three years, and 10 percent for the decade. Over the past five years, this fund has outperformed 60 percent of all mutual funds; within its general category it has done better than 85 percent of its peers. High-yield bond funds have averaged 8 percent annually over these same five years.

During the past five years, a $10,000 initial investment grew to $12,750 after taxes, assuming a 39.6 percent income tax bracket (state and federal combined) and a capital gains rate of 28 percent. This means that investors in this fund were able to preserve 84 percent of their total returns. Compared to other fixed-income funds, this fund's tax savings are considered to be very good.

Risk/Volatility   ★ ★ ★ ★ ★
Over the past five years, Vanguard High-Yield Corporate has been safer than 95 percent of all high-yield bond funds. Over the past decade, the fund has had two negative years, while the Lehman Brothers Aggregate Bond Index has had one (off 3 percent in 1994); the First Boston High-Yield Bond Index fell twice (off 6 percent in 1990 and 1 percent in 1994). The fund has underperformed the Lehman Brothers Aggregate Bond Index three times and the First Boston High-Yield Bond Index six times in the last ten years.

	last 5 years		last 10 years	
worst year	-2%	1994	-6%	1990
best year	19%	1995	29%	1991

In the past, Vanguard High-Yield Corporate has done better than 45 percent of its peer group in up markets and outperformed 100 percent of its competition in down markets. Consistency, or predictability, of returns for Vanguard High-Yield Corporate can be described as very good. This fund's risk-adjusted return is excellent.

Management   ★ ★ ★ ★ ★

There are 225 fixed-income securities in this $5.6 billion portfolio. The average high-yield bond fund today is $386 million in size. Close to 97 percent of the fund's holdings are in bonds. The average maturity of the bonds in this account is eight years; the weighted coupon rate averages 8.8 percent. The portfolio's fixed-income holdings can be categorized as intermediate-term, low-quality debt.

Earl McEvoy has managed this fund for the past fifteen years. There are sixty-eight funds besides High-Yield Corporate within the Vanguard family. Overall, the fund family's risk-adjusted performance can be described as very good.

Current Income   ★ ★

Over the past year, Vanguard High-Yield Corporate had a twelve-month yield of 8.3 percent. During this same twelve-month period, the typical high-yield bond fund had a yield that averaged 9.2 percent.

Expenses   ★ ★ ★ ★ ★

Vanguard High-Yield Corporate's expense ratio is .3 percent; it has also averaged .3 percent annually over the past three calendar years. The average expense ratio for the 300 funds in this category is 1.3 percent. This fund's turnover rate over the past year has been 45 percent, while its peer group average has been 125 percent.

Summary

Vanguard High-Yield Corporate rarely ends up in the top performance quartile for its category, but the fund's consistency is so good that its risk-adjusted returns over the past three, five, and ten years have been superb. Almost the entire portfolio is in bonds rated B or BB. Emerging market debt and zero-coupon issues are avoided in order to reduce risk and increase predictability. The fund typically keeps a modest portion of its assets in government securities. This is one of the top-rated high-yield corporate bond funds.

Profile

minimum initial investment $3,000	*IRA accounts available* . . . . yes
subsequent minimum investment . . $100	*IRA minimum investment* $1,000
available in all 50 states. . . . . yes	*date of inception.* . . . . Dec. 1978
telephone exchanges. . . . . yes	*dividend/income paid.* . . . . monthly
number of other funds in family 68	*average credit quality* . . . . BB

Metals and Natural Resources Funds

These funds purchase metals in one or more of the following forms: bullion, South African gold stocks, and non–South African mining stocks. The United States, Canada, and Australia are the three major stock-issuing producers of metals outside of South Africa. Metals funds, also referred to as gold funds, often own minor positions in other precious metals stocks, such as silver and platinum.

The proportion and type of metal held by a fund can have a great impact on its performance and volatility. Outright ownership of gold bullion is almost always less volatile than owning stock in a gold mining company. Thus, much greater gains or losses occur in metals funds that purchase only gold stocks, compared to funds that hold high levels of bullion, coins, and stock. Silver, incidentally, has nearly twice the volatility of gold yet has not enjoyed any greater returns over the long term.

Gold, or metals, funds can do well during periods of political uncertainty and inflationary concerns. Over the past several hundred years, gold and silver have served as hedges against inflation. Most readers will be surprised to learn that, historically, both metals have outperformed inflation by less than one percent annually.

Metals funds are the riskiest category of mutual funds described in this book, with a standard deviation of 33—about 15 percent higher than the standard deviation of aggressive growth funds. And yet, although this is certainly a high-risk investment when viewed on its own, ownership of a metals fund can actually reduce a portfolio's overall risk level and often enhance its total return. Why? Because gold usually has a negative correlation to other investments. When the other investments go down in value, gold may go up. Thus, a portfolio made up strictly of government bonds will actually exhibit more risk and less return than one made up of 90 percent government and 10 percent metals funds.

There are forty-five metals funds; total market capitalization is $3 billion. Turnover has averaged 75 percent. The p/e ratio for metals funds is 32, while dividend yield is one half of one percent. Over the past three years, these funds averaged –24.6 percent per year, –13.5 percent for the last five years, –4.8 percent for the past decade, and –4.2 percent for the last fifteen years.

Natural resources funds invest in the stocks of companies that deal in the ownership, production, transmission, transportation, refinement, and/or storage of oil, natural gas, and timber. These funds also invest in companies that either own or are involved in real estate.

There are sixty-five natural resources funds; total market capitalization is just under $5 billion. This group has had a standard deviation of 25.8 percent over the past three years. Beta, or market-related risk, has been 0.8 percent, but do not let this low number fool you. As you can see by the standard deviation, few equity categories are riskier. Turnover has averaged 90 percent per year. The p/e ratio for natural resources funds is 28; dividend yield is a little under one percent. Over the past three years, these funds have averaged –1.3 percent — 5.8 percent for the past five years, 6.7 percent for the last ten years, and 6.8 percent for the past fifteen years.

Metals and natural resources funds should be avoided by anyone who cannot tolerate wide price swings in any single part of his portfolio. These funds are designed as an integral part of a diversified portfolio, for investors who look at the overall return of their holdings.

Precious Metals Funds

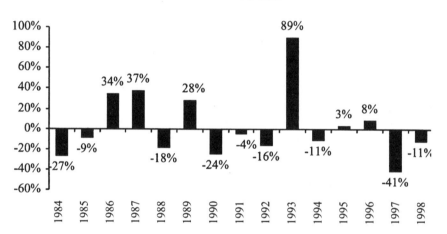

Natural Resources Funds

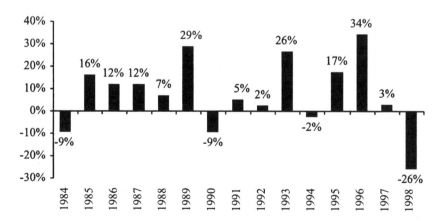

Franklin Gold A
777 Mariners Island Boulevard
San Mateo, CA 94403-777
800-342-5236

total return	★ ★
risk reduction	★ ★ ★ ★ ★
management	★ ★ ★ ★
tax minimization	★ ★ ★ ★ ★
expense control	★ ★ ★ ★ ★
symbol FKRCX	21 points
up-market performance	good
down-market performance	fair
predictability of returns	good

Total Return   ★ ★
Over the past five years, Franklin Gold A has taken $10,000 and turned it into $5,931 ($5,124 over three years and $8,641 over the past ten years). This translates into an average annual return of -10 percent over the past five years, -20 percent over the past three years, and -1 percent for the decade. Over the past five years, this fund has outperformed 1 percent of all mutual funds; within its general category it has done better than 80 percent of its peers. Metals and natural resources funds have averaged -5 percent annually over these same five years.

Risk/Volatility   ★ ★ ★ ★ ★
Over the past five years, Franklin Gold A has been safer than 90 percent of all metals and natural resources funds. Over the past decade, the fund has had six negative years, while the S&P 500 has had one (off 3 percent in 1990). The fund has underperformed the S&P 500 eight times in the last ten years.

	last 5 years		last 10 years	
worst year	-36%	1998	-36%	1998
best year	1%	1996	74%	1993

In the past, Franklin Gold A has done better than 60 percent of its peer group in up markets and outperformed 30 percent of its competition in down markets. Consistency, or predictability, of returns for Franklin Gold A can be described as good. This fund's risk-adjusted return is excellent.

Management   ★ ★ ★ ★
There are forty stocks in this $190 million portfolio. The average metals and natural resources fund today is $63 million in size. Close to 97 percent of the fund's holdings are in stocks. The stocks in this portfolio have an average price-earnings (p/e) ratio of 30 and a median market capitalization of $2.1 billion. The portfolio's equity holdings can be categorized as mid-cap and growth-oriented issues.

R. Martin Wiskemann and Suzanne Willoughby Killea have managed this fund for the past sixteen years. There are eighty funds besides Gold within the

Franklin-Templeton family. Overall, the fund family's risk-adjusted performance can be described as very good.

Tax Minimization   ★ ★ ★ ★ ★

During the past five years, a $10,000 initial investment grew to $5,610 after taxes, assuming a 39.6 percent income tax bracket (state and federal combined) and a capital gains rate of 28 percent. This means that investors in this fund were able to preserve 99 percent of their total returns. Compared to other equity funds, this fund's tax savings are considered to be excellent.

Expenses   ★ ★ ★ ★ ★

Franklin Gold A's expense ratio is 1.2 percent; it has averaged 1.1 percent annually over the past three calendar years. The average expense ratio for the 105 funds in this category is 1.8 percent. This fund's turnover rate over the past year has been 6 percent, while its peer group average has been 85 percent.

Summary

Franklin Gold A has ranked in the top performance quartile for its category frequently over the past 15 years. Manager Wiskemann concentrates the portfolio's gold allocation to long-life mining companies that have strong reserves; at least two-thirds of the fund's assets are in companies engaged in gold operations. This fund has ranked in the quartile over the past one, three, five, ten, and fifteen years. Over the past 20 years it is the number one ranked metals fund. The fund also receives excellent marks for its risk minimization.

Profile

minimum initial investment $1,000	*IRA accounts available* . . . . yes
subsequent minimum investment . . . $50	*IRA minimum investment* $250
available in all 50 states. . . . . yes	*date of inception.* . . . . May 1969
telephone exchanges. . . . . yes	*dividend/income paid* . . . . annually
number of other funds in family. 80	*largest sector weighting.* . . . . . industrial cyclicals

Scudder Gold
Two International Place
Boston, MA 02110
800-225-2470

total return	★ ★ ★ ★
risk reduction	★ ★ ★ ★ ★
management	★ ★ ★ ★
tax minimization	★ ★ ★ ★ ★
expense control	★ ★ ★
symbol SCGDX	21 points
up-market performance	very good
down-market performance	poor
predictability of returns	good

Total Return   ★ ★ ★ ★

Over the past five years, Scudder Gold has taken $10,000 and turned it into $6,681 ($4,823 over three years and $8,528 over the past ten years). This translates into an average annual return of -8 percent over the past five years, -22 percent over the past three years, and -2 percent for the decade. Over the past five years, this fund has outperformed 2 percent of all mutual funds; within its general category it has done better than 97 percent of its peers. Metals and natural resources funds have averaged -5 percent annually over these same five years.

Risk/Volatility   ★ ★ ★ ★ ★

Over the past five years, Scudder Gold has been safer than 90 percent of all metals and natural resources funds. Over the past decade, the fund has had six negative years, while the S&P 500 has had one (off 3 percent in 1990). The fund has under-performed the S&P 500 eight times in the last ten years.

	last 5 years		last 10 years	
worst year	-41%	1997	-41%	1997
best year	32%	1996	59%	1993

In the past, Scudder Gold has done better than 85 percent of its peer group in up markets and outperformed 15 percent of its competition in down markets. Consistency, or predictability, of returns for Scudder Gold can be described as good. This fund's risk-adjusted return is excellent.

Management   ★ ★ ★ ★

There are fifty-nine stocks in this $105 million portfolio. The average metals and natural resources fund today is $63 million in size. Close to 92 percent of the fund's holdings are in stocks. The stocks in this portfolio have an average price-earnings (p/e) ratio of 31 and a median market capitalization of $830 million. The port-folio's equity holdings can be categorized as small-cap and growth-oriented issues.

Clay Hoes and William Wallace have managed this fund for the past seven years. There are forty-five funds besides Gold within the Scudder family. Overall, the fund family's risk-adjusted performance can be described as very good.

Tax Minimization   ★ ★ ★ ★ ★

During the past five years, a $10,000 initial investment grew to $6,030 after taxes, assuming a 39.6 percent income tax bracket (state and federal combined) and a capital gains rate of 28 percent. This means that investors in this fund were able to preserve 88 percent of their total returns. Compared to other equity funds, this fund's tax savings are considered to be very good.

Expenses   ★ ★ ★

Scudder Gold's expense ratio is 1.8 percent; it has averaged 1.7 percent annually over the past three calendar years. The average expense ratio for the 105 funds in this category is 1.8 percent. This fund's turnover rate over the past year has been 68 percent, while its peer group average has been 85 percent.

Summary

Scudder Gold invests in companies that are in the business of exploration, mining, fabrication, processing, or distribution of gold, bullion, and coins. Co-managers Hoes and Wallace are concerned with the quality of metals mined, the costs associated with processing, as well as the amount of unmined reserves. Management also studies a company's labor relations, tax liabilities, expenditure plans, potential property development, and caliber of decision makers. Up to one-third of the fund's assets can be invested in metals-related companies other than gold. The fund's risk reduction is exceptional and this is just one of several recommended Scudder portfolios.

Profile

minimum initial investment $2,500	*IRA accounts available* . . . . yes
subsequent minimum investment . . $100	*IRA minimum investment* $1,000
available in all 50 states. . . . . yes	*date of inception* . . . . Sept. 1988
telephone exchanges. . . . . yes	*dividend/income paid* . . . . annually
number of other funds in family 45	*largest sector weighting*. . . . . industrial cyclicals

State Street Research Global Resources A

One Financial Center
Boston, MA 02111
800-882-0052

total return	★ ★ ★ ★
risk reduction	★
management	★ ★ ★
tax minimization	★ ★ ★
expense control	★ ★ ★
symbol SSGRX	14 points
up-market performance	poor
down-market performance	poor
predictability of returns	fair

Total Return   ★ ★ ★ ★

Over the past five years, State Street Research Global Resources A has taken $10,000 and turned it into $11,567 ($8,080 over three years). This translates into an average annual return of 3 percent over the past five years and -7 percent over the past three years. Over the past five years, this fund has outperformed 3 percent of all mutual funds; within its general category it has done better than 35 percent of its peers. Metals and natural resources funds have averaged -5 percent annually over these same five years.

Risk/Volatility   ★

Over the past five years, State Street Research Global Resources A has been safer than 20 percent of all metals and natural resources funds. Over the past decade, the fund has had three negative years, while the S&P 500 has had one (off 3 percent in 1990). The fund has underperformed the S&P 500 six times in the last ten years.

	last 5 years		since inception	
worst year	-48%	1998	-48%	1998
best year	70%	1996	70%	1996

In the past, State Street Research Global Resources A has done better than 15 percent of its peer group in up markets and outperformed 25 percent of its competition in down markets. Consistency, or predictability, of returns for State Street Research Global Resources A can be described as fair. This fund's risk-adjusted return is poor.

Management   ★ ★ ★

There are 115 stocks in this $40 million portfolio. The average metals and natural resources fund today is $63 million in size. Close to 100 percent of the fund's holdings are in stocks. The stocks in this portfolio have an average price-earnings (p/e) ratio of 159 and a median market capitalization of $290 million. The portfolio's equity holdings can be categorized as small-cap and value-oriented issues.

Daniel Rice, III has managed this fund for the past nine years. There are twenty-two funds besides Global Resources within the State Street Research family. Overall, the fund family's risk-adjusted performance can be described as good.

Tax Minimization ★ ★ ★

During the past five years, a $10,000 initial investment grew to $7,870 after taxes, assuming a 39.6 percent income tax bracket (state and federal combined) and a capital gains rate of 28 percent. This means that investors in this fund were able to preserve 73 percent of their total returns. Compared to other equity funds, this fund's tax savings are considered to be fair.

Expenses ★ ★ ★

State Street Research Global Resources A's expense ratio is 1.5 percent; it has averaged 1.4 percent annually over the past three calendar years. The average expense ratio for the 105 funds in this category is 1.8 percent. This fund's turnover rate over the past year has been 69 percent, while its peer group average has been 85 percent.

Summary

State Street Research Global Resources A invests in stocks of energy and natural resources companies. Prospective candidates are involved in the exploration, production and/or distribution of gas, oil, metals, or minerals. The fund's management prefers investing in small-cap issues in developed markets. This can be a highly volatile fund and is recommended as a diversification tool or for the investor who wants to add this sector to his portfolio.

Profile

minimum initial investment $2,500	*IRA accounts available* . . . . yes
subsequent minimum investment . . . $50	*IRA minimum investment* $2,000
available in all 50 states. . . . . yes	*date of inception* . . . . March 1990
telephone exchanges. . . . . yes	*dividend/income paid* . . . . annually
number of other funds in family 22	*largest sector weighting*. . . . . . . energy

Vanguard Energy
Vanguard Financial Center
P.O. Box 2600
Valley Forge, PA 19482
800-662-7447

total return	★ ★ ★ ★ ★
risk reduction	★ ★ ★
management	★ ★ ★ ★
tax minimization	★ ★ ★
expense control	★ ★ ★ ★ ★
symbol VGENX	20 points
up-market performance	poor
down-market performance	good
predictability of returns	excellent

Total Return   ★ ★ ★ ★ ★
Over the past five years, Vanguard Energy has taken $10,000 and turned it into
$16,775 ($12,299 over three years and $27,412 over the past ten years). This trans-
lates into an average annual return of 11 percent over the past five years, 7 percent
over the past three years, and 11 percent for the decade. Over the past five years,
this fund has outperformed 40 percent of all mutual funds; within its general category it has done better than 80 percent of its peers. Metals and natural resources
funds have averaged -5 percent annually over these same five years.

Risk/Volatility   ★ ★ ★
Over the past five years, Vanguard Energy has been safer than 65 percent of all
metals and natural resources funds. Over the past decade, the fund has had three
negative years, while the S&P 500 has had one (off 3 percent in 1990). The fund
has underperformed the S&P 500 six times in the last ten years.

	last 5 years		last 10 years	
worst year	-21%	1998	-21%	1998
best year	34%	1996	43%	1989

In the past, Vanguard Energy has done better than 25 percent of its peer group
in up markets and outperformed 55 percent of its competition in down markets.
Consistency, or predictability, of returns for Vanguard Energy can be described as
excellent. This fund's risk-adjusted return is poor.

Management   ★ ★ ★ ★
There are fifty-six stocks in this $750 million portfolio. The average metals and nat-
ural resources fund today is $63 million in size. Close to 96 percent of the fund's hold-
ings are in stocks. The stocks in this portfolio have an average price-earnings (p/e)
ratio of 30 and a median market capitalization of $7 billion. The portfolio's equity
holdings can be categorized as mid-cap and a blend of growth and value stocks.

Ernst von Metzsch has managed this fund for the past fifteen years. There are sixty-eight funds besides Energy within the Vanguard family. Overall, the fund family's risk-adjusted performance can be described as very good.

Tax Minimization   ★ ★ ★

During the past five years, a $10,000 initial investment grew to $12,490 after taxes, assuming a 39.6 percent income tax bracket (state and federal combined) and a capital gains rate of 28 percent. This means that investors in this fund were able to preserve 83 percent of their total returns. Compared to other equity funds, this fund's tax savings are considered to be good.

Expenses   ★ ★ ★ ★ ★

Vanguard Energy's expense ratio is .4 percent; it has also averaged .4 percent annually over the past three calendar years. The average expense ratio for the 105 funds in this category is 1.8 percent. This fund's turnover rate over the past year has been 19 percent, while its peer group average has been 85 percent.

Summary

Vanguard Energy, also known as Vanguard Specialized Energy, receives top marks for its returns and expense control. The energy/natural resources category is not a stable one and high returns are difficult to obtain. Management favors value over growth and seeks to reduce risk by investing domestically as well as overseas, maintaining a balance of oil and gas issues. Manager Metzsch mixes things up by investing in large- as well as small-cap issues and by owning shares of companies that are involved in pipeline operations, oil services, tanker companies plus refiners and producers. This fund also has a very appealing 10- and 15-year track record for its peer group.

Profile

minimum initial investment $3,000	*IRA accounts available* . . . . yes
subsequent minimum investment . . $100	*IRA minimum investment* $1,000
available in all 50 states. . . . . yes	*date of inception.* . . . . May 1984
telephone exchanges. . . . . yes	*dividend/income paid* . . . . annually
number of other funds in family 68	*largest sector weighting.* . . . . energy

Money Market Funds

Money market funds invest in securities that mature in less than one year. They are made up of one or more of the following instruments: Treasury bills, certificates of deposit, commercial paper, repurchase agreements, Euro-dollar CDs, and notes. There are four different categories of money market funds: all-purpose, government-backed, federally tax-free, and doubly tax-exempt. As of August 1999, the average maturity of taxable money market funds was 55 days, 44 days for the typical tax-exempt money fund.

The first money market fund was invented in 1972; by the end of that year there were fifty such funds. At the beginning of 1999, there were over 1,300 money market funds, with a cumulative value of $1.5 trillion. All-purpose funds are the most popular and make up the bulk of the money market universe. Fully taxable, they are composed of securities such as CDs, commercial paper, and T-bills.

Government-backed money funds invest only in short-term paper, directly or indirectly backed by the U.S. government. These funds are technically safer than the all-purpose variety, but only one money market fund has ever defaulted (a fund set up by a bank for banks). The yield on government-backed funds is somewhat lower than that of its all-purpose peers.

Federally tax-free funds are made up of municipal notes. Investors in these funds do not have to pay federal income taxes on the interest earned. The before-tax yield on federally tax-free funds is certainly lower than that of all-purpose and government-backed funds, but the after-tax return can be greater for the moderate- or high-tax-bracket investor.

Double-tax-exempt funds invest in the municipal obligations of a specific state. You must be a resident of that state in order to avoid paying state income taxes on any interest earned. Nonresident investors will still receive a federal tax exemption.

All money market funds are safer than any other mutual fund or category of funds in this book. Since their 1972 inception, the safety record for money market funds has been close to perfect. In 1990 two funds defaulted, but the parent companies stepped in and covered the $1.2 billion loss, thereby assuring that no investor lost a dime. Four years later, the first such fund did fail, due to investments in derivatives. Shortly thereafter, the SEC began to require higher quality standards for money market accounts, and there has not been a single problem since.

Investors can only make money in these interest-bearing accounts. The rate of return earned in a money market depends upon the average maturity of the fund's paper, the kinds of securities held, the quality rating of that paper, and how efficiently the fund is operated. A lean fund will almost always outperform a similar fund with high operating costs. Since 1975, average annual yields have ranged from a low of 2.7

percent (1993) to a high of 16.8 percent (1981). Since 1981, average annual yields for tax-free money market funds have been as low as 2.0 percent (1993) and as high as 7.1 percent (1981).

Investments such as United States Treasury bills and, for all practical purposes, money market funds, are often referred to as "risk-free." These kinds of investments are free from price swings and default risk because of their composition. However, as we have come to learn, there is more than one form of risk. Money market funds should never be considered as a medium- or long-term investment. The real return on this investment is poor. An investment's real return takes into account the effects of inflation and income taxes. During virtually every period of time, the after-tax, after-inflation return on all money market funds has been near zero or even negative.

Over the past fifty years, United States Treasury bills—an index often used as a substitute for money market funds—have outperformed inflation on average 78 percent of the time over one-year periods, 83 percent of the time over five-year periods, 78 percent of the time over ten-year periods, 92 percent of the time over fifteen-year periods, and 100 percent over any given twenty-year period of time. These figures are not adjusted for income taxes. Money market funds have rarely, if ever, outperformed inflation on an after-tax basis when looking at three-, five-, ten-, fifteen-, or twenty-year holding positions.

Investors often look back to the good old days of the early 1980s, when money market funds briefly averaged 18 percent, and wish such times would come again. Well, those were not good times. During the early 1980s the top tax bracket, state and federal combined, was 55 percent. If you began with an 18-percent return and deducted taxes, many taxpayers saw their 18-percent return knocked down to about 9 percent. This may look great, especially for a "risk-free" investment, but we are not through yet. During the partial year in which money market accounts paid 18 percent, inflation was 12 percent. Now, if you take the 9 percent return and subtract 12 percent for inflation; the real return was actually -3 percent for the year. So much for the good old days.

Money market funds are the best place to park your money while you are looking at other investment alternatives or if you will be using the money during the next year. These funds can provide the convenience of check writing and a yield that is highly competitive with interest rates in general. These incredibly safe funds should only be considered for short-term periods or for regular expenditures, the way you would use a savings or checking account.

Since money market funds only came into existence for the general public in the early 1970s, Treasury bills are often used as a substitute by those who wish to analyze the performance of these funds over a long period of time. The results are instructive. Since 1949, a dollar invested in T-bills grew to $11.90 by the end of 1998. By the end of 1997, you would have needed $6.80 to equal the purchasing power of $1 at the beginning of 1949.

To give you a better sense of the cumulative effects of inflation, consider what a $100,000 investment in a money market fund would have to yield at the beginning of 1999 to equal the same purchasing power as the interest (or yield) from a $100,000 investment in a money market fund twenty years ago (1979). At the beginning of 1999, for instance, a $100,000 account held since 1978 would need to generate $26,862 to equal the same purchasing power as a $100,000 account yielding approximately 11.1 percent in

1979 (the average interest rate for money market accounts that year). The reality, however, is that at the beginning of 1999, money market funds were yielding 5 percent ($5,000 a year versus the $26,862 that would be required to maintain purchasing power).

You may have avoided stock investing in the past because "stocks are too risky." Yet it all depends upon how you define risk. As an example, in 1969 a $100,000 CD generated enough interest ($7,900) to buy a new, "fully loaded" Cadillac ($5,936) plus take a week-long cruise. As of the beginning of 1999, that same $100,000 CD would not generate enough income (CD rates were 5 percent) to buy one-eighth of the Cadillac ($5,000 vs. $46,000 for the cost of a 1999 Cadillac Hardtop Sedan De Ville).

As a risk-reduction tool, the addition of a money market fund may be a worthwhile strategy. For the period between 1960 and 1996, a 50-50 mix of stocks and cash delivered 79 percent of the S&P's return, with half the volatility. A more aggressive mix of 60 percent stocks and 40 percent cash yielded 84 percent of the S&P's gains, with just 60 percent of the risk (as measured by standard deviation).

Over the past three years, taxable money market funds have had an average compound return of 5.0 percent per year. The annual return for the past five years has been 4.9 percent; 5.3 percent for the past ten years, 6.0 percent for the last fifteen years, and 7.5 percent for the last twenty years (all periods ending 12/31/98). The standard deviation for money market funds is lower than any other mutual fund category. This means that these funds have had less return variances than any other group.

Tax-Free Money Market Funds

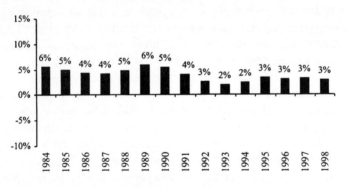

Taxable Money Market Funds

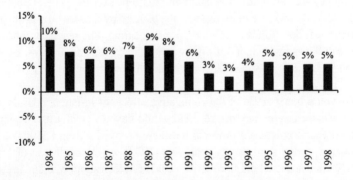

Aetna Money Market Fund A

Aetna Life Insurance and Annuity Company
242 Trumbull St., ALT 7
Hartford, CT 06103
(800) 367-7732

total return	★ ★ ★ ★ ★
risk reduction	★ ★ ★ ★ ★
management	★ ★ ★ ★ ★
expense control	★ ★ ★ ★
symbol AEMXX	19 points

Total Return   ★ ★ ★ ★ ★

Over the past five years (all periods ending 6/30/99), Aetna Money Market Fund A has taken $10,000 and turned it into $12,980 ($11,650 over three years). This translates into an average annual return of 5.4 percent over five years and 5.2 percent over the past three years. This is the number one performing noninstitutional taxable money market fund over the past five years.

Risk/Volatility   ★ ★ ★ ★ ★

During the last three and five years, the fund's standard deviation has been 0.1 percent.

	last 4 years		since inception	
worst year	5.3%	1998	5.3%	1998
best year	6.0%	1995	6.0%	1995

Management   ★ ★ ★ ★ ★

The average maturity of the paper in the portfolio is approximately sixty-six days. The fund has been managed by Len Carlson since April 1999. The fund has outperformed its peer group average over the past one, three, and five years.

Expense Control   ★ ★ ★ ★

The expense ratio for this $5 million fund is 0.5 percent. This means that for every $1,000 invested, $5 goes to paying overhead.

Summary

Aetna Money Market Fund A is highly recommended.

Profile

minimum initial investment $1,000	IRA accounts available . . . . yes
subsequent min. investment $100	IRA minimum investment $500
available in all 50 states. . . . . yes	IRA minimum additions $100
telephone exchanges. . . . . yes	dividend/income paid. . . . . monthly
number of other funds in family 16	quality of annual reports . . . . n/a

Dreyfus Basic Municipal Money Market

Dreyfus Service Corp.
Pan Am Building
200 Park Ave., 7th Floor
New York, NY 10166
(800) 645-6561

total return	★ ★ ★ ★ ★
risk reduction	★ ★ ★ ★ ★
management	★ ★ ★ ★ ★
expense control	★ ★ ★ ★
symbol DBMXX	19 points

Total Return   ★ ★ ★ ★ ★

Over the past five years (all periods ending 6/30/99), Dreyfus Basic Municipal Money Market has taken $10,000 and turned it into $11,800 ($10,990 over three years). This translates into an average annual return of 3.3 percent over five years and 3.2 percent over the past three years. This is the number three performing non-institutional municipal money market fund over the past three and five years.

Risk/Volatility   ★ ★ ★ ★ ★

During the last three and five years, the fund's standard deviation has been 0.1 percent.

	last 5 years		since inception	
worst year	2.9%	1994	2.6%	1993
best year	3.9%	1995	3.9%	1995

Management   ★ ★ ★ ★ ★

The average maturity of the paper in the portfolio is approximately sixty-two days. The fund has been managed by Douglas J. Gaylor since January 1996. The fund has outperformed its peer group average over the past one, three, and five years.

Expense Control   ★ ★ ★ ★

The expense ratio for this $5 million fund is 0.5 percent. This means that for every $1,000 invested, $5 goes to paying overhead.

Summary

Dreyfus Basic Municipal Money Market is highly recommended.

Profile

minimum initial investment $25,000	*IRA accounts available* .... n/a
subsequent min. investment..... $1,000	*IRA minimum investment*......... n/a
available in all 50 states.......... yes	*IRA minimum additions* .... n/a
telephone exchanges............. yes	*dividend/income paid*........ monthly
number of other funds in family..... 63	*quality of annual reports* .... n/a

Freemont Money Market

Freemont Investment Advisors
333 Market St.
San Francisco, CA 94105
(800) 548-4539

total return	★ ★ ★ ★ ★
risk reduction	★ ★ ★ ★ ★
management	★ ★ ★ ★ ★
expense control	★ ★ ★ ★ ★
symbol FRMXX	20 points

Total Return ★ ★ ★ ★ ★
Over the past five years (all periods ending 6/30/99), Freemont Money Market has taken $10,000 and turned it into $12,980 ($11,670 over three years and $16,670 over ten years). This translates into an average annual return of 5.4 percent over five years, 5.3 percent over three years, and 5.2 percent over ten years. This is the number two performing noninstitutional taxable money market fund over the past five years.

Risk/Volatility ★ ★ ★ ★ ★
During the last three and five years, the fund's standard deviation has been 0.1 percent.

	last 5 years		last 10 years	
worst year	4.0%	1994	2.6%	1993
best year	5.9%	1995	8.9%	1989

Management ★ ★ ★ ★ ★
The average maturity of the paper in the portfolio is approximately seventy-one days. The fund has been managed by Norman Gee since November 1988. The fund has outperformed its peer group average over the past one, three, five, and ten years.

Expense Control ★ ★ ★ ★ ★
The expense ratio for this $800 million fund is 0.3 percent. This means that for every $1,000 invested, $3 goes to paying overhead.

Summary
Freemont Money Market is highly recommended.

Profile
minimum initial investment $2,000
subsequent min. investment $100
available in all 50 states. . . . . yes
telephone exchanges. . . . . yes
number of other funds in family 11

IRA accounts available . . . . yes
IRA minimum investment $1,000
IRA minimum additions $100
dividend/income paid. . . . . monthly
quality of annual reports . . . . n/a

JP Morgan Prime Money Market
Morgan Guaranty Trust
522 5th Ave., 11th Floor
New York, NY 10036
(800) 521-5411

total return	★ ★ ★ ★ ★
risk reduction	★ ★ ★ ★ ★
management	★ ★ ★ ★ ★
expense control	★ ★ ★ ★
symbol PPMXX	19 points

Total Return   ★ ★ ★ ★ ★
Over the past five years (all periods ending 6/30/99), JP Morgan Prime Money Market has taken $10,000 and turned it into $12,940 ($11,660 over three years and $16,760 over ten years). This translates into an average annual return of 5.3 percent over three, five and ten years. This is the number six performing noninstitutional taxable money market fund over the past five years.

Risk/Volatility   ★ ★ ★ ★ ★
During the last three and five years, the fund's standard deviation has been 0.1 percent.

	last 5 years		last 10 years	
worst year	3.9%	1994	2.9%	1993
best year	5.8%	1995	9.1%	1989

Management   ★ ★ ★ ★
The average maturity of the paper in the portfolio is approximately fifty-one days. The fund has been managed by Skip Johnson since June 1988. The fund has outperformed its peer group average over the past one, three, five, and ten years.

Expense Control   ★ ★ ★ ★
The expense ratio for this $3 billion fund is 0.4 percent. This means that for every $1,000 invested, $4 goes to paying overhead.

Summary
JP Morgan Prime Money Market is highly recommended.

Profile

minimum initial investment $2,000	*IRA accounts available* . . . . yes
subsequent min. investment $100	*IRA minimum investment* $2,500
available in all 50 states. . . . . yes	*IRA minimum additions* $500
telephone exchanges. . . . . yes	*dividend/income paid.* . . . . monthly
number of other funds in family 20	*quality of annual reports* . . . . n/a

Marshall Money Market Y

Federated Securities Corp.
Federated Investors Tower / 1001 Liberty Ave.
Pittsburgh, PA 15222
(800) 236-3863

total return	★ ★ ★ ★ ★
risk reduction	★ ★ ★ ★ ★
management	★ ★ ★ ★ ★
expense control	★ ★ ★
symbol MABXX	18 points

Total Return   ★ ★ ★ ★ ★

Over the past five years (all periods ending 6/30/99), Marshall Money Market Y has taken $10,000 and turned it into $12,960 ($11,670 over three years). This translates into an average annual return of 5.3 percent over the past three and five years. This is the number five performing noninstitutional taxable money market fund over the past five years.

Risk/Volatility   ★ ★ ★ ★ ★

During the last three and five years, the fund's standard deviation has been 0.1 percent.

	last 5 years		since inception	
worst year	4.1%	1994	3.0%	1993
best year	5.8%	1995	5.8%	1995

Management   ★ ★ ★ ★ ★

The average maturity of the paper in the portfolio is approximately thirty-nine days. The fund has been managed by Richard Rokus since January 1994. The fund has outperformed its peer group average over the past one, three, and five years.

Expense Control   ★ ★ ★

The expense ratio for this $3 billion fund is 0.7 percent. This means that for every $1,000 invested, $7 goes to paying overhead.

Summary

Marshall Money Market Y is highly recommended.

Profile

minimum initial investment $1,000	*IRA accounts available* . . . . yes
subsequent min. investment $50	*IRA minimum investment* $1,000
available in all 50 states. . . . . yes	*IRA minimum additions* $50
telephone exchanges. . . . . yes	*dividend/income paid.* . . . . monthly
number of other funds in family. 9	*quality of annual reports* . . . . n/a

Monetta Government Money Market

Monetta Financial Services, Inc.
1776 A South Naperville R, Suite 100
Wheaton, IL 60187
(800) 537-6001

total return	★ ★ ★ ★ ★
risk reduction	★ ★ ★ ★ ★
management	★ ★ ★ ★ ★
expense control	★ ★ ★ ★ ★
symbol MONXX	20 points

Total Return   ★ ★ ★ ★ ★

Over the past five years (all periods ending 6/30/99), Monetta Government Money Market has taken $10,000 and turned it into $12,880 ($11,610 over three years). This translates into an average annual return of 5.2 percent over five years and 5.1 percent over the past three years. This is the number three performing noninstitutional government money market fund over the past three and five years.

Risk/Volatility   ★ ★ ★ ★ ★

During the last three and five years, the fund's standard deviation has ranged between 0.1 percent and 0.2 percent.

	last 5 years		since inception	
worst year	4.1%	1994	4.1%	1994
best year	5.9%	1995	5.9%	1995

Management   ★ ★ ★ ★ ★

The average maturity of the paper in the portfolio is approximately forty-five days. The fund has been managed by Robert Bacarella and Kevin Moore since November 1996. The fund has outperformed its peer group average over the past one, three, and five years.

Expense Control   ★ ★ ★ ★ ★

The expense ratio for this $5 million fund is 0.3 percent. This means that for every $1,000 invested, $3 goes to paying overhead.

Summary

Monetta Government Money Market is highly recommended.

Profile

minimum initial investment $250	IRA accounts available .... yes
subsequent minimum investment $1	IRA minimum investment $250
available in all 50 states.......... yes	IRA minimum additions $1
telephone exchanges............. yes	dividend/income paid........ monthly
number of other funds in family...... 5	quality of annual reports .... n/a

Strong Money Market
Strong Capital Mgmt.
P.O. Box 2936
Milwaukee, WI 53201
(800) 368-3863

total return	★ ★ ★ ★ ★
risk reduction	★ ★ ★ ★ ★
management	★ ★ ★ ★ ★
expense control	★ ★ ★
symbol SICRE	18 points

Total Return ★ ★ ★ ★ ★
Over the past five years (all periods ending 6/30/98), Strong Money Market has taken $10,000 and turned it into $12,970 ($11,620 over three years and $16,850 over ten years). This translates into an average annual return of 5.3 percent over five years, 5.1 percent over three years, and 5.4 percent over the past ten years. This is the number two performing noninstitutional taxable money market fund over the past three and five years.

Risk/Volatility ★ ★ ★ ★ ★
During the last three and five years, the fund's standard deviation has been 0.1 percent.

	last 5 years		last 10 years	
worst year	4.0%	1994	2.9%	1993
best year	6.2%	1995	9.2%	1989

Management ★ ★ ★ ★ ★
The average maturity of the paper in the portfolio is approximately seventy-seven days. The fund has been managed by Jay N. Mueller since September 1991. The fund has outperformed its peer group average over the past one, three, five, and ten years.

Expense Control ★ ★ ★
The expense ratio for this $1.9 billion fund is 0.6 percent. This means that for every $1,000 invested, $6 goes to paying overhead.

Summary
Strong Municipal Money Market is highly recommended, despite its somewhat high expense ratio.

Profile

minimum initial investment	$1,000	IRA accounts available	yes
subsequent minimum investment	$50	IRA minimum investment	$250
available in all 50 states	yes	IRA minimum additions	$50
telephone exchanges	yes	dividend/income paid	monthly
number of other funds in family	35	quality of annual reports	n/a

USAA Tax Exempt Money Market
USAA Investment Mgmt. Co.
USAA Bld.
San Antonio, TX 78288
(800) 531-8722

total return	★ ★ ★ ★ ★
risk reduction	★ ★ ★ ★ ★
management	★ ★ ★ ★ ★
expense control	★ ★ ★ ★
symbol USEXX	19 points

Total Return   ★ ★ ★ ★ ★
Over the past five years (all periods ending 6/30/99), USAA Tax Exempt Money Market has taken $10,000 and turned it into $11,800 ($11,030 over three years and $14,440 over ten years). This translates into an average annual return of 3.4 percent over five years, 3.3 percent over the past three years, and 3.7 percent over the past ten years. This is the number four performing noninstitutional municipal money market fund over the past three and five years.

Risk/Volatility   ★ ★ ★ ★ ★
During the last three and five years, the fund's standard deviation has been 0.1 percent.

	last 5 years		since inception	
worst year	2.6%	1994	2.4%	1993
best year	3.7%	1995	6.3%	1989

Management   ★ ★ ★ ★ ★
The average maturity of the paper in the portfolio is approximately forty-one days. The fund has been managed by Thomas G. Ramos since August 1994. The fund has outperformed its peer group average over the past one, three, five, and ten years.

Expense Control   ★ ★ ★ ★
The expense ratio for this $1.8 billion fund is 0.4 percent. This means that for every $1,000 invested, $4 goes to paying overhead.

Summary
USAA Tax Exempt Money Market is highly recommended.

Profile

minimum initial investment $3,000	IRA accounts available . . . . n/a
subsequent min. investment $50	IRA minimum investment . . . . n/a
available in all 50 states. . . . . yes	IRA minimum additions . . . . n/a
telephone exchanges. . . . . yes	dividend/income paid. . . . . monthly
number of other funds in family 25	quality of annual reports . . . . n/a

Vanguard Municipal Tax-Exempt Money Market
Vanguard Group
P.O. Box 2600
Valley Forge, PA 19482
(800) 635-1511

total return	★ ★ ★ ★ ★
risk reduction	★ ★ ★ ★ ★
management	★ ★ ★ ★ ★
expense control	★ ★ ★ ★ ★
symbol VMSXX	20 points

Total Return   ★ ★ ★ ★ ★
Over the past five years (all periods ending 6/30/99), Vanguard Municipal Money Market has taken $10,000 and turned it into $11,830 ($11,040 over three years). This translates into an average annual return of 3.4 percent over five years and 3.4 percent over the past three years. This is the number two performing noninstitutional municipal money market fund over the past five years.

Risk/Volatility   ★ ★ ★ ★ ★
During the last three and five years, the fund's standard deviation has been 0.1 percent.

	last 5 years		last 10 years	
worst year	2.4%	1993	2.4%	1993
best year	3.8%	1995	6.3%	1989

Management   ★ ★ ★ ★ ★
The average maturity of the paper in the portfolio is approximately forty-three days. The fund has been managed by Pamela W. Tynan since May 1988. The fund has outperformed its peer group average over the past one, three, five, and ten years.

Expense Control   ★ ★ ★ ★ ★
The expense ratio for this $6.7 billion fund is 0.2 percent. This means that for every $1,000 invested, $2 goes to paying overhead.

Summary
Vanguard Municipal Money Market is highly recommended. This money market fund is exempt from federal income taxes.

Profile

minimum initial investment $3,000	IRA accounts available . . . . n/a
subsequent minimum investment . . $100	IRA minimum investment . . . . n/a
available in all 50 states. . . . . yes	IRA minimum additions . . . . n/a
telephone exchanges. . . . . yes	dividend/income paid. . . . . monthly
number of other funds in family 68	quality of annual reports . . . . n/a

Zurich Money Government Money
Scudder Kemper Investments, Inc.
Two International Place
Boston, MA 02110
(800) 537-6001

total return	★ ★ ★ ★ ★
risk reduction	★ ★ ★ ★ ★
management	★ ★ ★ ★ ★
expense control	★ ★ ★ ★
symbol KEGXX	19 points

Total Return   ★ ★ ★ ★ ★
Over the past five years (all periods ending 6/30/99), Zurich Money Government Money has taken $10,000 and turned it into $12,890 ($11,620 over three years and $16,780 over ten years). This translates into an average annual return of 5.2 percent over five years, 5.1 percent over three years, and 5.3 percent over the past ten years. This is the number two performing noninstitutional government money market fund over the past three and five years.

Risk/Volatility   ★ ★ ★ ★ ★
During the last three and five years, the fund's standard deviation has been 0.1 percent.

	last 5 years		last 10 years	
worst year	4.0%	1994	2.9%	1993
best year	5.7%	1995	9.2%	1989

Management   ★ ★ ★ ★ ★
The average maturity of the paper in the portfolio is approximately twenty-six days. The fund has been managed by Frank J. Rachwalski since November 1981. The fund has outperformed its peer group average over the past one, three, five, and ten years.

Expense Control   ★ ★ ★ ★
The expense ratio for this $710 million fund is 0.4 percent. This means that for every $1,000 invested, $4 goes to paying overhead.

Summary
Zurich Money Government Money is highly recommended.

Profile
minimum initial investment $1,000	IRA accounts available . . . . yes
subsequent minimum investment . . $100	IRA minimum investment $250
available in all 50 states. . . . . yes	IRA minimum additions $50
telephone exchanges. . . . . yes	dividend/income paid. . . . . monthly
number of other funds in family 43	quality of annual reports . . . . n/a

Municipal Bond Funds

Municipal bond funds invest in securities issued by municipalities, political subdivisions, and U.S. territories. The type of security issued is either a note or bond, both of which are interest-bearing instruments that are exempt from federal income taxes. There are three different categories of municipal bond funds: national, state-free, and high-yield.

National municipal bond funds are made up of debt instruments issued by a wide range of states. These funds are exempt from federal income taxes only. To determine what small percentage is also exempt from state income taxes, consult the fund's prospectus and look for the weighting of U.S. territory issues (U.S. Virgin Islands, Guam, Puerto Rico), District of Columbia items, and obligations from your state of residence.

State-free funds, sometimes referred to as "double tax-free funds" invest only in bonds and notes issued in a particular state. You must be a legal resident of that state in order to avoid paying state income taxes on the fund's return. For example, most California residents who are in a high tax bracket will only want to consider purchasing a municipal bond fund that has the name "California" in it. Residents of New York who purchase a California tax-free fund will escape federal income taxes but not state taxes.

High-yield tax-free funds invest in the same kinds of issues found in a national municipal bond fund but with one important difference. By seeking higher returns, high-yield funds look for lower-rated or nonrated notes and bonds. A municipality may decide not to obtain a rating for its issue because of the costs involved compared to the relatively small size of the bond or note being floated. Many nonrated issues are very safe. High-yield municipal bond funds are relatively new but should not be overlooked by the tax-conscious investor. These kinds of tax-free funds have demonstrated less volatility and higher return than their other tax-free counterparts.

Prospective investors need to compare tax-free bond yields to after-tax yields on corporate or government bond funds. To determine which of these three fund categories is best for you, use your marginal tax bracket, subtract this amount from one, and multiply the resulting figure by the taxable investment. For instance, suppose you were in the 35 percent bracket, state and federal combined. By subtracting this figure from 1, you are left with 0.65. Multiply 0.65 by the fully taxable yield you could get, let us say 7 percent. Sixty-five percent of 7 percent is 4.55 percent. The 4.55 percent represents what you get on a 7 percent investment after you have paid state and federal income taxes on it. This means that if you can get 4.55 percent or higher from a tax-free investment, take it.

Interest paid on tax-free investments is generally lower than interest paid on taxable investments like corporate bonds and bank CDs. But you should compare the yields on tax-free investments to taxable investments only after you have considered the municipal bond fund's tax-free advantage. The result will be the taxable equivalent yield—the yield you will have to get on a similar taxable investment to equal the tax-free yield. If the example above was not clear, look at the next table.

1999 income tax brackets

bracket	15%	28%	31%	36%	39.6%
jt. return	$0–$43,050	$43,051–$104,050	$104,051–$158,550	$158,551–283,150	over $283,150
single return	$0–25,750	$25,751–62450	$62,451–$130,250	$130,251–$283,150	over $283,150

tax-exempt yield %	taxable equivalent yield %				
2.5	2.9	3.5	3.6	3.9	4.1
3.0	3.5	4.2	4.4	4.7	5.0
3.5	4.1	4.9	5.1	5.5	5.8
4.0	4.7	5.6	5.8	6.3	6.6
4.5	5.3	6.3	6.5	7.0	7.5
5.0	5.9	6.9	7.3	7.8	8.3
5.5	6.5	7.6	8.0	8.6	9.1
6.0	7.1	8.3	8.7	9.4	9.9
6.5	7.7	9.0	9.4	10.2	10.8
7.0	8.2	9.7	10.1	10.9	11.6
7.5	8.8	10.4	10.9	11.7	12.4
8.0	10.6	12.5	13.0	14.0	14.9

As you can see from the table above, if you are in the 36 percent federal tax bracket, a taxable investment would have to yield 7.8 percent to give you the same after-tax income as a tax-free yield of 5.0 percent.

Municipal bond funds are not for investors who are in a low tax bracket. If such investors want to be in bonds, they would be better off in corporate or government issues. Furthermore, municipals should never be used in a retirement plan. There is only one way to make tax-free income taxable and that is to put it into an IRA, pension, 403(b), 401(k) or profit-sharing plan. Everything that comes out of these plans is fully taxable by the federal government.

Over the past three and five years, the typical municipal bond fund has had an average compounded annual return of 6.3 and 6.4 percent respectively. They have averaged a total annual return (current yield plus bond appreciation or minus bond depreciation) of 7.3 percent over the past ten years and 8.4 percent annually for the last fifteen years. Municipal bond fund returns have been fairly stable over the past three years, having a standard deviation of 2.9 percent (all periods ending 3/31/99).

A little less than two thousand funds make up the municipal bond category. Total market capitalization of all municipal bond funds is $320 billion. Close to 98 percent of a typical municipal bond fund's portfolio is in tax-free bonds, with the balance in tax-free money market instruments. Close to 1,000 of the 2,000 municipal bond funds offered are single-state funds.

The typical municipal bond fund yields 4.4 percent in tax-free income each year. The average weighted maturity is fifteen years. Expenses for this category are 1.1 percent each year.

As you read through the descriptions of the municipal bond funds selected, you will notice a paragraph in each describing the tax efficiency of the portfolio. This may surprise you, since municipal bonds are supposed to be tax-free. Keep in mind that only the income (current yield) from these instruments is free from federal income taxes (and often state income taxes, depending on the fund in question and your state of residence). Since bond funds generally have a high turnover rate (which triggers a potential capital gain or loss upon each sale of a security by the portfolio manager), there are capital gains considerations with municipal bonds.

Municipal Bond Funds

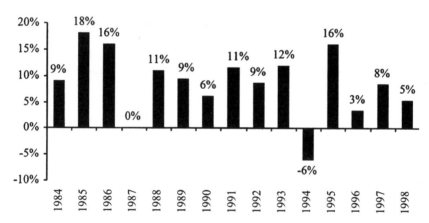

Alliance Municipal Income CA A

P.O. Box 1520
Secaucus, NJ 07096
800-227-4618

total return	★ ★ ★ ★ ★
risk reduction	★ ★ ★
management	★ ★ ★ ★ ★
current income	★ ★ ★ ★ ★
expense control	★ ★ ★ ★ ★
symbol ALCAX	23 points
up-market performance	excellent
down-market performance	fair
predictability of returns	good

Total Return   ★ ★ ★ ★ ★

Over the past five years, Alliance Municipal Income CA A has taken $10,000 and turned it into $14,981 ($12,819 over three years and $22,402 over the past ten years). This translates into an average annual return of 8 percent over the past five years, 9 percent over the past three years, and 8 percent for the decade. Over the past five years, this fund has outperformed 55 percent of all mutual funds; within its general category it has done better than 92 percent of its peers. Municipal bond funds have averaged 6 percent annually over these same five years.

During the past five years, a $10,000 initial investment grew to $14,100 after taxes, assuming a 39.6 percent income tax bracket (state and federal combined) and a capital gains rate of 28 percent. This means that investors in this fund were able to preserve 100 percent of their total returns. Compared to other fixed-income funds, this fund's tax savings are considered to be excellent.

Risk/Volatility   ★ ★ ★

Over the past five years, Alliance Municipal Income CA A has been safer than 55 percent of all municipal bond funds. Over the past decade, the fund has had one negative year, while the Lehman Brothers Aggregate Bond Index has had one (off 3 percent in 1994); the Lehman Brothers Municipal Bond Index also fell once (off 5 percent in 1994). The fund has underperformed the Lehman Brothers Aggregate Bond Index five times and the Lehman Brothers Municipal Bond Index six times in the last ten years.

	last 5 years		last 10 years	
worst year	-10%	1994	-10%	1994
best year	24%	1995	24%	1995

In the past, Alliance Municipal Income CA A has done better than 90 percent of its peer group in up markets and outperformed 45 percent of its competition in down markets. Consistency, or predictability, of returns for Alliance Municipal Income CA A can be described as good. This fund's risk-adjusted return is excellent.

Management
★ ★ ★ ★ ★

There are eighty-three fixed-income securities in this $620 million portfolio. The average municipal bond fund today is $166 million in size. Close to 100 percent of the funds holdings are in bonds. The average maturity of the bonds in this account is twenty-two years; the weighted coupon rate averages 5.6 percent. The portfolio's fixed-income holdings can be categorized as intermediate-term, high-quality debt.

Susan Keenan has managed this fund for the past thirteen years. There are forty-nine funds besides Municipal Income CA within the Alliance family. Overall, the fund family's risk-adjusted performance can be described as good.

Current Income
★ ★ ★ ★ ★

Over the past year, Alliance Municipal Income CA A had a twelve-month yield of 5.2 percent. During this same twelve-month period, the typical municipal bond fund had a yield that averaged 4.4 percent.

Expenses
★ ★ ★ ★ ★

Alliance Municipal Income CA A's expense ratio is .7 percent; it has also averaged .7 percent annually over the past three calendar years. The average expense ratio for the 1,900 funds in this category is 1.1 percent. This fund's turnover rate over the past year has been 22 percent, while its peer group average has been 41 percent.

Summary

Alliance Municipal Income CA A has ranked in the top performance quartile for each of the past four calendar years. Risk-adjusted returns over the past three, five, and ten years have ranged from very good to excellent. Even though current yield figures have been quite impressive for a tax-free fund, manager Keenan is more concerned with total return. This concern is reflected by the top marks it receives. This is the top-rated California municipal bond fund but is also recommended for residents of other states. The fund has an overall score of 23 out of 25 possible points.

Profile

minimum initial investment $250	*IRA accounts available*. . . . . no
subsequent minimum investment . . . $50	*IRA minimum investment* . . . . n/a
available in all 50 states . . . . no	*date of inception*. . . . . Dec. 1986
telephone exchanges. . . . . yes	*dividend/income paid*. . . . . . . monthly
number of other funds in family 49	*average credit quality*. . . . . AA

Alliance Municipal Income National A

P.O. Box 1520
Secaucus, NJ 07096
800-227-4618

total return	★ ★ ★ ★ ★
risk reduction	★
management	★ ★ ★ ★
current income	★ ★ ★ ★ ★
expense control	★ ★ ★ ★
symbol ALTHX	19 points
up-market performance	excellent
down-market performance	poor
predictability of returns	good

Total Return   ★ ★ ★ ★ ★

Over the past five years, Alliance Municipal Income National A has taken $10,000 and turned it into $14,714 ($12,657 over three years and $22,299 over the past ten years). This translates into an average annual return of 8 percent over the past five years, 8 percent over the past three years, and 8 percent for the decade. Over the past five years, this fund has outperformed 45 percent of all mutual funds; within its general category it has done better than 85 percent of its peers. Municipal bond funds have averaged 6 percent annually over these same five years.

During the past five years, a $10,000 initial investment grew to $13,450 after taxes, assuming a 39.6 percent income tax bracket (state and federal combined) and a capital gains rate of 28 percent. This means that investors in this fund were able to preserve 100 percent of their total returns. Compared to other fixed-income funds, this fund's tax savings are considered to be excellent.

Risk/Volatility   ★

Over the past five years, Alliance Municipal Income National A has been safer than 20 percent of all municipal bond funds. Over the past decade, the fund has had one negative year, while the Lehman Brothers Aggregate Bond Index has had one (off 3 percent in 1994); the Lehman Brothers Municipal Bond Index also fell once (off 5 percent in 1994). The fund has underperformed the Lehman Brothers Aggregate Bond Index five times and the Lehman Brothers Municipal Bond Index five times in the last ten years.

	last 5 years		last 10 years	
worst year	-10%	1994	-10%	1994
best year	22%	1995	22%	1995

In the past, Alliance Municipal Income National A has done better than 90 percent of its peer group in up markets and outperformed 15 percent of its competition in down markets. Consistency, or predictability, of returns for Alliance Municipal Income National A can be described as good. This fund's risk-adjusted return is excellent.

Management   ★ ★ ★ ★
There are one hundred fixed-income securities in this $400 million portfolio. The average municipal bond fund today is $166 million in size. Close to 100 percent of the funds holdings are in bonds. The average maturity of the bonds in this account is twenty-two years; the weighted coupon rate averages 5.9 percent. The portfolio's fixed-income holdings can be categorized as intermediate-term, high-quality debt.

Susan Keenan has managed this fund for the past thirteen years. There are forty-nine funds besides Municipal Income National within the Alliance family. Overall, the fund family's risk-adjusted performance can be described as good.

Current Income   ★ ★ ★ ★ ★
Over the past year, Alliance Municipal Income National A had a twelve-month yield of 5.2 percent. During this same twelve-month period, the typical municipal bond fund had a yield that averaged 4.4 percent.

Expenses   ★ ★ ★ ★
Alliance Municipal Income National A's expense ratio is .7 percent; it has also averaged .7 percent annually over the past three calendar years. The average expense ratio for the 1,900 funds in this category is 1.1 percent. This fund's turnover rate over the past year has been 56 percent, while its peer group average has been 41 percent.

Summary
Alliance Municipal Income National A has ranked in the top performance quartile for four of the past five years. Risk-adjusted returns have been very good since the fund's 1986 inception. Manager Keenan is not afraid to load up on a single issue if she really likes it. No single issue represents more than 7 percent of the portfolio currently, but the fund has had as much as 20 percent of its holdings with a single issuer in the past. Call-protected issues are favored in order to cash in on level or declining interest rates. There are a large number of tax-free funds that boast better risk figures, but few that can match this fund's returns.

Profile
minimum initial investment . . . . . . $250   *IRA accounts available*. . . . . no
subsequent minimum investment . . . $50   *IRA minimum investment* . . . . n/a
available in all 50 states. . . . . yes   *date of inception*. . . . . Dec. 1986
telephone exchanges. . . . . yes   *dividend/income paid*. . . . . monthly
number of other funds in family. 49   *average credit quality* . . . . AAA

Calvert Tax-Free Reserves Limited-Term Portfolio A

4550 Montgomery Avenue, Suite 1000N
Bethesda, MD 20814
800-368-2748

total return	★ ★
risk reduction	★ ★ ★ ★ ★
management	★ ★ ★ ★
current income	★ ★
expense control	★ ★ ★ ★
symbol CTFLX	17 points
up-market performance	very good
down-market performance	excellent
predictability of returns	excellent

Total Return ★ ★

Over the past five years, Calvert Tax-Free Reserves Limited-Term Portfolio A has taken $10,000 and turned it into $12,184 ($11,213 over three years and $15,997 over the past ten years). This translates into an average annual return of 4 percent over the past five years, 4 percent over the past three years, and 5 percent for the decade. Over the past five years, this fund has outperformed 10 percent of all mutual funds; within its general category it has done better than 20 percent of its peers. Municipal bond funds have averaged 6 percent annually over these same five years.

During the past five years, a $10,000 initial investment grew to $12,150 after taxes, assuming a 39.6 percent income tax bracket (state and federal combined) and a capital gains rate of 28 percent. This means that investors in this fund were able to preserve 100 percent of their total returns. Compared to other fixed-income funds, this fund's tax savings are considered to be excellent.

Risk/Volatility ★ ★ ★ ★ ★

Over the past five years, Calvert Tax-Free Reserves Limited-Term Portfolio A has been safer than 99 percent of all municipal bond funds. Over the past decade, the fund has not had a negative year, while the Lehman Brothers Aggregate Bond Index has had one (off 3 percent in 1994); the Lehman Brothers Municipal Bond Index also fell once (off 5 percent in 1994). The fund has underperformed the Lehman Brothers Aggregate Bond Index eight times and the Lehman Brothers Municipal Bond Index nine times in the last ten years.

	last 5 years		last 10 years	
worst year	2%	1994	2%	1994
best year	6%	1995	7%	1989

In the past, Calvert Tax-Free Reserves Limited-Term Portfolio A has done better than 75 percent and outperformed 90 percent of its competition in down markets. Consistency, or predictability, of returns for Calvert Tax-Free Reserves Limited-Term Portfolio A can be described as excellent. This fund's risk-adjusted return is good.

Management
★ ★ ★ ★

There are fifty-one fixed-income securities in this $580 million portfolio. The average municipal bond fund today is $166 million in size. Close to 82 percent of the funds holdings are in bonds. The average maturity of the bonds in this account is .seven years; the weighted coupon rate averages 4.8 percent. The portfolio's fixed-income holdings can be categorized as short-term, medium-quality debt.

A team has managed this fund for the past eleven years. There are fourteen funds besides Tax-Free Reserves within the Calvert family. Overall, the fund family's risk-adjusted performance can be described as very good.

Current Income
★ ★

Over the past year, Calvert Tax-Free Reserves Limited-Term Portfolio A had a twelve-month yield of 3.6 percent. During this same twelve-month period, the typical municipal bond fund had a yield that averaged 4.4 percent.

Expenses
★ ★ ★ ★

Calvert Tax-Free Reserves Limited-Term Portfolio A's expense ratio is .7 percent; it has also averaged .7 percent annually over the past three calendar years. The average expense ratio for the 1,900 funds in this category is 1.1 percent. This fund's turnover rate over the past year has been 52 percent, while its peer group average has been 41 percent.

Summary
Calvert Tax-Free Reserves Limited-Term Portfolio A has had risk-adjusted returns that have ranged from very good to superb over the past three, five, and ten years. This is one of the lowest risk funds you can own. Return figures are in line with such a short-term portfolio. The fund is an excellent choice for high tax bracket investors looking for returns greater than a tax-free money market but with very little additional risk.

Profile

minimum initial investment $2,000	IRA accounts available. . . . . no
subsequent minimum investment . . $250	IRA minimum investment . . . . n/a
available in all 50 states. . . . . yes	date of inception . . . . March 1981
telephone exchanges. . . . . yes	dividend/income paid. . . . . monthly
number of other funds in family 14	average credit quality . . . . A

Excelsior Long-Term Tax-Exempt
114 West 47th Street
New York, NY 10036-1532
800-446-1012

total return	★ ★ ★ ★ ★
risk reduction	★
management	★ ★ ★
current income	★ ★ ★
expense control	★ ★
symbol UMLTX	14 points
up-market performance	poor
down-market performance	very good
predictability of returns	fair

Total Return   ★ ★ ★ ★ ★

Over the past five years, Excelsior Long-Term Tax-Exempt has taken $10,000 and turned it into $15,141 ($12,475 over three years and $24,045 over the past ten years). This translates into an average annual return of 9 percent over the past five years, 8 percent over the past three years, and 9 percent for the decade. Over the past five years, this fund has outperformed 55 percent of all mutual funds; within its general category it has done better than 97 percent of its peers. Municipal bond funds have averaged 6 percent annually over these same five years.

During the past five years, a $10,000 initial investment grew to $13,750 after taxes, assuming a 39.6 percent income tax bracket (state and federal combined) and a capital gains rate of 28 percent. This means that investors in this fund were able to preserve 98 percent of their total returns. Compared to other fixed-income funds, this fund's tax savings are considered to be excellent.

Risk/Volatility   ★

Over the past five years, Excelsior Long-Term Tax-Exempt has been safer than 15 percent of all municipal bond funds. Over the past decade, the fund has had one negative year, while the Lehman Brothers Aggregate Bond Index has had one (off 3 percent in 1994); the Lehman Brothers Municipal Bond Index also fell once (off 5 percent in 1994). The fund has underperformed the Lehman Brothers Aggregate Bond Index six times and the Lehman Brothers Municipal Bond Index four times in the last ten years.

	last 5 years		last 10 years	
worst year	-6%	1994	-6%	1994
best year	23%	1995	23%	1995

In the past, Excelsior Long-Term Tax-Exempt has done better than 15 percent of its peer group in up markets and outperformed 80 percent of its competition in down markets. Consistency, or predictability, of returns for Excelsior Long-Term Tax-Exempt can be described as fair. This fund's risk-adjusted return is very good.

Management   ★ ★ ★

There are thirty fixed-income securities in this $200 million portfolio. The average municipal bond fund today is $166 million in size. Close to 100 percent of the funds holdings are in bonds. The average maturity of the bonds in this account is twenty-four years; the weighted coupon rate averages 4.9 percent. The portfolio's fixed-income holdings can be categorized as long-term, high-quality debt.

Kenneth McAlley has managed this fund for the past thirteen years. There are twenty-six funds besides Long-Term Tax-Exempt within the Excelsior family. Overall, the fund family's risk-adjusted performance can be described as good.

Current Income   ★ ★ ★

Over the past year, Excelsior Long-Term Tax-Exempt had a twelve-month yield of 4.2 percent. During this same twelve-month period, the typical municipal bond fund had a yield that averaged 4.4 percent.

Expenses   ★ ★

Excelsior Long-Term Tax-Exempt's expense ratio is .7 percent; it has also averaged .7 percent annually over the past three calendar years. The average expense ratio for the 1,900 funds in this category is 1.1 percent. This fund's turnover rate over the past year has been 83 percent, while its peer group average has been 41 percent.

Summary

Excelsior Long-Term Tax-Exempt excels when it comes to performance but is one of the riskier municipal bond fund offerings. Decisions as to quality, coupon rate, and maturity are based on manager McAlley's interest-rate outlook. Making correct calls on the direction of interest rates is extremely difficult but management has been right much more often than it has been wrong. The fund has always been in the top performance half or quartile for each of the past ten or more years.

Profile

minimum initial investment $500	*IRA accounts available*. . . . . no
subsequent minimum investment . . . $50	*IRA minimum investment* . . . . n/a
available in all 50 states. . . . . yes	*date of inception* . . . . Feb. 1986
telephone exchanges. . . . . yes	*dividend/income paid*. . . . . monthly
number of other funds in family 26	*average credit quality* . . . . AAA

Smith Barney CA Municipals A

388 Greenwich Street, 37th Floor
New York, NY 10013
800-451-2010

total return	★ ★ ★ ★ ★
risk reduction	★ ★ ★
management	★ ★ ★ ★
current income	★ ★ ★
expense control	★ ★ ★ ★
symbol SHRCX	19 points
up-market performance	very good
down-market performance	good
predictability of returns	fair

Total Return   ★ ★ ★ ★ ★

Over the past five years, Smith Barney CA Municipals A has taken $10,000 and turned it into $14,926 ($12,674 over three years and $22,485 over the past ten years). This translates into an average annual return of 8 percent over the past five years, 8 percent over the past three years, and 8 percent for the decade. Over the past five years, this fund has outperformed 60 percent of all mutual funds; within its general category it has done better than 98 percent of its peers. Municipal bond funds have averaged 6 percent annually over these same five years.

During the past five years, a $10,000 initial investment grew to $14,050 after taxes, assuming a 39.6 percent income tax bracket (state and federal combined) and a capital gains rate of 28 percent. This means that investors in this fund were able to preserve 100 percent of their total returns. Compared to other fixed-income funds, this fund's tax savings are considered to be excellent.

Risk/Volatility   ★ ★ ★

Over the past five years, Smith Barney CA Municipals A has been safer than 45 percent of all municipal bond funds. Over the past decade, the fund has had one negative year, while the Lehman Brothers Aggregate Bond Index has had one (off 3 percent in 1994); the Lehman Brothers Municipal Bond Index also fell once (off 5 percent in 1994). The fund has underperformed the Lehman Brothers Aggregate Bond Index five times and the Lehman Brothers Municipal Bond Index six times in the last ten years.

	last 5 years		last 10 years	
worst year	-7%	1994	-7%	1994
best year	22%	1995	22%	1995

In the past, Smith Barney CA Municipals A has done better than 90 percent of its peer group in up markets and outperformed 65 percent of its competition in down markets. Consistency, or predictability, of returns for Smith Barney CA Municipals A can be described as fair. This fund's risk-adjusted return is very good.

Management   ★ ★ ★ ★

There are 277 fixed-income securities in this $800 million portfolio. The average municipal bond fund today is $166 million in size. Close to 99 percent of the funds holdings are in bonds. The average maturity of the bonds in this account is nine-teen years; the weighted coupon rate averages 5.3 percent. The portfolio's fixed-income holdings can be categorized as long-term, high-quality debt.

Joseph Deane has managed this fund for the past eleven years. There are forty-one funds besides CA Municipals within the Smith Barney family. Overall, the fund family's risk-adjusted performance can be described as very good.

Current Income   ★ ★ ★

Over the past year, Smith Barney CA Municipals A had a twelve-month yield of 4.6 percent. During this same twelve-month period, the typical municipal bond fund had a yield that averaged 4.4 percent.

Expenses   ★ ★ ★ ★

Smith Barney CA Municipals A's expense ratio is .7 percent; it has also averaged .7 percent annually over the past three calendar years. The average expense ratio for the 1,900 funds in this category is 1.1 percent. This fund's turnover rate over the past year has been 60 percent, while its peer group average has been 41 percent.

Summary

Smith Barney CA Municipals A has excellent returns, low overhead costs, minimal risk as well as highly regarded management. But this is a fund that requires just a little patience. Manager Ragus is ahead of the crowd when he positions his port-folio and the fruits of his decisions are often not reflected in the fund's performance for several quarters. Ragus has demonstrated real insight and true leadership, traits that are not common among his peers.

Profile

minimum initial investment $1,000	*IRA accounts available*. . . . . no
subsequent minimum investment . . . $50	*IRA minimum investment* . . . . n/a
available in all 50 states. . . . . yes	*date of inception* . . . . April 1984
telephone exchanges. . . . . yes	*dividend/income paid*. . . . . monthly
number of other funds in family 41	*average credit quality*. . . . . AA

Strong High-Yield Municipal Bond

P.O. Box 2936
Milwaukee, WI 53201-2936
800-368-1030

total return	★ ★ ★ ★ ★
risk reduction	★ ★ ★ ★ ★
management	★ ★ ★ ★ ★
current income	★ ★ ★ ★ ★
expense control	★ ★ ★
symbol SHYLX	23 points
up-market performance	very good
down-market performance	poor
predictability of returns	good

Total Return   ★ ★ ★ ★ ★

Over the past five years, Strong High-Yield Municipal Bond has taken $10,000 and turned it into $14,789 ($13,079 over three years). This translates into an average annual return of 8 percent over the past five years and 9 percent over the past three years. Over the past five years, this fund has outperformed 60 percent of all mutual funds; within its general category it has done better than 98 percent of its peers. Municipal bond funds have averaged 6 percent annually over these same five years.

During the past five years, a $10,000 initial investment grew to $14,250 after taxes, assuming a 39.6 percent income tax bracket (state and federal combined) and a capital gains rate of 28 percent. This means that investors in this fund were able to preserve 100 percent of their total returns. Compared to other fixed-income funds, this fund's tax savings are considered to be excellent.

Risk/Volatility   ★ ★ ★ ★ ★

Over the past five years, Strong High-Yield Municipal Bond has been safer than 98 percent of all municipal bond funds. Over the past decade, the fund has had one negative year, while the Lehman Brothers Aggregate Bond Index has had one (off 3 percent in 1994); the Lehman Brothers Municipal Bond Index also fell once (off 5 percent in 1994). The fund has underperformed the Lehman Brothers Aggregate Bond Index twice and the Lehman Brothers Municipal Bond Index twice in the last ten years.

	last 5 years		since inception	
worst year	-1%	1994	-1%	1994
best year	15%	1995	15%	1995

In the past, Strong High-Yield Municipal Bond has done better than 75 percent of its peer group in up markets and outperformed 20 percent of its competition in down markets. Consistency, or predictability, of returns for Strong High-Yield Municipal Bond can be described as good. This fund's risk-adjusted return is excellent.

Management   ★ ★ ★ ★ ★

There are 191 fixed-income securities in this $700 million portfolio. The average municipal bond fund today is $166 million in size. Close to 99 percent of the funds holdings are in bonds. The average maturity of the bonds in this account is twelve years; the weighted coupon rate averages 6.3 percent. The portfolio's fixed-income holdings can be categorized as long-term, low-quality debt.

Mary-Kay Bourbulas has managed this fund for the past six years. There are thirty-five funds besides High-Yield Municipal within the Strong family. Overall, the fund family's risk-adjusted performance can be described as very good.

Current Income   ★ ★ ★ ★ ★

Over the past year, Strong High-Yield Municipal Bond had a twelve-month yield of 5.6 percent. During this same twelve-month period, the typical municipal bond fund had a yield that averaged 4.4 percent.

Expenses   ★ ★ ★

Strong High-Yield Municipal Bond's expense ratio is .7 percent; it has also averaged .7 percent annually over the past three calendar years. The average expense ratio for the 1,900 funds in this category is 1.1 percent. This fund's turnover rate over the past year has been 67 percent, while its peer group average has been 41 percent.

Summary

Strong High-Yield Municipal Bond has had excellent risk-adjusted returns since its 1993 inception. This is one of the most highly-rated tax-free funds and earns an almost perfect score across the board. This fund specializes in nonrated bonds which are considered to have the equivalent of a B or BB rating. In order to reduce such credit risk, management limits its exposure to no more than 2 percent per issuer; roughly 75 percent of the portfolio is in nonrated issues. This unique approach to bond selection has paid off handsomely in the past and is a recommended strategy for investors—assuming they benefit from manager Mary-Kay Bourbulas' skills.

Profile

minimum initial investment $2,500	*IRA accounts available.* . . . . no
subsequent minimum investment . . . $50	*IRA minimum investment* . . . . n/a
available in all 50 states. . . . . yes	*date of inception* . . . . Oct. 1993
telephone exchanges. . . . . yes	*dividend/income paid.* . . . . monthly
number of other funds in family 35	*average credit quality* . . . . n/a

United Municipal High-Income A
6300 Lamar Avenue
Shawnee Mission, KS 66201-9217
800-366-5465

total return	★ ★ ★ ★ ★
risk reduction	★ ★ ★ ★ ★
management	★ ★ ★ ★ ★
current income	★ ★ ★ ★ ★
expense control	★ ★ ★ ★
symbol UMUHX	24 points
up-market performance	excellent
down-market performance	fair
predictability of returns	very good

Total Return ★ ★ ★ ★ ★

Over the past five years, United Municipal High-Income A has taken $10,000 and turned it into $15,162 ($12,922 over three years and $23,848 over the past ten years). This translates into an average annual return of 9 percent over the past five years, 9 percent over the past three years, and 9 percent for the decade. Over the past five years, this fund has outperformed 60 percent of all mutual funds; within its general category it has done better than 99 percent of its peers. Municipal bond funds have averaged 6 percent annually over these same five years.

During the past five years, a $10,000 initial investment grew to $14,450 after taxes, assuming a 39.6 percent income tax bracket (state and federal combined) and a capital gains rate of 28 percent. This means that investors in this fund were able to preserve 100 percent of their total returns. Compared to other fixed-income funds, this fund's tax savings are considered to be excellent.

Risk/Volatility ★ ★ ★ ★ ★

Over the past five years, United Municipal High-Income A has been safer than 99 percent of all municipal bond funds. Over the past decade, the fund has had one negative year, while the Lehman Brothers Aggregate Bond Index has had one (off 3 percent in 1994); the Lehman Brothers Municipal Bond Index also fell once (off 5 percent in 1994). The fund has underperformed the Lehman Brothers Aggregate Bond Index six times and the Lehman Brothers Municipal Bond Index three times in the last ten years.

	last 5 years		last 10 years	
worst year	-3%	1994	-3%	1994
best year	17%	1995	17%	1995

In the past, United Municipal High-Income A has done better than 90 percent of its peer group in up markets and outperformed 45 percent of its competition in down markets. Consistency, or predictability, of returns for United Municipal High-Income A can be described as very good. This fund's risk-adjusted return is excellent.

Management ★★★★★

There are 191 fixed-income securities in this $550 million portfolio. The average municipal bond fund today is $166 million in size. Close to 100 percent of the funds holdings are in bonds. The average maturity of the bonds in this account is twenty years; the weighted coupon rate averages 6.5 percent. The portfolio's fixed-income holdings can be categorized as long-term, medium-quality debt.

John Holliday has managed this fund for the past thirteen years. There are sixteen funds besides Municipal High-Income within the United family. Overall, the fund family's risk-adjusted performance can be described as very good.

Current Income ★★★★★

Over the past year, United Municipal High-Income A had a twelve-month yield of 5.6 percent. During this same twelve-month period, the typical municipal bond fund had a yield that averaged 4.4 percent.

Expenses ★★★★

United Municipal High-Income A's expense ratio is .8 percent; it has also averaged .8 percent annually over the past three calendar years. The average expense ratio for the 1,900 funds in this category is 1.1 percent. This fund's turnover rate over the past year has been 35 percent, while its peer group average has been 41 percent.

Summary

United Municipal High-Income A has landed in the top performance quartile for its peer group for each of the past four years. The fund's risk adjusted returns have been fantastic since its 1986 inception. This is the number one tax-free bond fund. The fund receives 24 out of 25 possible points, a score that only a modest number of funds has achieved in all categories combined. This fund is highly recommended for anyone looking for tax relief and/or a very attractive current income.

Profile

minimum initial investment $500	*IRA accounts available.* . . . . no
subsequent minimum investment $1	*IRA minimum investment* . . . . n/a
available in all 50 states. . . . . yes	*date of inception* . . . . Jan. 1986
telephone exchanges . . . . no	*dividend/income paid.* . . . . monthly
number of other funds in family 16	*average credit quality* . . . . n/a

Vanguard Short-Term Tax-Exempt
Vanguard Financial Center
P.O. Box 2600
Valley Forge, PA 19482
800-662-7447

total return	★ ★
risk reduction	★ ★ ★ ★ ★
management	★ ★ ★ ★
current income	★ ★
expense control	★ ★ ★ ★ ★
symbol VWSTX	18 points
up-market performance	excellent
down-market performance	poor
predictability of returns	excellent

Total Return   ★ ★

Over the past five years, Vanguard Short-Term Tax-Exempt has taken $10,000 and turned it into $12,219 ($11,265 over three years and $16,119 over the past ten years). This translates into an average annual return of 4 percent over the past five years, 4 percent over the past three years, and 5 percent for the decade. Over the past five years, this fund has outperformed 10 percent of all mutual funds; within its general category it has done better than 20 percent of its peers. Municipal bond funds have averaged 6 percent annually over these same five years.

During the past five years, a $10,000 initial investment grew to $12,140 after taxes, assuming a 39.6 percent income tax bracket (state and federal combined) and a capital gains rate of 28 percent. This means that investors in this fund were able to preserve 100 percent of their total returns. Compared to other fixed-income funds, this fund's tax savings are considered to be excellent.

Risk/Volatility   ★ ★ ★ ★ ★

Over the past five years, Vanguard Short-Term Tax-Exempt has been safer than 98 percent of all municipal bond funds. Over the past decade, the fund has not had a negative year, while the Lehman Brothers Aggregate Bond Index has had one (off 3 percent in 1994); the Lehman Brothers Municipal Bond Index also fell once (off 5 percent in 1994). The fund has underperformed the Lehman Brothers Aggregate Bond Index eight times and the Lehman Brothers Municipal Bond Index nine times in the last ten years.

	last 5 years		last 10 years	
worst year	2%	1994	2%	1994
best year	6%	1995	6%	1995

In the past, Vanguard Short-Term Tax-Exempt has done better than 100 percent of its peer group in up markets and outperformed 20 percent of its competition in down markets. Consistency, or predictability, of returns for Vanguard

Short-Term Tax-Exempt can be described as excellent. This fund's risk-adjusted return is good.

Management   ★ ★ ★ ★

There are 160 fixed-income securities in this $1.8 billion portfolio. The average municipal bond fund today is $166 million in size. Close to 90 percent of the funds holdings are in bonds. The average maturity of the bonds in this account is one year; the weighted coupon rate averages 5.9 percent. The portfolio's fixed-income holdings can be categorized as short-term, high-quality debt.

A team has managed this fund for the past ten years. There are sixty-eight funds besides Short-Term Tax-Exempt within the Vanguard family. Overall, the fund family's risk-adjusted performance can be described as very good.

Current Income   ★ ★

Over the past year, Vanguard Short-Term Tax-Exempt had a twelve-month yield of 3.8 percent. During this same twelve-month period, the typical municipal bond fund had a yield that averaged 4.4 percent.

Expenses   ★ ★ ★ ★ ★

Vanguard Short-Term Tax-Exempt's expense ratio is .2 percent; it has also averaged .2 percent annually over the past three calendar years. The average expense ratio for the 1,900 funds in this category is 1.1 percent. This fund's turnover rate over the past year has been 36 percent, while its peer group average has been 41 percent.

Summary

Vanguard Short-Term Tax-Exempt does not have a particularly high level of current income and the fund's total return figures are not impressive but safety is fantastic. This fund is the perfect choice for the high bracket taxpayer who wants tax-free income that is greater than that found with municipal money market funds. For all practical purposes, the real risk level of this fund is not much different than that found with "risk free" investments.

Profile

minimum initial investment $3,000	*IRA accounts available*. . . . . no
subsequent minimum investment . . $100	*IRA minimum investment*. . . . . n/a
available in all 50 states. . . . . yes	*date of inception* . . . . Sept. 1977
telephone exchanges. . . . . yes	*dividend/income paid*. . . . . monthly
number of other funds in family 68	*average credit quality*. . . . . AA

Utility Stock Funds

Utility stock funds look for both growth and income, investing in common stocks of utility companies across the country. Historically, somewhere between one-third and half of these funds' total returns come from common stock dividends. Utility funds normally stay away from speculative issues, focusing instead on well-established companies with solid histories of paying good dividends. Surprisingly, the goal of most of these funds is long-term growth.

Utility, metals, and natural resources funds are the only three sector, or specialty, fund categories in this book. Funds that invest in a single industry, or sector, should be avoided by most investors for two reasons. First, you limit the fund manager's ability to find attractive stocks or bonds if he or she is only able to choose securities from one particular geographic area or industry. Second, as a general category, these specialty funds represent the worst of both worlds: above-average risk and substandard returns. If you find the term "aggressive growth" unappealing, then the words "sector fund" should positively appall you.

Utility funds are the one exception. They sound safe and they are safe (-8.8 percent for 1994 notwithstanding). Any category of stocks that relies moderately or heavily on dividends generated automatically has a built-in safety cushion. A comparatively high dividend income means that you have to worry less about the appreciation of the underlying issues.

Four factors generally determine the profitability of a utility company: (1) how much it pays for energy, (2) the general level of interest rates, (3) its expected use of nuclear power, and (4) the political climate.

The prices of oil and gas are passed directly on to the consumer, but the utility companies are sensitive to this issue. Higher fuel prices mean that the utility industry has less latitude to increase its profit margins. Thus, higher fuel prices can mean smaller profits and/or dividends to investors.

Next to energy costs, interest is the industry's greatest expense. Utility companies are heavily debt-laden. Their interest costs directly affect their profitability. When rates go down and companies are able to refinance their debt, the savings can be staggering. Paying 7 percent interest on a couple of hundred million dollars worth of bonds each year is much more appealing than having to pay 10 percent on the same amount of debt. A lower-interest-rate environment translates into more money being left over for shareholders.

Depending on how you look at it, nuclear power has been an issue or problem for the United States for a few decades now. Other countries seem to have come to grips with the matter, yet we remain divided. Although new power plants have not been successfully proposed or built in this country for several years, no one knows what the future may hold. Venturing into nuclear power always seems to be much more expensive than anticipated by the utility companies and the independent experts they rely on for advice. Because of these uncertainties, mutual fund managers try to seek out utility companies that have no foreseeable plans to develop any or more nuclear power facilities. Whether this will help the nation in the long term remains to be seen, but such avoidance keeps share prices more stable and predictable.

Finally, the political climate is an important concern when calculating whether utility funds should be part of your portfolio. The Public Utilities Commission (PUC) is a political animal and can directly reflect the views of a state's government. Utility bills are something most of us are concerned with and aware of; the powers that be are more likely to be reelected if they are able to keep rate increases to a minimum. Modest, or minimum, increases can be healthy for the utility companies; freezing rates for a couple of years is a bad sign.

One hundred and five funds make up the utilities category. Total market capitalization of this category is just over $25 billion. Over 85 percent of a typical utility fund's portfolio is in common stocks, with the balance in bonds, convertibles, and money market instruments. The typical utilities fund has about 13 percent of its holdings in foreign utility stocks.

Over the past three years, utility funds have had an average compound return of 15.7 percent per year; the annual return for the past five years has been 14.0 percent. For the last ten years, these funds have averaged 13.3 percent per year; 13.0 percent per year for the last fifteen years. The standard deviation for these funds has been 14.2 percent over the past three years. This means that utility funds have been less volatile than any other stock category and have been only slightly less stable than balanced and convertible funds (all periods ending 3/31/99).

Usually, utility stock prices closely follow the long-term bond market. If the economy surges and long-term interest rates go up, utility stock prices are likely to go down. Utility stocks are also vulnerable to a general stock market decline, although they are considered less risky than other types of common stock because of their dividends and the monopoly position of most utilities. Typically, utilities have fallen about two-thirds as much as other common stocks during market downturns.

Worldwide, there is a tremendous opportunity for growth in this industry. The average per-capita production of electricity in many developing countries is only one-fifth that of the United States. The electrical output per capita in the United States is 12,100 kilowatt hours, compared to 2,500 kilowatt hours for developing nations. This disparity may well be on the way out. All over the world, previously underdeveloped countries are making economic strides as they move toward free market systems.

When emerging countries become developed economically, their citizens demand higher standards of living. As a result, their requirements for electricity, water, and telephones tend to rise dramatically. Moreover, many countries are selling their utility companies to public owners, opening a new arena for investors. The net result of all of this for you, the investor, is that fund groups are beginning to offer global utility funds. This increased diversification—allowing a fund to invest in utility companies all over the world instead of just in the United States—coupled with tremendous long-term growth potential, should make this a dynamic industry group. Utility funds are a good choice for the investor who wants a hedge against inflation but is still afraid or distrustful of the stock market in general.

Beta, which measures the market-related risk of a stock, is only 0.5 percent for utility funds as a group (compared to 1.0 for the S&P 500). This means that when it comes to stock market risk, utilities have only 50 percent the risk of the Dow Jones Industrial Average (DJIA) or the S&P 500. Keep in mind, however, that there are other risks, such as rising interest rates and the price of oil, that also need to be considered whenever utilities are being considered.

Utility Stock Funds

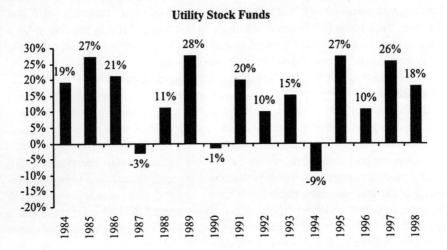

Global Utility A
One Seaport Plaza
New York, NY 10292
800-225-1852

total return	★ ★ ★
risk reduction	★ ★ ★ ★ ★
management	★ ★ ★ ★
tax minimization	★ ★ ★
expense control	★ ★ ★ ★ ★
symbol GLUAX	20 points
up-market performance	excellent
down-market performance	excellent
predictability of returns	very good

Total Return   ★ ★ ★
Over the past five years, Global Utility A has taken $10,000 and turned it into $20,166 ($16,632 over three years). This translates into an average annual return of 15 percent over the past five years and 18 percent over the past three years. Over the past five years, this fund has outperformed 80 percent of all mutual funds; within its general category it has done better than 75 percent of its peers. Utility stock funds have averaged 14 percent annually over these same five years.

Risk/Volatility
Over the past five years, Global Utility A has been safer than 85 percent of all utility stock funds. Over the past decade, the fund has had one negative year, while the S&P 500 has had one (off 3 percent in 1990). The fund has underperformed the S&P 500 six times in the last ten years.

	last 5 years		since inception	
worst year	-8%	1994	-8%	1994
best year	24%	1997	24%	1997

In the past, Global Utility A has done better than 100 percent of its peer group in up markets and outperformed 100 percent of its competition in down markets. Consistency, or predictability, of returns for Global Utility A can be described as very good. This fund's risk-adjusted return is excellent.

Management
There are fifty-five stocks in this $150 million portfolio. The average utility stock fund today is $240 million in size. Close to 77 percent of the fund's holdings are in stocks. The stocks in this portfolio have an average price-earnings (p/e) ratio of 23 and a median market capitalization of $19.9 billion. The portfolio's equity holdings can be categorized as large-cap and value-oriented issues.

William Hicks and Earl McEvoy have managed this fund for the past five years. There are fifty-five funds besides Global Utility A within the Prudential family. Overall, the fund family's risk-adjusted performance can be described as good.

Tax Minimization   ★★★

During the past five years, a $10,000 initial investment grew to $17,160 after taxes, assuming a 39.6 percent income tax bracket (state and federal combined) and a capital gains rate of 28 percent. This means that investors in this fund were able to preserve 89 percent of their total returns. Compared to other equity funds, this fund's tax savings are considered to be excellent.

Expenses   ★★★★★

Global Utility A's expense ratio is 1.2 percent; it has also averaged 1.2 percent annually over the past three calendar years. The average expense ratio for the 110 funds in this category is 1.5 percent. This fund's turnover rate over the past year has been 20 percent, while its peer group average has been 55 percent.

Summary

Global Utility A uses an aggressive approach to investing. Manager Hicks has most of the portfolio in fast-growing global utilities. Roughly half of the portfolio is in telecommunication stocks. Portfolio risk is reduced by having close to one-fifth of the fund's assets in high quality bonds. This is the number one rated utilities fund and is highly recommended.

Profile

minimum initial investment $1,000	IRA accounts available . . . . yes
subsequent minimum investment . . $100	IRA minimum investment $1
available in all 50 states. . . . . yes	date of inception . . . . Jan. 1990
telephone exchanges. . . . . yes	dividend/income paid . . . . quarterly
number of other funds in family 55	largest sector weighting . . . . . . services

Merrill Lynch Global Utility B

Box 9011
Princeton, NJ 08543-9011
800-637-3863

total return	★ ★ ★
risk reduction	★
management	★ ★ ★
tax minimization	★ ★ ★ ★
expense control	★ ★ ★ ★
symbol MBGUX	15 points
up-market performance	good
down-market performance	poor
predictability of returns	good

Total Return   ★ ★ ★

Over the past five years, Merrill Lynch Global Utility B has taken $10,000 and turned it into $19,654 ($16,686 over three years). This translates into an average annual return of 14 percent over the past five years and 19 percent over the past three years. Over the past five years, this fund has outperformed 75 percent of all mutual funds; within its general category it has done better than 70 percent of its peers. Utility stock funds have averaged 14 percent annually over these same five years.

Risk/Volatility   ★

Over the past five years, Merrill Lynch Global Utility B has been safer than 15 percent of all utility stock funds. Over the past decade, the fund has had one negative year, while the S&P 500 has had one (off 3 percent in 1990). The fund has underperformed the S&P 500 six times in the last ten years.

	last 5 years		since inception	
worst year	-11%	1994	-11%	1994
best year	25%	1998	25%	1998

In the past, Merrill Lynch Global Utility B has done better than 65 percent of its peer group in up markets and outperformed 25 percent of its competition in down markets. Consistency, or predictability, of returns for Merrill Lynch Global Utility B can be described as good. This fund's risk-adjusted return is good.

Management   ★ ★ ★

There are eighty-one stocks in this $350 million portfolio. The average utility stock fund today is $240 million in size. Close to 93 percent of the fund's holdings are in stocks. The stocks in this portfolio have an average price-earnings (p/e) ratio of 25 and a median market capitalization of $17.4 billion. The portfolio's equity holdings can be categorized as large-cap and value-oriented issues.

Walter Rogers has managed this fund for the past nine years. There are seventy funds besides Global Utility within the Merrill Lynch family. Overall, the fund family's risk-adjusted performance can be described as good.

Tax Minimization   ★ ★ ★ ★
During the past five years, a $10,000 initial investment grew to $17,720 after taxes, assuming a 39.6 percent income tax bracket (state and federal combined) and a capital gains rate of 28 percent. This means that investors in this fund were able to preserve 93 percent of their total returns. Compared to other equity funds, this fund's tax savings are considered to be excellent.

Expenses   ★ ★ ★ ★
Merrill Lynch Global Utility B's expense ratio is 1.6 percent; it has also averaged 1.6 percent annually over the past three calendar years. The average expense ratio for the 110 funds in this category is 1.5 percent. This fund's turnover rate over the past year has been 7 percent, while its peer group average has been 55 percent.

Summary
Merrill Lynch Global Utility B invests at least two-thirds of its assets in domestic and foreign companies that generate, transmit, or distribute electricity, telecommunications, gas, or water. Any bonds purchased by the fund must be investment grade. Management invests in over 20 countries; U.S. companies for their income and foreign securities for their appreciation potential. Manager Rogers concentrates on industry-specific events, corporate fundamentals, financial resources, caliber of management, as well as economic and currency stability. This fund's strong suit is tax minimization.

Profile
minimum initial investment $1,000	IRA accounts available . . . . yes
subsequent minimum investment . . . $50	IRA minimum investment $100
available in all 50 states. . . . . yes	date of inception. . . . . Dec. 1990
telephone exchanges. . . . . yes	dividend/income paid . . . . quarterly
number of other funds in family 70	largest sector weighting . . . . . . services

MFS Utilities A

500 Boylston Street
Boston, MA 02116
800-637-2929

total return	★ ★ ★ ★ ★
risk reduction	★ ★ ★ ★ ★
management	★ ★ ★ ★
tax minimization	★ ★ ★ ★ ★
expense control	★ ★ ★
symbol MMUFX	22 points
up-market performance	good
down-market performance	fair
predictability of returns	good

Total Return   ★ ★ ★ ★ ★

Over the past five years, MFS Utilities A has taken $10,000 and turned it into $24,196 ($18,190 over three years). This translates into an average annual return of 19 percent over the past five years and 22 percent over the past three years. Over the past five years, this fund has outperformed 85 percent of all mutual funds; within its general category it has done better than 96 percent of its peers. Utility stock funds have averaged 14 percent annually over these same five years.

Risk/Volatility   ★ ★ ★ ★ ★

Over the past five years, MFS Utilities A has been safer than 90 percent of all utility stock funds. Over the past decade, the fund has had one negative year, while the S&P 500 has had one (off 3 percent in 1990). The fund has underperformed the S&P 500 five times in the last ten years.

	last 5 years		since inception	
worst year	-5%	1994	-5%	1994
best year	33%	1995	33%	1995

In the past, MFS Utilities A has done better than 65 percent of its peer group in up markets and outperformed 45 percent of its competition in down markets. Consistency, or predictability, of returns for MFS Utilities A can be described as good. This fund's risk-adjusted return is excellent.

Management   ★ ★ ★ ★

There are 113 stocks in this $400 million portfolio. The average utility stock fund today is $240 million in size. Close to 75 percent of the fund's holdings are in stocks. The stocks in this portfolio have an average price-earnings (p/e) ratio of 20 and a median market capitalization of $4.7 billion. The portfolio's equity holdings can be categorized as mid-cap and value-oriented issues.

Maura Shaughnessy has managed this fund for the past seven years. There are sixty-one funds besides Utilities A within the MFS family. Overall, the fund family's risk-adjusted performance can be described as good.

Tax Minimization   ★ ★ ★ ★ ★

During the past five years, a $10,000 initial investment grew to $19,140 after taxes, assuming a 39.6 percent income tax bracket (state and federal combined) and a capital gains rate of 28 percent. This means that investors in this fund were able to preserve 82 percent of their total returns. Compared to other equity funds, this fund's tax savings are considered to be good.

Expenses   ★ ★ ★

MFS Utilities A's expense ratio is 1.1 percent; it has also averaged 1.1 percent annually over the past three calendar years. The average expense ratio for the 110 funds in this category is 1.5 percent. This fund's turnover rate over the past year has been 124 percent, while its peer group average has been 55 percent.

Summary

MFS Utilities A invests in stocks and bonds of domestic and foreign utility companies such as electric, energy water services, and telecommunications. Manager Shaughnessy is an eclectic investor who uses a bottom-up approach to security selection. The fund's performance places it in the top 5 percent of its peer group for the past three and five years. It ties for second place as the best utility fund. Risk minimization has also been exceptional.

Profile

minimum initial investment $1,000	*IRA accounts available* . . . . yes
subsequent minimum investment . . . $50	*IRA minimum investment* $250
available in all 50 states. . . . . yes	*date of inception* . . . . Jan. 1992
telephone exchanges. . . . . yes	*dividend/income paid.* . . . . monthly
number of other funds in family 61	*largest sector weighting* . . . . . . utilities

MSDW Utilities B

Two World Trade Center, 72nd Floor
New York, NY 10048
800-869-3863

total return	★ ★ ★
risk reduction	★ ★ ★ ★
management	★ ★ ★ ★
tax minimization	★ ★ ★
expense control	★ ★ ★ ★
symbol UTLBX	18 points
up-market performance	fair
down-market performance	very good
predictability of returns	excellent

Total Return   ★ ★ ★

Over the past five years, MSDW Utilities B has taken $10,000 and turned it into $19,279 ($15,722 over three years and $32,043 over the past ten years). This translates into an average annual return of 14 percent over the past five years, 16 percent over the past three years, and 12 percent for the decade. Over the past five years, this fund has outperformed 75 percent of all mutual funds; within its general category it has done better than 60 percent of its peers. Utility stock funds have averaged 14 percent annually over these same five years.

Risk/Volatility   ★ ★ ★ ★

Over the past five years, MSDW Utilities B has been safer than 75 percent of all utility stock funds. Over the past decade, the fund has had two negative years, while the S&P 500 has had one (off 3 percent in 1990). The fund has underperformed the S&P 500 seven times in the last ten years.

	last 5 years		last 10 years	
worst year	-9%	1994	-9%	1994
best year	28%	1995	28%	1995

In the past, MSDW Utilities B has done better than 45 percent of its peer group in up markets and outperformed 70 percent of its competition in down markets. Consistency, or predictability, of returns for MSDW Utilities B can be described as excellent. This fund's risk-adjusted return is good.

Management   ★ ★ ★ ★

There are ninety stocks in this $2.6 billion portfolio. The average utility stock fund today is $240 million in size. Close to 87 percent of the fund's holdings are in stocks. The stocks in this portfolio have an average price-earnings (p/e) ratio of 22 and a median market capitalization of $11 billion. The portfolio's equity holdings can be categorized as large-cap and value-oriented issues.

Edward Gaylor has managed this fund for the past eleven years. There are sixty-five funds besides Utilities B within the Morgan Stanley Dean Witter family. Overall, the fund family's risk-adjusted performance can be described as very good.

Tax Minimization   ★ ★ ★
During the past five years, a $10,000 initial investment grew to $16,900 after taxes, assuming a 39.6 percent income tax bracket (state and federal combined) and a capital gains rate of 28 percent. This means that investors in this fund were able to preserve 90 percent of their total returns. Compared to other equity funds, this fund's tax savings are considered to be excellent.

Expenses   ★ ★ ★ ★
MSDW Utilities B's expense ratio is 1.7 percent; it has also averaged 1.7 percent annually over the past three calendar years. The average expense ratio for the 110 funds in this category is 1.5 percent. This fund's turnover rate over the past year has been 6 percent, while its peer group average has been 55 percent.

Summary
MSDW Utilities B is part of the Morgan Stanley Dean Witter group and is just one of several recommended funds from a very good fund family. Tax minimization has been superb, a difficult accomplishment for any fund in the utility sector. Manager Gaylor reduces portfolio risk in a number of ways: (1) it is rare for a single position to represent more than 3 percent of the fund and (2) corporate and government bonds are included. Management favors companies that have room for flexible pricing and quality leadership. This fund scores well across the board and has done a particularly good job at minimizing taxes.

Profile
minimum initial investment $1,000	*IRA accounts available* . . . . yes
subsequent minimum investment . . $100	*IRA minimum investment* $500
available in all 50 states. . . . . yes	*date of inception* . . . . April 1988
telephone exchanges. . . . . yes	*dividend/income paid* . . . . annually
number of other funds in family 65	*largest sector weighting* . . . . . . utilities

Strong American Utilities

P.O. Box 2936
Milwaukee, WI 53201-2936
800-368-1030

total return	★ ★ ★ ★
risk reduction	★ ★ ★ ★
management	★ ★ ★ ★
tax minimization	★ ★ ★ ★ ★
expense control	★ ★ ★ ★
symbol SAMUX	21 points
up-market performance	fair
down-market performance	excellent
predictability of returns	good

Total Return   ★ ★ ★ ★

Over the past five years, Strong American Utilities has taken $10,000 and turned it into $21,803 ($15,589 over three years). This translates into an average annual return of 17 percent over the past five years and 16 percent over the past three years. Over the past five years, this fund has outperformed 85 percent of all mutual funds; within its general category it has done better than 90 percent of its peers. Utility stock funds have averaged 14 percent annually over these same five years.

Risk/Volatility   ★ ★ ★ ★

Over the past five years, Strong American Utilities has been safer than 75 percent of all utility stock funds. Over the past decade, the fund has had one negative year, while the S&P 500 has had one (off 3 percent in 1990). The fund has underperformed the S&P 500 five times in the last ten years.

	last 5 years		since inception	
worst year	-3%	1994	-3%	1994
best year	37%	1995	37%	1995

In the past, Strong American Utilities has done better than 40 percent of its peer group in up markets and outperformed 90 percent of its competition in down markets. Consistency, or predictability, of returns for Strong American Utilities can be described as good. This fund's risk-adjusted return is fair.

Management   ★ ★ ★ ★

There are forty-nine stocks in this $250 million portfolio. The average utility stock fund today is $240 million in size. Close to 93 percent of the fund's holdings are in stocks. The stocks in this portfolio have an average price-earnings (p/e) ratio of 22 and a median market capitalization of $16 billion. The portfolio's equity holdings can be categorized as large-cap and value-oriented issues.

A team has managed this fund for the past six years. There are thirty-five funds besides American Utilities within the Strong family. Overall, the fund family's risk-adjusted performance can be described as very good.

Tax Minimization ★ ★ ★ ★ ★

During the past five years, a $10,000 initial investment grew to $19,350 after taxes, assuming a 39.6 percent income tax bracket (state and federal combined) and a capital gains rate of 28 percent. This means that investors in this fund were able to preserve 87 percent of their total returns. Compared to other equity funds, this fund's tax savings are considered to be very good.

Expenses ★ ★ ★ ★

Strong American Utilities' expense ratio is 1 percent; it has averaged 1.1 percent annually over the past three calendar years. The average expense ratio for the 110 funds in this category is 1.5 percent. This fund's turnover rate over the past year has been 69 percent, while its peer group average has been 55 percent.

Summary

Strong American Utilities invests at least two-thirds of its assets in common, preferred, and convertible securities of domestic utility companies. The remaining third can be invested in non-related industries, both domestic and foreign. Management favors those companies that have returns on equity of at least 12 percent and an increasing dividend stream. They are always on the look out for any catalyst that could result in a jump in revenues. This is one of the very few funds in the book that receives a "very good" rating in every single category.

Profile

minimum initial investment $2,500	*IRA accounts available* . . . . yes
subsequent minimum investment . . . $50	*IRA minimum investment* $250
available in all 50 states. . . . . yes	*date of inception* . . . . July 1993
telephone exchanges. . . . . yes	*dividend/income paid* . . . . quarterly
number of other funds in family 35	*largest sector weighting* . . . . . . utilities

World Bond Funds

Global, or world, funds invest in securities issued all over the world, including the United States. A global bond fund usually invests in bonds issued by stable governments from a handful of countries. These funds try to avoid purchasing foreign government debt instruments from politically or economically unstable nations. Foreign, also known as international, bond funds invest in debt instruments from countries other than the United States.

International funds purchase securities issued in a foreign currency, such as the Japanese yen or the British pound. Prospective investors need to be aware of the potential changes in the value of the foreign currency relative to the U.S. dollar. As an example, if you were to invest in U.K. pound-denominated bonds with a yield of 8 percent and the British currency appreciated 5 percent against the U.S. dollar, your total return for the year would be 13 percent. If the British pound declined by 9 percent against the U.S. dollar, your total return would be -1 percent (8 percent yield minus 9 percent).

Since foreign markets do not necessarily move in tandem with U.S. markets, each country represents varying investment opportunities at different times. As of the beginning of 1999, the countries with the largest percent of the global government bond marketplace were: the United States (36%), Japan (19%), Germany (9%), France (9%), Italy (8.5%), and the United Kingdom (7.5%). The typical global bond *fund* has roughly 40 percent of its holdings in European bonds, followed by the United States and Canada (27%) and Latin America (17%).

Assessing the economic environment to evaluate its effects on interest rates and bond values requires an understanding of two important factors: inflation and supply. During inflationary periods, when there is too much money chasing too few goods, government tightening of the money supply helps create a balance between an economy's cash resources and its available goods. Money supply refers to the amount of cash made available for spending, borrowing, or investing. Controlled by the central banks of each nation, it is a primary tool used to manage inflation, interest rates, and economic growth.

A prudent tightening of the money supply can help bring on disinflation: decelerated loan demand, reduced durable goods orders, and falling prices. During disinflationary times, interest rates also fall, strengthening the underlying value of existing bonds. While such factors ultimately contribute to a healthier economy, they also mean lower yields for government bond investors. A trend toward disinflation currently exists in markets around the world. The worldwide growth in money supply is at its lowest level in twenty years.

As the United States and other governments implement policies designed to reduce inflation, interest rates are stabilizing. This disinflation can be disquieting to the individual who specifically invests for high monthly income. In reality, falling interest rates mean higher bond values, and investors seeking long-term growth or high total returns can therefore benefit from declining rates. Inflation, which drives interest rates higher, is the true enemy of bond investors. It diminishes bond values and, in addition, erodes the buying power of the interest income investors receive.

Income-seeking investors need to find economies where inflation is coming under control yet where interest rates are still high enough to provide favorable bond yields. An investor who has only U.S. bonds is not taking advantage of such opportunities. If global disinflationary trends continue, those who remain invested only in the United States can lose out on opportunities for high income and total return elsewhere. The gradually decreasing yields on U.S. bonds compel the investor who seeks high income to think globally.

While not all bond markets will peak at the same level, they do tend to follow patterns. Targeting those countries where interest rates are at peak levels and inflation is falling not only results in higher income but also creates significant potential for capital appreciation as rates ultimately decline and bond prices increase.

Even with high income as the primary goal, investors must consider credit and market risk. By investing primarily in mutual funds that purchase government-guaranteed bonds from the world's most creditworthy nations, you can get an extra measure of credit safety for payment of interest and repayment of principal. By diversifying across multiple markets, fund managers can significantly reduce market risk as well. Diversification is a proven technique for controlling market risk.

The long-term success of a global bond manager depends on expertise in assessing economic trends from country to country, as well as protecting the U.S. valuation of foreign holdings. The most effective way to protect the U.S. dollar value of international holdings is through active currency management. Although its effects over a ten-year period are nominal at best, currency fluctuation can substantially help returns over a one-, three-, or five-year period.

In the simplest terms, effective currency management provides exposure to bond markets worldwide, while reducing the affects of adverse currency changes that can lower bond values. If a portfolio manager anticipates that the U.S. dollar will strengthen, he or she can lock in a currency exchange rate to protect the fund against a decline in the value of its foreign holdings. (A strong dollar means that other currencies are declining in value.) This strategy is commonly referred to as hedging the exposure of the portfolio. If, on the other hand, the manager expects the U.S. dollar to weaken, the fund can stay unhedged to allow it to benefit from the increasing value of foreign currencies.

Investing in global bonds gives you the potential for capital appreciation during periods of declining interest rates. An inverse relationship exists between bond values and interest rates. When interest rates fall, as is the case in most bond markets in the world today, existing bond values climb. Conversely, as interest rates rise, the value of existing bonds declines (they are less desirable since new bonds have a higher current yield).

Over the past three and five years, global bond funds have had an average compound return of 6.0 and 6.5 percent per year respectively; the annual returns for the past ten and fifteen years have been 7.6 and 10.5 percent, respectively. U.S. bonds have outperformed their foreign counterparts over the past one, three, five, and ten years and only slightly underperformed foreign bonds over the past fifteen years. The standard deviation for global bond funds has been 9.2 percent over the past three years (all periods ending 3/31/99). This means that these funds have been less volatile than any equity fund but more volatile than government bond funds (standard deviation of 3.4). Just 250 funds make up the global bond category. Total market capitalization of this category is $22 billion.

Global bond funds, particularly those with high concentrations in foreign issues, can be an excellent risk-reduction tool that should be utilized by the vast majority of investors, particularly when U.S. interest rates are increasing.

World Bond Funds

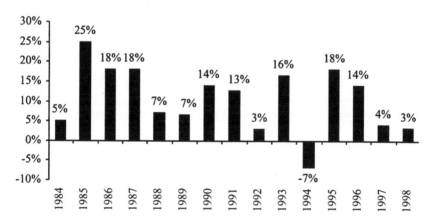

Alliance Global Dollar Government A
P.O. Box 1520
Secaucus, NJ 07096
800-227-4618

total return	★ ★ ★ ★
risk reduction	★
management	★ ★ ★
current income	★ ★ ★ ★ ★
expense control	★ ★ ★ ★
symbol AGDAX	17 points
up-market performance	excellent
down-market performance	poor
predictability of returns	poor

Total Return   ★ ★ ★ ★
Over the past five years, Alliance Global Dollar Government A has taken $10,000 and turned it into $14,625 ($11,666 over three years). This translates into an average annual return of 8 percent over the past five years and 5 percent over the past three years. Over the past five years, this fund has outperformed 10 percent of all mutual funds; within its general category it has done better than 60 percent of its peers. World bond funds have averaged 6 percent annually over these same five years.

During the past five years, a $10,000 initial investment grew to $7,230 after taxes, assuming a 39.6 percent income tax bracket (state and federal combined) and a capital gains rate of 28 percent. This means that investors in this fund were able to preserve 48 percent of their total returns. Compared to other fixed-income funds, this fund's tax savings are considered to be poor.

Risk/Volatility   ★
Over the past five years, Alliance Global Dollar Government A has been safer than 20 percent of all world bond funds. Over the past decade, the fund has had one negative year, while the Lehman Brothers Aggregate Bond Index has had one (off 3 percent in 1994); the Saloman Brothers World Government Bond Index fell twice (off 3 percent in 1989 and 4 percent in 1997). The fund has underperformed the Lehman Brothers Aggregate Bond Index once and the Saloman Brothers World Government Bond Index once in the last ten years.

	last 5 years		since inception	
worst year	-22%	1998	-22%	1998
best year	39%	1996	39%	1996

In the past, Alliance Global Dollar Government A has done better than 100 percent of its peer group in up markets and outperformed 15 percent of its competition in down markets. Consistency, or predictability, of returns for Alliance Global Dollar Government A can be described as poor. This fund's risk-adjusted return is very good.

Management ★ ★ ★

There are thirty-seven fixed-income securities in this $55 million portfolio. The average world bond fund today is $90 million in size. Close to 100 percent of the funds holdings are in bonds. The average maturity of the bonds in this account is fifteen years; the weighted coupon rate averages 9 percent. The portfolio's fixed-income holdings can be categorized as long-term, high-quality debt.

Wayne Lyski has managed this fund for the past five years. There are forty-nine funds besides Global Dollar Government within the Alliance family. Overall, the fund family's risk-adjusted performance can be described as good.

Current Income ★ ★ ★ ★ ★

Over the past year, Alliance Global Dollar Government A had a twelve-month yield of 14.5 percent. During this same twelve-month period, the typical world bond fund had a yield that averaged 6.9 percent.

Expenses ★ ★ ★ ★

Alliance Global Dollar Government A's expense ratio is 1.5 percent; it has also averaged 1.5 percent annually over the past three calendar years. The average expense ratio for the funds in this category is 1.5 percent. This fund's turnover rate over the past year has been 188 percent, while its peer group average has been 260 percent.

Summary

Alliance Global Dollar Government A has the vast majority of its assets invested in emerging market debt. The three most represented countries in the portfolio are Argentina, Brazil, and Mexico. Despite these descriptions, the portfolio's overall credit rating averages AAA. Current income is particularly attractive. Investors looking for diversification by being in emerging markets that offer a yield higher than any of its category peers in the book will love this fund.

Profile

minimum initial investment $250	IRA accounts available . . . . yes
subsequent minimum investment . . . $50	IRA minimum investment $250
available in all 50 states. . . . . yes	date of inception . . . . Feb. 1994
telephone exchanges. . . . . yes	dividend/income paid. . . . . monthly
number of other funds in family 49	average credit quality . . . . AAA

Capital World Bond
333 South Hope Street
Los Angeles, CA 90071
800-421-4120

total return	★ ★ ★
risk reduction	★ ★ ★ ★
management	★ ★ ★ ★
current income	★ ★
expense control	★ ★ ★ ★ ★
symbol CWBFX	18 points
up-market performance	fair
down-market performance	good
predictability of returns	excellent

Total Return   ★ ★ ★
Over the past five years, Capital World Bond has taken $10,000 and turned it into $14,019 ($11,560 over three years and $21,632 over the past ten years). This translates into an average annual return of 7 percent over the past five years, 5 percent over the past three years, and 8 percent for the decade. Over the past five years, this fund has outperformed 50 percent of all mutual funds; within its general category it has done better than 70 percent of its peers. World bond funds have averaged 6 percent annually over these same five years.

During the past five years, a $10,000 initial investment grew to $12,030 after taxes, assuming a 39.6 percent income tax bracket (state and federal combined) and a capital gains rate of 28 percent. This means that investors in this fund were able to preserve 86 percent of their total returns. Compared to other fixed-income funds, this fund's tax savings are considered to be very good.

Risk/Volatility   ★ ★ ★ ★
Over the past five years, Capital World Bond has been safer than 65 percent of all world bond funds. Over the past decade, the fund has had two negative years, while the Lehman Brothers Aggregate Bond Index has had one (off 3 percent in 1994); the Saloman Brothers World Government Bond Index fell twice (off 3 percent in 1989 and 4 percent in 1997). The fund has underperformed the Lehman Brothers Aggregate Bond Index four times and the Saloman Brothers World Government Bond Index four times in the last ten years.

	last 5 years		last 10 years	
worst year	-1%	1994	-1%	1994
best year	21%	1995	21%	1995

In the past, Capital World Bond has done better than 45 percent of its peer group in up markets and outperformed 65 percent of its competition in down markets. Consistency, or predictability, of returns for Capital World Bond can be described as excellent. This fund's risk-adjusted return is excellent.

Management ★ ★ ★ ★

There are 178 fixed-income securities in this $650 million portfolio. The average world bond fund today is $90 million in size. Close to 71 percent of the funds holdings are in bonds. The average maturity of the bonds in this account is nine years ; the weighted coupon rate averages 6.9 percent. The portfolio's fixed-income holdings can be categorized as intermediate-term, high-quality debt.

A team has managed this fund for the past six years. There are twenty-eight funds besides Capital World Bond within the American Funds family. Overall, the fund family's risk-adjusted performance can be described as very good.

Current Income ★ ★

Over the past year, Capital World Bond had a twelve-month yield of 5.0 percent. During this same twelve-month period, the typical world bond fund had a yield that averaged 6.9 percent.

Expenses ★ ★ ★ ★ ★

Capital World Bond's expense ratio is 1.1 percent; it has also averaged 1.1 percent annually over the past three calendar years. The average expense ratio for the funds in this category is 1.5 percent. This fund's turnover rate over the past year has been 101 percent, while its peer group average has been 260 percent.

Summary

Capital World Bond, a member of the much-respected American Funds family, will be the global bond fund of choice for most investors. This is one of the few fund families that really understands foreign markets. Management typically underweights emerging market debt and further reduces risk by being sensitive to interest rate as well as currency changes. Approximately one-third of the portfolio is in high quality U.S. bonds; German debt is the number two position, followed by the U.K. and New Zealand. This is a very attractive fund and management company.

Profile

minimum initial investment $1,000	*IRA accounts available* . . . . yes
subsequent minimum investment . . . $50	*IRA minimum investment* $250
available in all 50 states. . . . . yes	*date of inception* . . . . Aug. 1987
telephone exchanges. . . . . yes	*dividend/income paid* . . . . quarterly
number of other funds in family 28	*average credit quality* . . . . AA

Goldman Sachs Global A
4900 Sears Tower
Chicago, IL 60606
800-526-7384

total return	★ ★ ★ ★ ★
risk reduction	★ ★ ★ ★ ★
management	★ ★ ★ ★ ★
current income	★
expense control	★ ★ ★ ★
symbol GSGIX	20 points
up-market performance	fair
down-market performance	very good
predictability of returns	excellent

Total Return   ★ ★ ★ ★ ★
Over the past five years, Goldman Sachs Global A has taken $10,000 and turned it into $15,422 ($13,216 over three years). This translates into an average annual return of 9 percent over the past five years and 10 percent over the past three years. Over the past five years, this fund has outperformed 60 percent of all mutual funds; within its general category it has done better than 90 percent of its peers. World bond funds have averaged 6 percent annually over these same five years.

During the past five years, a $10,000 initial investment grew to $13,050 after taxes, assuming a 39.6 percent income tax bracket (state and federal combined) and a capital gains rate of 28 percent. This means that investors in this fund were able to preserve 89 percent of their total returns. Compared to other fixed-income funds, this fund's tax savings are considered to be excellent.

Risk/Volatility   ★ ★ ★ ★ ★
Over the past five years, Goldman Sachs Global A has been safer than 95 percent of all world bond funds. Over the past decade, the fund has had one negative year, while the Lehman Brothers Aggregate Bond Index has had one (off 3 percent in 1994); the Saloman Brothers World Government Bond Index fell twice (off 3 percent in 1989 and 4 percent in 1997). The fund has underperformed the Lehman Brothers Aggregate Bond Index three times and the Saloman Brothers World Government Bond Index four times in the last ten years.

	last 5 years		since inception	
worst year	-5%	1994	-5%	1994
best year	18%	1995	18%	1995

In the past, Goldman Sachs Global A has done better than 45 percent of its peer group in up markets and outperformed 75 percent of its competition in down markets. Consistency, or predictability, of returns for Goldman Sachs Global A can be described as excellent. This fund's risk-adjusted return is excellent.

Management ★ ★ ★ ★ ★

There are 136 fixed-income securities in this $250 million portfolio. The average world bond fund today is $90 million in size. Close to 93 percent of the funds holdings are in bonds. The average maturity of the bonds in this account is thirteen years; the weighted coupon rate averages 6.9 percent. The portfolio's fixed-income holdings can be categorized as intermediate-term, high-quality debt.

Stephen Fitzgerald and Andrew Wilson have managed this fund for the past five years. There are twenty funds besides Global A within the Goldman Sachs family. Overall, the fund family's risk-adjusted performance can be described as good.

Current Income ★

Over the past year, Goldman Sachs Global A had a twelve-month yield of 4.1 percent. During this same twelve-month period, the typical world bond fund had a yield that averaged 6.9 percent.

Expenses ★ ★ ★ ★

Goldman Sachs Global A's expense ratio is 1.3 percent; it has averaged 1.2 percent annually over the past three calendar years. The average expense ratio for the funds in this category is 1.5 percent. This fund's turnover rate over the past year has been 230 percent, while its peer group average has been 260 percent.

Summary

Goldman Sachs Global A has had risk-adjusted returns that have been superb since the fund's 1991 inception. Co-managers Fitzgerald and Wilson are more concerned with total return than current yield; a philosophy that is somewhat different than their peer group which is often yield driven. The entire portfolio is currency hedged. Management uses the JP Morgan Global Government Bond Index as a benchmark. This fund gets a perfect score in the three most important categories: total return, risk reduction, and management.

Profile

minimum initial investment $1,000	*IRA accounts available* . . . . yes
subsequent minimum investment . . . $50	*IRA minimum investment* $250
available in all 50 states. . . . . yes	*date of inception* . . . . Aug. 1991
telephone exchanges. . . . . yes	*dividend/income paid.* . . . . monthly
number of other funds in family 20	*average credit quality* . . . . AA

IDS Global Bond A

IDS Tower 10
Minneapolis, MN 55440-0010
800-328-8300

total return	★ ★ ★
risk reduction	★ ★ ★
management	★ ★ ★ ★
current income	★ ★
expense control	★ ★ ★ ★ ★
symbol IGBFX	17 points
up-market performance	good
down-market performance	good
predictability of returns	excellent

Total Return   ★ ★ ★

Over the past five years, IDS Global Bond A has taken $10,000 and turned it into $13,973 ($11,937 over three years and $24,708 over the past ten years). This translates into an average annual return of 7 percent over the past five years, 6 percent over the past three years, and 9 percent for the decade. Over the past five years, this fund has outperformed 50 percent of all mutual funds; within its general category it has done better than 65 percent of its peers. World bond funds have averaged 6 percent annually over these same five years.

During the past five years, a $10,000 initial investment grew to $12,060 after taxes, assuming a 39.6 percent income tax bracket (state and federal combined) and a capital gains rate of 28 percent. This means that investors in this fund were able to preserve 88 percent of their total returns. Compared to other fixed-income funds, this fund's tax savings are considered to be excellent.

Risk/Volatility   ★ ★ ★

Over the past five years, IDS Global Bond A has been safer than 50 percent of all world bond funds. Over the past decade, the fund has had one negative year, while the Lehman Brothers Aggregate Bond Index has had one (off 3 percent in 1994); the Saloman Brothers World Government Bond Index fell twice (off 3 percent in 1989 and 4 percent in 1997). The fund has underperformed the Lehman Brothers Aggregate Bond Index four times and the Saloman Brothers World Government Bond Index six times in the last ten years.

	last 5 years		last 10 years	
worst year	-5%	1994	-5%	1994
best year	19%	1995	19%	1995

In the past, IDS Global Bond A has done better than 55 percent of its peer group in up markets and outperformed 55 percent of its competition in down markets. Consistency, or predictability, of returns for IDS Global Bond A can be described as excellent. This fund's risk-adjusted return is excellent.

Management ★ ★ ★ ★

There are ninety-one fixed-income securities in this $700 million portfolio. The average world bond fund today is $90 million in size. Close to 90 percent of the funds holdings are in bonds. The average maturity of the bonds in this account is eleven years; the weighted coupon rate averages 8.1 percent. The portfolio's fixed-income holdings can be categorized as intermediate-term, high-quality debt.

Ray Goodner has managed this fund for the past ten years. There are forty-five funds besides Global Bond within the IDS family. Overall, the fund family's risk-adjusted performance can be described as good.

Current Income ★ ★

Over the past year, IDS Global Bond A had a twelve-month yield of 4.6 percent. During this same twelve-month period, the typical world bond fund had a yield that averaged 6.9 percent.

Expenses ★ ★ ★ ★ ★

IDS Global Bond A's expense ratio is 1.2 percent; it has also averaged 1.2 percent annually over the past three calendar years. The average expense ratio for the funds in this category is 1.5 percent. This fund's turnover rate over the past year has been 56 percent, while its peer group average has been 260 percent.

Summary

IDS Global Bond A is one of only a handful of global or foreign bond funds to make the cut. This intermediate-term portfolio of high quality debt instruments is just one of several IDS recommended offerings. The fund is one of the most consistent in its category and is therefore a good choice for the typical investor who has had little or no exposure in this area.

Profile

minimum initial investment $2,000	*IRA accounts available* . . . . yes
subsequent minimum investment . . $100	*IRA minimum investment* $1
available in all 50 states. . . . . yes	*date of inception* . . . . March 1989
telephone exchanges. . . . . yes	*dividend/income paid* . . . . quarterly
number of other funds in family 45	*average credit quality.* . . . . AA

Payden & Rygel Global Fixed-Income R
333 South Grand Avenue, 32nd Floor
Los Angeles, CA 90071-0000
800-572-9336

total return	★ ★ ★ ★ ★
risk reduction	★ ★ ★ ★ ★
management	★ ★ ★ ★ ★
current income	★ ★ ★
expense control	★ ★ ★ ★
symbol PYGFX	22 points
up-market performance	good
down-market performance	very good
predictability of returns	excellent

Total Return   ★ ★ ★ ★ ★

Over the past five years, Payden & Rygel Global Fixed-Income R has taken $10,000 and turned it into $15,414 ($13,090 over three years). This translates into an average annual return of 9 percent over the past five years and 9 percent over the past three years. Over the past five years, this fund has outperformed 60 percent of all mutual funds; within its general category it has done better than 90 percent of its peers. World bond funds have averaged 6 percent annually over these same five years.

During the past five years, a $10,000 initial investment grew to $12,740 after taxes, assuming a 39.6 percent income tax bracket (state and federal combined) and a capital gains rate of 28 percent. This means that investors in this fund were able to preserve 86 percent of their total returns. Compared to other fixed-income funds, this fund's tax savings are considered to be very good.

Risk/Volatility   ★ ★ ★ ★ ★

Over the past five years, Payden & Rygel Global Fixed-Income R has been safer than 95 percent of all world bond funds. Over the past decade, the fund has had one negative year, while the Lehman Brothers Aggregate Bond Index has had one (off 3 percent in 1994); the Saloman Brothers World Government Bond Index fell twice (off 3 percent in 1989 and 4 percent in 1997). The fund has underperformed the Lehman Brothers Aggregate Bond Index three times and the Saloman Brothers World Government Bond Index four times in the last ten years.

	last 5 years		since inception	
worst year	-3%	1994	-3%	1994
best year	18%	1995	18%	1995

In the past, Payden & Rygel Global Fixed-Income R has done better than 55 percent of its peer group in up markets and outperformed 75 percent of its competition in down markets. Consistency, or predictability, of returns for Payden & Rygel Global Fixed-Income R can be described as excellent. This fund's risk-adjusted return is excellent.

Management   ★ ★ ★ ★ ★

There are twenty-two fixed-income securities in this $550 million portfolio. The average world bond fund today is $90 million in size. Close to 100 percent of the funds holdings are in bonds. The average maturity of the bonds in this account is nine years; the weighted coupon rate averages 6.7 percent. The portfolio's fixed-income holdings can be categorized as long-term, high-quality debt.

A team has managed this fund for the past seven years. There are seventeen funds besides Global Fixed-Income R within the Payden & Rygel family. Overall, the fund family's risk-adjusted performance can be described as fair.

Current Income   ★ ★ ★

Over the past year, Payden & Rygel Global Fixed-Income R had a twelve-month yield of 5.8 percent. During this same twelve-month period, the typical world bond fund had a yield that averaged 6.9 percent.

Expenses   ★ ★ ★ ★

Payden & Rygel Global Fixed-Income R's expense ratio is .5 percent; it has also averaged .5 percent annually over the past three calendar years. The average expense ratio for the funds in this category is 1.5 percent. This fund's turnover rate over the past year has been 223 percent, while its peer group average has been 260 percent.

Summary

Payden & Rygel Global Fixed-Income R is the most highly regarded global or foreign bond fund in the book. The portfolio has excellent three- and five-year risk-adjusted returns. Management is also rated superb. Over one-third of the fund's assets are in U.S. securities, German bonds make up just under one-third of the portfolio, while the U.K. represents the third largest position at 15 percent. Not only is this the best fund in its category, its overall score of 22 out of 25 possible points makes it one of the better mutual funds regardless of type or description.

Profile

minimum initial investment $5,000	IRA accounts available . . . . yes
subsequent minimum investment . $1,000	IRA minimum investment $2,000
available in all 50 states. . . . . yes	date of inception . . . . Sept. 1992
telephone exchanges. . . . . yes	dividend/income paid. . . . . monthly
number of other funds in family 17	average credit quality . . . . AAA

XII.
Summary

Aggressive Growth Funds (11)
1. Alger Capital Appreciation B
2. Baron Asset
3. Citizens Emerging Growth
4. Evergreen Omega A
5. Franklin Small Cap Growth A
6. Legg Mason Special Investment Trust—Primary Shares
7. Royce Total Return
8. Selected Special
9. Smith Barney Aggressive Growth A
10. United New Concepts A
11. Value Line Leveraged Growth Investors

Balanced Funds (10)
12. Flex-Funds Muirfield
13. Gabelli Westwood Balanced Fund—Retail Class
14. Invesco Total Return
15. Oppenheimer Quest Opportunity Value Fund A
16. Preferred Asset Allocation
17. Stagecoach Asset Allocation A
18. Value Line Asset Allocation
19. Vanguard Asset Allocation
20. Vanguard Balanced Index
21. Vanguard Wellington

Corporate Bond Funds (6)
22. Fremont Bond
23. Invesco Select Income
24. Lebenthal Taxable Municipal Bond
25. New England Bond Income A
26. Vanguard Long-Term Corporate Bond
27. Vanguard Preferred Stock

Global Equity Funds (8)
   28. Bartlett Europe A
   29. Capital World Growth & Income
   30. Idex JCC Global A
   31. Invesco European
   32. Janus Worldwide
   33. New Perspective
   34. Pioneer Europe A
   35. Vanguard European Stock Index

Government Bond Funds (5)
   36. Franklin U.S. Government Securities A
   37. Principal Government Securities Income A
   38. Vanguard GNMA
   39. Vanguard Intermediate-Term U.S. Treasury
   40. Vanguard Long-Term U.S. Treasury

Growth Funds (9)
   41. Enterprise Growth A
   42. Harbor Capital Appreciation
   43. Janus Mercury
   44. Legg Mason Value Trust—Primary Class
   45. Merger
   46. Spectra
   47. Vanguard Growth Index
   48. Vanguard U.S. Growth
   49. White Oak Growth Stock

Growth and Income Funds (11)
   50. Domini Social Equity
   51. Dreyfus Disciplined Stock
   52. Fidelity
   53. Gateway
   54. Pioneer A
   55. Schwab 1000 Investors
   56. Smith Breeden U.S. Equity Market Plus
   57. Vanguard 500 Index
   58. Vanguard Growth & Income
   59. Victory Diversified Stock A
   60. Washington Mutual Investors

High-Yield Funds (8)
   61. Fidelity Advisor High-Yield Fund T
   62. Franklin's AGE High Income A
   63. Invesco High-Yield
   64. Legg Mason High-Yield Portfolio Primary Shares

65. MainStay High-Yield Corporate Bond B
66. Northeast Investors
67. Seligman High-Yield Bond A
68. Vanguard High-Yield Corporate

Metals and Natural Resources Funds (4)
69. Franklin Gold A
70. Scudder Gold
71. State Street Research Global Resources A
72. Vanguard Energy

Money Market Funds (10)
73. Aetna Money Market Fund A
74. Dreyfus Basic Municipal Money Market
75. Freemont Money Market
76. JP Morgan Prime Money Market
77. Marshall Money Market Y
78. Monetta Government Money Market
79. Strong Money Market
80. USAA Tax Exempt Money Market
81. Vanguard Municipal Tax-Exempt Money Market
82. Zurich Money Government Money

Municipal Bond Funds (8)
83. Alliance Municipal Income CA A
84. Alliance Municipal Income National A
85. Calvert Tax-Free Reserves Limited-Term Portfolio A
86. Excelsior Long-Term Tax-Exempt
87. Smith Barney CA Municipals A
88. Strong High-Yield Municipal Bond
89. United Municipal High-Income A
90. Vanguard Short-Term Tax-Exempt

Utility Stock Funds (5)
91. Global Utility A
92. Merrill Lynch Global Utility B
93. MFS Utilities A
94. MSDW Utilities B
95. Strong American Utilities

World Bond Funds (5)
96. Alliance Global Dollar Government A
97. Capital World Bond
98. Goldman Sachs Global A
99. IDS Global Bond A
100. Payden & Rygel Global Fixed-Income R

Appendix A
Glossary of Mutual Fund Terms

Advisor—The individual or organization employed by a mutual fund to give professional advice on the fund's investments and asset management practices (also called the "investment advisor").

Asked or Offering Price—The price at which a mutual fund's shares can be purchased. The asked, or offering, price means the current net asset value per share plus sales charge, if any.

BARRA Growth Index—An index of 152 large-capitalization stocks that are all part of the S&P 500; specifically those with above-average sales and earnings growth.

BARRA Value Index—An index of 363 large-capitalization stocks that are all part of the S&P 500; specifically those with above-average dividend yields and relatively low prices considering their book values.

Bid or Sell Price—The price at which a mutual fund's shares are redeemed (bought back) by the fund. The bid or redemption price usually means the current net asset value per share.

Board Certified—Designation given to someone who has become certified in: insurance, estate planning, income taxes, securities, mutual funds, or financial planning. To obtain additional information about the board certified programs or to get the name of a board certified advisor in your area, call (800) 848-2029.

Bottom Up—Refers to a type of security analysis. Management that follows the bottom-up approach is more concerned with the company than with the economy in general. (For a contrasting style, see **Top Down.**)

Broker/Dealer—A firm that buys and sells mutual fund shares and other securities to the public.

Capital Gains Distributions—Payments to mutual fund shareholders of profits (long-term gains) realized on the sale of the fund's portfolio securities. These amounts are usually paid once a year.

Capital Growth—An increase in the market value of a mutual fund's securities, as reflected in the net asset value of fund shares. This is a specific long-term objective of many mutual funds.

Broker/Dealer—A firm that buys and sells mutual fund shares and other securities to the public.

Cash Reserves—Short-term, interest-bearing securities that can easily and quickly be converted to cash. Some funds keep cash levels at a minimum and always remain in stocks and/or bonds; other funds hold up to 25 percent or more of their assets in cash reserves (money market instruments) as either a defensive play or as a buying opportunity to be used when securities become depressed in price.

CFS—Also known as Certified Fund Specialist, this is the only designation awarded to brokers, financial planners, CPAs, insurance agents, and other investment advisors who either recommend or sell mutual funds. Fewer than 7,000 people across the country have passed this certification program. To obtain additional information about the CFS program or to get the name of a CFS in your area, call (800) 848-2029.

CPI—The Consumer Price Index (CPI) is the most commonly used yardstick for measuring the rate of inflation in the United States.

Custodian—The organization (usually a bank) that keeps custody of securities and other assets of a mutual fund.

Derivatives—A financial contract whose value is based on, or "derived," from a traditional security, such as a stock or bond. The most common examples of derivatives are futures contracts and options.

Diversification—The policy of all mutual funds to spread investments among a number of different securities in order to reduce the risk inherent in investing.

Dollar-Cost Averaging—The practice of investing equal amounts of money at regular intervals regardless of whether securities markets are moving up or down. This procedure reduces average share costs to the investor, who acquires more shares in the periods of lower securities prices and fewer shares in periods of higher prices.

EAFE—An equity index (EAFE stands for Europe, Australia, and the Far East) used to measure stock market performance outside of the United States. The EAFE is a sort of S&P 500 Index for overseas or foreign stocks. As of the middle of 1997, the EAFE was weighted as follows: 59.5% Europe, 28.8% Japan, 10.6% Pacific Rim, and 1.1% "other."

Exchange Privilege—An option enabling mutual fund shareholders to transfer their investment from one fund to another within the same fund family as their needs or objectives change. Typically, funds allow investors to use the exchange privilege several times a year for a low fee or no fee per exchange.

Expense Ratio—A figure expressed as a percentage of a fund's assets. The main element is the management fee. Administrative fees cover a fund's day-to-day operations, including printing materials, keeping records, paying staff, and renting office space. Sometimes administrative fees are included in the management fee; a number of funds list such fees separately. Roughly half of all funds charge a

12b-1 fee, which pays for a fund's distribution and advertising costs. The 12b-1 fee can be higher than the management or administrative fee.

Indexing—In contrast to the traditional approach to investing that tries to outperform market averages, index investing is a strategy that seeks to match the performance of a group of securities that form a recognized market measure, known as an index.

Investment Company—A corporation, trust, or partnership that invests pooled funds of shareholders in securities appropriate to the fund's objective. Among the benefits of investment companies, compared to direct investments, are professional management and diversification. Mutual funds (also known as open-ended and close-ended investment companies) are the most popular type of investment company.

Investment Objective—The goal that the investor and mutual fund pursue together (e.g., growth of capital or current income).

Large-Cap Stocks—Equities issued by companies with a net worth of at least $7.5 billion dollars.

Long-Term Funds—An industry designation for funds that invest primarily in securities with remaining maturities of more than one year. In this book the term means fifteen years or more. Long-term funds are broadly divided into bond and income funds.

Management Fee—The amount paid by a mutual fund to the investment advisor for its services. The average annual fee industrywide is about 0.7 percent of fund assets.

"Market-Neutral" Funds—A strategy that seeks to neutralize market movements by running two portfolios simultaneously—one buys stocks that are predicted to rise, and the other invests an equal amount in a similar assortment of other stocks that are predicted to decline.

Mid-Cap Stocks—Equities issued by companies with a net worth between $1 billion and $7.5 billion dollars.

Mutual Fund—An investment company that pools money from shareholders and invests in a variety of securities, including stocks, bonds, and money market instruments. A mutual fund stands ready to buy back (redeem) its shares at their current net asset value; this value depends on the market value of the fund's portfolio securities at the time of redemption. Most mutual funds continuously offer new shares to investors.

Net Asset Value Per Share—The market worth of one share of a mutual fund. This figure is derived by taking a fund's total assets—securities, cash, and any accrued earnings—deducting liabilities, and dividing by the number of shares outstanding.

No-Load Fund—A mutual fund selling its shares at net asset value without the addition of sales charges.

Passive Management—A portfolio that tries to match the performance of a target index, such as the S&P 500.

Portfolio—A collection of securities owned by an individual or an institution (such as a mutual fund). A fund's portfolio may include a combination of stocks, bonds, and money market securities.

Portfolio Diversification—The average U.S. stock fund has about 30 percent of its assets invested in its ten largest holdings.

Prospectus—The official booklet that describes a mutual fund, which must be furnished to all investors. It contains information required by the U.S. Securities and Exchange Commission on such subjects as the fund's investment objectives, services, and fees. A more detailed document, known as "Part B" of the prospectus or the "Statement of Additional Information," is available at no charge upon request.

Redemption Price—The amount per share (shown as the "bid" in newspaper tables) that mutual fund shareholders receive when they cash in the shares. The value of the shares depends on the market value of the fund's portfolio securities at the time. This value is the same as net asset value per share.

Reinvestment Privilege—An option available to mutual fund shareholders in which fund dividends and capital gains distributions are automatically turned back into the fund to buy new shares, without charge (meaning no sales fee or commission), thereby increasing holdings.

Russell 2000—An index that represents 2,000 small domestic companies (less than 8 percent of the U.S. equity market).

Sales Charge—An amount charged to purchase shares in many mutual funds sold by brokers or other sales agents. The maximum charge is 8.5 percent of the initial investment; the vast majority of funds now have a maximum charge of 4.75 percent or less. The charge is added to the net asset value per share when determining the offering price.

Short-Term Funds—An industry designation for funds that invest primarily in securities with maturities of less than one year; the term means five years or less in this book. Short-term funds include money market funds and certain municipal bond funds.

Small-Cap Stocks—Equities issued by companies with a net worth of less than $1 billion.

Top Down—Refers to a type of security analysis. Management that follows the top-down approach is very concerned with the general level of the economy and any fiscal policy being followed by the government.

Turnover—The percentage of a fund's portfolio that is sold during the year, a percentage rate that can range from 0 to 300 percent or more. The average turnover rate for U.S. stock funds is approximately 80 percent (10 percent for domestic stock index funds).

Transfer Agent—The organization employed by a mutual fund to prepare and maintain records relating to the accounts of its shareholders. Some funds serve as their own transfer agents.

12b-1 Fee—The distribution fee charged by some funds, named after a federal government rule. Such fees pay for marketing costs, such as advertising and dealer compensation. The fund's prospectus outlines 12b-1 fees, if applicable.

Underwriter—The organization that acts as the distributor of a mutual fund's shares to broker/dealers and investors.

Value Stocks—Stocks that most investors view as unattractive for some reason. They tend to be priced low relative to some measure of the company's worth, such as earnings, book value, or cash flow. Value stock managers try to identify companies whose prices are depressed for temporary reasons that may bounce back strongly if investor sentiment improves.

■ ■ ■

The Securities Act of 1933 requires a fund's shares to be registered with the Securities and Exchange Commission (SEC) prior to their sale. In essence, the Securities Act ensures that the fund provides potential investors with a current prospectus. This law also limits the types of advertisements that may be used by a mutual fund.

The Securities Exchange Act of 1934 regulates the purchase and sale of all types of securities, including mutual fund shares.

The Investment Advisors Act of 1940 is a body of law that regulates certain activities of the investment advisors to mutual funds.

The Investment Company Act of 1940 is a highly detailed regulatory statute applying to mutual fund companies. This act contains numerous provisions designed to prevent self-dealing by employees of the mutual fund company, as well as other conflicts of interest. It also provides for the safekeeping of fund assets and prohibits the payment of excessive fees and charges by the fund and its shareholders.

Appendix B
Who Regulates Mutual Funds?

Mutual funds are highly regulated businesses that must comply with some of the toughest laws and rules in the financial services industry. All funds are regulated by the U.S. Securities and Exchange Commission (SEC). With its extensive rule-making and enforcement authority, the SEC oversees mutual fund compliance chiefly by relying on the four major federal securities statutes mentioned in Appendix A.

Fund assets must generally be held by an independent custodian. There are strict requirements for fidelity bonding to ensure against the misappropriation of shareholder monies. In addition to federal statutes, almost every state has its own set of regulations governing mutual funds.

Although federal and state laws cannot guarantee that a fund will be profitable, they are designed to ensure that all mutual funds are operated and managed in the interests of their shareholders. Here are some specific investor protections that every fund must follow:

- Regulations concerning what may be claimed or promised about a mutual fund and its potential
- Requirements that vital information about a fund be made readily available (such as a prospectus, the "Statement of Additional Information," also known as "Part B" of the prospectus, and annual and semiannual reports)
- Requirements that a fund operate in the interest of its shareholders, rather than any special interests of its management
- Rules dictating diversification of the fund's portfolio over a wide range of investments to avoid too much concentration in a particular security

Appendix C
Dollar-Cost Averaging

Investors often believe that the market will go down as soon as they get in. For these people, and anyone concerned with reducing risk, the solution is dollar-cost averaging.

Dollar-cost averaging is a simple yet effective way to reduce risk, whether you are investing in stocks or bonds. The premise behind dollar-cost averaging (DCA) is that if several purchases of a fund are made over an extended period of time, the unpredictable highs and lows will average out. The investor ends up with buying some shares at a comparatively low price, others at perhaps a much higher price.

DCA assumes that investors are willing to sacrifice the possibility of having bought all of their shares at the lowest price in return for knowing that they did not also buy every share at the highest price. In short, we are willing to accept a compromise—a sort of *risk-adjusted* decision.

DCA is based on investing a fixed amount of money in a given fund at specific intervals. Typically, an investor will add a few hundred dollars at the beginning of each month into the XYZ mutual fund. DCA works best if you invest and continue to invest on an established schedule, *regardless of price fluctuations*. You will be buying more shares when the price is down than when it is up. Most investors do not mind buying shares when prices are increasing, since this means that their existing shares are also going up. When this program is followed, losses during market declines are limited, while the ability to participate in good markets is maintained.

Another advantage of DCA is that it increases the likelihood that you will follow an investment program. As with other aspects of our life, it is important to have goals. However, DCA is not something that should be universally recommended. Your risk level determines whether you should use dollar-cost averaging.

From its beginnings well over one hundred years ago, there has been an upward bias in the performance of the stock market. More often than not, the market goes up, not down. Therefore, it hardly makes sense to apply dollar-cost averaging to an investment vehicle, knowing that historically one would be paying a higher and higher price per share over time.

Studies done by the Institute of Business & Finance (800-848-2029) show that over the past fifty years, a dollar-cost averaging program produced inferior returns compared to a lump-sum investment. The institute's studies conclude the following: (1) a DCA program is a good idea for a conservative investor (the person or couple who gives more weight or importance to risk than reward); (2) for investor's whose risk level is anything but conservative, an immediate, one-time investment resulted in better returns the great majority of the time; and (3) there have certainly been periods of time when a DCA program would have benefitted even the extremely aggressive investor, but such periods have not been very common over the past half century and have been quite rare over the past twenty, fifteen, ten, five, and three years.

Example of Dollar-Cost Averaging
($1,000 invested per period)

Period (1)	Cost per share (2)	Number of shares bought with $1,000 (3)	Total shares owned (4)	Total amount invested (5)	Current value of shares (2) x (4) (6)	Net gain or loss (percentage) (6) x (5) (7)
1	$100	10.0	10.0	$1,000	$1,000	0
2	$80	12.5	22.5	$2,000	$1,800	−10.0%
3	$70	14.3	36.8	$3,000	$2,576	−14.1%
4	$60	16.7	53.5	$4,000	$3,210	−19.7%
5	$50	20.0	73.5	$5,000	$3,675	−26.5%
6	$70	14.3	87.8	$6,000	$6,146	+2.4%
7	$80	12.5	100.3	$7,000	$8,024	+14.6%
8	$100	10.0	110.3	$8,000	$11,030	+37.9%

Appendix D
Systematic Withdrawal Plan

A systematic withdrawal plan (SWP) allows you to have a check for a specified amount sent monthly or quarterly to you, or anyone you designate, from your mutual fund account. There is no charge for this service.

This method of getting monthly checks is ideal for the income-oriented investor. It is also a risk reduction technique—a kind of dollar-cost averaging in reverse. A set amount is sent to you each month. In order to send you a check for a set amount, shares of one or more of your mutual funds must be sold, which, in turn, will most likely trigger a taxable event, but only for those shares redeemed.

When the market is low, the number of mutual fund shares being liquidated will be higher than when the market is high, since the fund's price per share will be lower. If you need $500 a month and the fund's price is $25.00 per share, twenty shares must be liquidated; if the price per share is $20.00 per share, twenty-five shares must be sold.

Shown below is an example of a SWP from the Investment Company of America (ICA), a conservative growth and income fund featured in previous editions of this book. The example assumes an initial investment of $100,000 in the fund at its inception, the beginning of 1934. A greater or smaller dollar amount could be used. The example shows what happens to the investor's principal over a sixty-six-year period (Jan. 1, 1934 through May 31, 1999). It assumes that $10,000 is withdrawn from the fund at the end of the first year. At the end of the first year, the $10,000 withdrawal *is increased by 4 percent each year thereafter* to offset the effects of inflation, which averaged less than 4 percent during this sixty-six-year period. This means that the withdrawal for the second year was $10,400 ($10,000 multiplied by 1.04), for the third year $10,816 ($10,400 x 1.04), and so on.

Compare this example to what would have happened if the money had been placed in an average fixed-income account at a bank. The $100,000 depositor who took out only $9,000 each year would be in a far different situation. His (or her) original $100,000 was fully depleted by the end of 1948. All the principal and interest payments could not keep up with an annual withdrawal of $9,000.

The difference between ICA and the savings account is over $8.1 million. The savings account had a total return of $26,300 (plus distribution of the original $100,000 principal); the ICA account had a total return of $6,012,000 ($2,950,000 distributed over sixty-six years plus a remaining principal, or account balance, of $5,353,000). This difference becomes even more disturbing when you consider that the bank depositor's withdrawals were not increasing each year to offset the effects of inflation. The interest rates used in this example came from the *U.S. Savings & Loan League Fact Book.*

SWP from The Investment Company of America (ICA)
initial investment: $100,000
annual withdrawals of: $10,000 (10%)
the first check is sent: 12/31/34
withdrawals annually increased by: 4%

date	amount withdrawn	value of remaining shares
12/31/34	$10,000	$109,000
12/31/35	$10,400	$185,000
12/31/40	$12,700	$151,000
12/31/45	$15,400	$241,000
12/31/50	$18,700	$204,000
12/31/55	$22,800	$354,000
12/31/60	$27,700	$431,000
12/31/65	$33,700	$612,000
12/31/70	$41,000	$649,000
12/31/75	$50,000	$552,000
12/31/80	$60,700	$762,000
12/31/85	$73,900	$1,225,000
12/31/86	$76,900	$1,415,000
12/31/87	$79,900	$1,411,000
12/31/88	$83,100	$1,515,000
12/31/89	$86,500	$1,872,000
12/31/90	$89,900	$1,794,000
12/31/91	$93,500	$2,170,000
12/31/92	$86,500	$2,224,000
12/31/93	$101,200	$2,379,000
12/31/94	$105,200	$2,277,000
12/31/95	$109,400	$2,865,000
12/31/96	$113,780	$3,900,000
12/31/97	$118,330	$4,200,000
12/31/98	$123,060	$4,995,000
5/31/99	————	$5,353,000

If the ICA systematic withdrawal plan were 8 percent annually instead of 10 percent (but still increased by 4 percent each year to offset the effects of inflation), the investor would have ended up with remaining shares worth $89.6 million, plus withdrawals that totaled $2.36 million.

Next time some broker or banker tells you that you should be buying bonds or CDs for current income, tell them about a systematic withdrawal plan (SWP), a program designed to maximize your income and offset something the CD, T-bill, and bond advocates never mention: inflation.

Appendix E
Load or No-Load—Which is Right for You?

As the amount of information available on mutual funds continues to grow almost exponentially, the load versus no-load debate has intensified. What makes the issue difficult to evaluate is the continued absence of neutrality on either side. Before you learn the real truth, let us first examine who is advocating what, what their biases are, and how each side argues its point.

A number of publications, including *Money, Forbes, Fortune, Kiplinger Personal Investor*, and *Business Week*, favor the no-load camp. Although these publications appear neutral, they are not. First, each one derives the overwhelming majority of its mutual fund advertisements from funds that charge no commission. Second, all of these publications are trying to increase readership; they are in the business of selling copy, not information. A good way to increase or maintain a healthy circulation is by having their readership rely on them for advice instead of going to a broker or investment advisor.

On the other side is the financial services industry, whose most vocal load supporters include the brokerage, banking, and insurance industries. That's not much of a surprise. These groups are also biased. Like the publication that only makes money by getting you to purchase a copy or having an editorial board whose policy favors no-load funds, much of the financial services community supports a sales charge because that is how they are compensated.

No-load proponents argue that a fund that charges any kind of commission or ongoing marketing fee (which is known as a 12b-1 charge) inherently cannot be as good as a similar investment that has no entry or exit fee or ongoing 12b-1 charge. On its surface, this argument appears logical. After all, if one investor starts off with a dollar invested and the other starts off with somewhere between 99 and 92 cents (commissions range from 1 to 8.5 percent; most are in the 3 to 5 percent range), all other things being equal, the person who has all of his money working for him will do better than someone who has an initial deduction. The press and the no-load funds say that there is no reason to pay a commission because you can do as well or better than the broker or advisor whose job it is to provide you with suggestions and guidance.

The commission-oriented community says you should pay a sales charge because you get what you pay for—good advice and ongoing service. After all, brokers, financial planners, banks that include mutual fund desks, and insurance agents are all highly trained professionals who know things you do not. Moreover, they study the markets on a continuous basis, ensuring that they have more information than any weekend investor. In short, they ask, do you want someone managing your money who has experience and works full-time in this area, or someone such as yourself who has no formal training and whose time and resources are limited?

There is no clear-cut solution. Valid points are raised by both sides. To gain more insight into what course of action (or type of fund) is best for you, let us take a neutral approach. I believe I can give you valid reasons why both kinds of funds make sense, because I have no hidden agenda. True, I am a licensed broker and branch manager of a national securities firm; however, it is also true that the great majority of my compensation is based on a fee for service, meaning that clients who invest solely in no-load funds pay me an annual management fee.

First, you should never pay a commission to someone who knows no more about investing than you do. There is no value added in such a situation, except perhaps during uncertain or negative periods in the market. (This point will be discussed later.) After all, if your broker's advice and mutual fund experience are based solely on the same financial publications you have access to, you are not getting your money's worth by paying a sales charge. I raise this point first because the financial services industry is filled with a tremendous number of inexperienced and ignorant brokers. These people may make a lot of money, but this is usually the result of their connections (they know a lot of people) or marketing skills (they know how to get new business)—neither of which have anything to do with investment knowledge.

Brokerage firms, banks, and insurance companies hire stockbrokers based on their sales ability, not their knowledge or analytical ability. The financial analysts at the home office are the ones involved in research and managing money. The fact that your broker has a couple of dozen years' experience in the securities industry or is a vice president may actually be hazardous to your financial health. Extensive experience could mean that the advisor is less inclined to learn about new products or studies because he already has an established client base. Brokers obtain titles such as "vice president" because they outsell their peers. Contests (awards, trips, prizes, and enhanced payouts) are based on how much is sold, period. There has never been an instance of a brokerage firm, bank, or insurance company giving an award to someone based on knowledge or how well a client's account performed.

Second, if your investment time horizon is less than a couple of years, it is a mistake to pay anything more than a nominal fee, something in the 1 percent range. Even though the advice you are receiving may be great, it is hard to justify a 3 to 5 percent commission over the short haul. Sales charges in this range can only be rationalized if they can be amortized over a number of years. Thus, worthwhile advice becomes a bargain if you stay with the investment or within the same family of mutual funds for at least three years.

Third, if you are purchasing a fund that charges a fee, find out what you are getting for your money. Question the advisor; find out about his or her training, experience, education, and designations. Equally important, get a clear understanding as to what you will be receiving on an ongoing basis. What kind of continuing education does the broker engage in (attending conferences, reading books, seeking a designation, and so forth)? Finally, make sure your advisor or broker tells you how your investments will be monitored. It is important to know how often you will be contacted and how a buy, hold, or sell decision will be made.

So far, it looks as if I've been pretty tough on my fellow brokers. Well, believe me, I'm even harder on about 99 percent of those do-it-yourself investors. I have been in this business for close to twenty years, and I can tell you that I have rarely met an investor who was better off on his or her own. Here's why.

First, it is extremely difficult to be objective about your own investments. Decisions based on what you have read from a newsletter or magazine or what you learned at a seminar are often a response to current news, such as trade relations with Japan, the value of the U.S. dollar, the state of the economy, or the direction of interest rates. This kind of knee-jerk reaction has proven to be wrong in most cases.

Mind you, out of fairness to those who manage their own investments, amateurs aren't the only ones who make investment errors. As an example, the majority of the major brokerage firms gave a sell signal just before the war in the Persian Gulf. It turned out that this would have been about the perfect time to buy. E.F. Hutton was forced to merge with another brokerage firm because they incorrectly predicted the direction of interest rates (and lost tens of millions of dollars in their own portfolio).

The mutual fund industry itself deserves a healthy part of the blame, as evidenced by their timing of new funds. Take my advice: When you see a number of new mutual funds coming out with the same timely theme (government plus or optioned-enhanced bond funds in the mid-eighties, Eastern European funds after German reunification, health care funds a few years ago, derivatives and hedge funds last year), run for cover. By the time these funds come out, the party is about to end. Investors who got into these funds often do well for a number of months but soon face devastating declines.

Your favorite financial publications are also to blame. Their advice is based on a herd instinct: What do our readers think? Instead of providing leadership, they simply reinforce what is most likely incorrect information. For example, for over a year after the 1987 stock market crash, the most popular of these mainstream publications, *Money*, had cover stories that recommended (and extolled the virtues of) safe investments. For almost a year and a half after the crash, this magazine was giving out bad advice. When something goes on sale (stocks, in this case) you should be a buyer, not a seller. Since *Money* routinely surveys (or polls) their readers for feature articles, such behavior (the herd instinct) is understandable but not forgivable.

Besides the lack of objectivity and the constant bombardment of what I call "daily noise" (what the market is doing at the moment, comments from the financial gurus, etc.), there is also the question of your competence. Presumably, you and I could figure out how to fix our own plumbing, sew our own clothes, fix the car when it breaks down, or avoid paying a lawyer by purchasing "do-it-yourself" books. The question then becomes whether it is worth going through the learning curve and, even supposing we are successful, whether the task would have been better accomplished by someone else—perhaps for less money or better use of our own time. I think the answer is obvious. Each of us has our own area or areas of expertise or skill. You and I rely on others either because they know more than we do about the topic or task at hand or because having someone else help is a more efficient use of our time.

If you're going to seek the services of an investment advisor or broker, it should be because he or she knows more than you do, because he or she is more objective, or because you can make more money doing whatever you do than in taking the time to make complex investment decisions yourself. This is what makes sense. The fact that there are brokers and advisors who put their interests before yours is simply a reality that you must deal with. And the proper way to deal with these conflicts of interest or ignorant counselors is by doing your homework. Ask questions. Just as there are great plumbers, mechanics, lawyers, and doctors, so too are there exceptional investment advisors and brokers. Your job is to find them.

Eliminating load or no-load funds from your investing universe is not the answer. If you are determined never to pay a commission, then you may miss out on the next John Templeton (the Franklin-Templeton family of funds), Peter Lynch (Fidelity Magellan Fund), or Jean-Marie Eveillard (SoGen Funds). You will also miss out on some of the very best mutual fund families: American Funds (large), Fidelity-Advisor (medium), and SoGen (small). A better way to proceed is to try to separate good funds from bad ones. After all, an investor is clearly far better off in a good load fund than in a bad no-load one.

The bottom line is that performance, as well as *risk-adjusted returns*, for load funds often exceeds the returns on no-load funds, and vice versa. The "top ten" list (or whatever number you want to use) for one period may have been dominated by funds that charge a commission, but in just a year or two the top ten list may be heavily populated by mutual funds with no sales charge or commission.

It might seem strange to be questioning the benefits of financial planning when our society places professions like law and accountancy in such high regard. And certainly I am not suggesting that investors should consider only load funds. But with all the load-fund bashing in recent years, it is important to recognize that no-load funds are not the perfect answer for a large percentage of investors. Approaching the mutual fund industry with an us versus them mentality results in a great deal of misleading information and unfairly discredits the work of skilled financial planners and brokers.

Appendix F
The Best and Worst Days

Many would-be stock investors fear investing at the wrong time—when market prices are *highest*. Suppose you invested $10,000 in the Standard & Poor's 500 Stock Index every year for the last twenty years on the day the market peaked. How much would your total investment of $100,000 be worth versus an investment made each year when prices were *lowest*? The results may surprise you.

Month of Market High	Cumulative Investment	Value of Acct. on 12/31	Month of Market Low	Cumulative Investment	Value of Acct. on 12/31
10/5/79	$10,000	$9,835	11/7/79	$10,000	$10,957
11/20/80	20,000	22,808	4/21/80	20,000	28,635
4/27/81	30,000	31,117	9/25/81	30,000	38,415
12/27/82	40,000	47,820	8/12/82	40,000	60,774
11/29/83	50,000	68,489	1/3/83	50,000	86,872
1/6/84	60,000	83,098	7/24/84	60,000	103,849
12/16/85	70,000	119,453	1/4/85	70,000	150,161
12/2/86	80,000	151,306	1/22/86	80,000	190,431
8/25/87	90,000	166,596	10/19/87	90,000	211,382
10/21/88	100,000	203,957	1/20/88	100,000	258,117
10/9/89	110,000	278,288	1/3/89	110,000	352,929
7/16/90	120,000	278,744	10/11/90	120,000	353,218
12/31/91	130,000	373,302	1/9/91	130,000	474,187
6/1/92	140,000	412,381	10/9/92	140,000	521,159
12/29/93	150,000	463,738	1/20/93	150,000	584,516
1/31/94	160,000	479,851	4/4/94	160,000	603,147
12/13/95	170,000	669,494	1/30/95	170,000	842,467
12/27/96	180,000	832,645	1/10/96	180,000	1,048,039
8/6/97	190,000	1,120,234	4/11/97	190,000	1,410,522
11/23/98	$200,000	1,450,111	8/31/98	$200,000	1,825,749

As you can see, even if you had the worst luck in the world, by investing $10,000 at the high point of the market each year (meaning you had the worst possible luck), you would still end up with $1,450,111 after twenty years. This is not as good as having perfect timing (buying at the market low each year), but the difference is certainly not as great as one might first suspect. Perfect timing resulted in an average annual rate of return of 19.1 percent over each of the past twenty years. Investing on each of the worst possible days still resulted in an average annual rate of return of 17.5 percent.

Appendix G
Investing in the Face of Fear

What do you do when the market declines? When the Iraqis invaded Kuwait, the market retreated from fears of rising interest rates and inflation. The Dow Jones Industrial Average (DJIA) had reached a new high on July 16, 1990 at 2999.75 and by August 22, 1990 had fallen to 2560—a decline of almost 15 percent. For some insight on how to respond to a drop in the market, let us look back at the first Arab oil embargo in 1973. Oil prices tripled, as did the Consumer Price Index and interest rates. And the DJIA fell from 947 on September 30, 1973, to 616 on December 31, 1974, a drop of 35 percent.

Suppose you had placed $10,000 in AIM Weingarten Fund (a fund featured in a previous edition of this book) on September 30, 1973. By December 31, 1974, your investment had dropped in value to $5,725—a decrease of 43 percent. What would you have done with your shares, and how would you have fared?

Let's look at several scenarios:
1. Sell now! Take the loss and put the money in a bank certificate of deposit.
2. Wait until the mutual fund breaks even, then sell it, and put the money in a certificate of deposit.
3. Hold on to your shares. It was a long-term investment, and time will win out.
4. Invest an additional $10,000 in Weingarten, capitalizing on the opportunity to buy more shares at a lower price.

Which scenario did you choose?
1. If you sold your AIM Weingarten Fund shares on December 31, 1974 in reaction to the declining market and placed the remaining money in a bank CD, your investment as of June 30, 1999 would have been worth (depending on the interest rate): $23,180 at 6 percent, $29,034 at 7 percent, and $36,321 at 8 percent.
2. If you had waited for Weingarten's value to return to $10,000, sold the shares on December 31, 1977, and then placed the money in a bank CD, the $10,000 as of June 30, 1999 would have been worth: $34,001 at 6 percent, $41,411 at 7 percent, and $50,342 at 8 percent.
3. If you had sat tight and left your money in the fund, your $10,000 would have been worth $584,973 as of July 31, 1999.

4(a). If you had an additional $10,000 to invest in Weingarten on December 31, 1974, your $20,000 total investment would have been worth $1,550,659 as of July 31, 1999.

4(b). Assuming you did not have another $10,000 lump sum to place in Weingarten, but started investing $100 each month beginning December 31, 1974, your total investment of $32,300 would have been worth $1,110,628 as of July 31, 1999.

Did you end up with $23,180, $34,001, $584,973, $1,550,659 or $1,110,628? Smart money does not panic! When confidence is low and emotion is high, there are opportunities for the smart investor.

Appendix H
U.S. Compared to Foreign Markets

Investing worldwide gives you exposure to different stages of economic market cycles—which has given international investors an advantage in the past. Foreign equities and bonds have generally offered higher levels of short-, intermediate-, and long-term growth than their domestic counterparts. Not once during the past twelve years was the U.S. stock market the world's top performer.

Top-Performing World Stock Markets: An Twelve-year Review: 1987–1998

year	1st	2nd	3rd	4th	5th
1998	Finland 121%	Belgium 68%	Italty 52%	Spain 50%	France 42%
1997	Portugal 47%	Switzerland 45%	Italty 36%	Denmark 35%	USA + 34%
1996	Spain 37%	Sweden 35%	Finland 32%	Hong Kong 29%	Ireland 29%
1995	Switzerland 44%	USA 37%	Sweden 33%	Spain 30%	Netherlands 28%
1994	Finland 52%	Norway 24%	Japan 22%	Sweden 19%	Ireland 15%
1993	Malaysia 114%	Hong Kong 110%	Finland 101%	Singapore 62%	Ireland 60%
1992	Hong Kong 37%	Switzerland 17%	USA 6%	Singapore 6%	France 3%
1991	Hong Kong 43%	Australia 39%	USA 30%	Singapore 23%	France 16%
1990	United Kingdom 6%	Austria 5%	Hong Kong 4%	Norway (1%)	Denmark (2%)
1989	Austria 105%	Germany 49%	Norway 46%	Denmark 45%	Singapore 42%
1988	Belgium 54%	Denmark 53%	Sweden 48%	Norway 42%	France 38%
1987	Japan 43%	Spain 41%	United Kingdom 35%	Canada 14%	Denmark 13%

The U.S. stock market has ranked among the five top performers only four times in the past eleven years. During this same period, the U.S. bond market has never claimed the number one spot against other world markets.

Global Market Performance

Twenty years ago, the U.S. represented 57 percent of the world's stock market capitalization; today, that figure has dropped to 43 percent—although the size of the pie is substantially bigger. By limiting a portfolio to just U.S. stocks, an investor would be ignoring: (1) ten of the world's ten largest real estate companies; (2) nine of the world's ten largest construction and housing companies; (3) eight of the world's largest electrical and electronics companies; (4) eight of the world's largest insurance companies; and (5) seven of the world's largest automobile companies.

The table below shows the average annual total returns, in U.S. dollars, of many of the world's major equity markets for the ten-year period ending December 31, 1997.

country	returns	country	returns
Netherlands	19.8%	United Kingdom	14.0%
Switzerland	19.4%	France	13.9%
Hong Kong	19.2%	Spain	11.6%
United States	**19.4%**	Singapore	10.7%
Sweden	18.4%	Australia	10.6%
Belgium	15.7%	Canada	10.0%
Germany	14.3%	Italy	7.0%

Appendix I
The Power of Dividends

The table below shows how important common stock dividends can be. The figures assume a one-time investment of $100,000 in the S&P 500 at the beginning of 1977. The table shows that dividends have increased for each of the past twenty-three years.

Viewed from a different perspective, if you were strictly income-oriented and invested $100,000 in the S&P 500 at the beginning of 1977, you would have received a 4.3 percent return on your investment ($4,310 divided by $100,000). For the 1997 calendar year, this same investment returned 31.9 percent for the year ($31,934 divided by $100,000); for 1998 the figure increases to 39.5 percent ($39,495 divided by $100,000). These figures assume that dividends received each year were spent and not reinvested. Moreover, these numbers do not include the over *twenty-four-fold* growth of capital (the original $100,000 grew to $2,495,000 without dividends) that also took place.

As a point of comparison for the figures described in the previous paragraph, consider what would have happened if the same investor had invested in a twenty-three-year U.S. government bond in 1977. By the end of 1998, twenty-three years later, the original $100,000 worth of bonds would have matured and had an ending value of $100,000. Additionally, the investor would have received approximately 7 percent for each of these twenty-three years—a far cry from the increased dividend stream and capital appreciation the S&P 500 experienced over the same period. Perhaps more important, the bond investor could have taken his $100,000 at the beginning of 1999 and invested the money for another twenty to thirty years, getting a 5.4 percent return for each of those years (versus the S&P 500 investor who just finished receiving over 39.5 percent, based on $100,000, and presumably will be receiving even greater dividend returns for each or most of the next twenty years).

Annual Dividends from $100,000 Invested in the S&P 500

year	S&P 500 dividend	year	S&P 500 dividend
1977	$4,310	1988	$16,017
1978	$4,946	1989	$17,275
1979	$5,647	1990	$19,824
1980	$9,798	1991	$21,824
1981	$7,564	1992	$22,598
1982	$8,112	1993	$22,725
1983	$8,955	1994	$24,906
1984	$10,005	1995	$26,039
1985	$11,893	1996	$31,234
1986	$11,523	1997	$31,934
1987	$13,286	1998	$39,495

Appendix J
Growth Stocks vs. Value Stocks

Throughout the different equity sections (e.g., growth, growth and income, global equity, etc.), the end of each stock fund's "Management" paragraph often mentions whether the fund manager seeks out "growth" or "value" issues. The differences and possible consequences of these two forms of equity selection are shown in the table below.

Value means that the stocks are inexpensive relative to their earnings potential. *Growth* refers to stocks of companies whose earnings per share are expected to grow significantly faster than the market average.

As you can see by the table, the performance of these two types of stocks can vary from year to year. On a monthly or quarterly basis, the difference is often much more significant than on an annual basis.

The table below shows performance of the S&P Barra Value Index and the S&P Barra Growth Index (dividends reinvested in both indexes). Over the past thirteen plus years, an investment in both growth stocks and value stocks would have been less volatile than an investment in only one equity style.

Year	Growth Stocks	Value Stocks
1985	33.3%	29.7%
1986	14.5%	21.7%
1987	6.5%	3.7%
1988	12.0%	21.7%
1989	36.0%	26.1%
1990	0.2%	−6.9%
1991	38.4%	22.6%
1992	5.1%	10.5%
1993	1.7%	18.6%
1994	3.1%	−0.6%
1995	38.1%	37.0%
1996	24.0%	22.0%
1997	36.5%	30.0%
1998	42.2%	14.7%
1999 (1st qtr.)	6.9%	2.9%

Source: S&P 500 Barra Value Index and the S&P 500 Barra Growth Index.

The table below shows the annualized returns of growth versus value funds, as categorized by Morningstar.

Total Returns through 3/31/99

mutual fund category	3 year	5 year	10 year
large growth	26.3%	23.2%	18.1%
large value	17.9%	18.8%	14.9%
mid-cap growth	14.2%	16.6%	15.2%
mid-cap value	12.7%	14.4%	12.4%
small growth	7.7%	12.0%	13.9%
small value	8.1%	10.5%	10.3%

Appendix K
Stock Volatility in Perspective

As of the middle of 1999, U.S. households held over to $30 trillion in financial assets, which represents an 120 percent increase from $13.8 trillion at year-end 1991. Currently, stocks comprise about 45 percent of household financial assets, up from earlier this decade but still below the level seen in the early 1970s, when interest rates were at comparable levels. And, although there have certainly been quite a few negative years for stocks during the twentieth century, the number of really bad years has been modest (as shown in the following table).

Since 1900, U.S. stocks have had thirty-one down years, averaging a negative 13.4 percent return per year—but the sixty-eight positive years have averaged over 23 percent annually. Furthermore, the market has had back-to-back negative years only once since World War II.

U.S. Stocks: The Bad Years from 1900 to 1997

up to a 5% loss		5–10% loss		10–25% loss		more than a 25% loss	
1939	−0.4%	1914	−5.11%	1966	−10.1%	1974	−26.5%
1953	−1.0	1977	−7.2	1913	−10.3	1920	−32.9
1934	−1.4	1946	−8.1	1957	−10.8	1937	−35.0
1906	−1.9	1932	−8.2	1941	−11.6	1907	−37.7
1990	−3.2	1929	−8.4	1973	−14.7	1931	−43.3
1923	−3.3	1969	−8.5	1910	−17.9		
1916	−4.2	1901	−8.7	1917	−21.7		
1981	−4.9	1962	−8.7	1903	−23.6		
		1940	−9.8	1930	−24.9		

Since 1900 there have been fifty-five occasions (not necessarily calendar years) when stocks have "corrected"—meaning that they fell by 10 percent or more from their most recent peak. In the past forty years, there have been fourteen bear markets—drops of 15 percent or more. The average duration of these fourteen bear markets has been just eight months; in most cases, the market fully recovered in less than one year (the average recovery period was thirteen months).

Sometimes the question is asked, "If the stock market is going down (or "expected" to go down in the near future), why not sit on the sidelines until it passes?" The reason you do not want to try and time the stock market is that missing out on just a few good days can make a tremendous difference to a portfolio's performance. According to a study by the University of Michigan, an investor who was on the sidelines during the best 1.2 percent of all trading days from 1963 to 1998 missed 95 percent of the market's gains.

Appendix L
Does Foreign Diversification Really Reduce Risk?

As you can see by the table below, whether you are looking at a purely U.S. portfolio (the S&P 500) or one that has 30 percent of its holdings in foreign stocks (as measured by the EAFE Index), being "global" has done little to enhance returns or reduce risk. The best case for a global portfolio under the heading "average annual return" shows only a 0.2 percent advantage for the more diversified portfolio (100 percent stocks). Looking at the "largest one-year gain," the best one-year period for a global portfolio was a portfolio that was evenly divided between stocks and bonds (25.0 percent for United States versus 27.3 percent for global).

Looking at risk reduction over all one-year calendar periods over the past twenty-five years (ending 12/31/96), the "best" global portfolio only reduced the loss by just 0.6 percent (100 percent stock). Looking back at the October 19, 1987 stock market crash, one of the few benefits of owning foreign stocks was that each country bounced back at different times; Japanese stocks took just over a year to recover while U.S. stocks took nineteen months. **Evidence suggests that a rising market is local, while a declining market is global. A large decline in U.S. stocks has frequently caused a big loss in foreign markets.**

During the 1973–74 bear market, the biggest cumulative loss U.S. stocks have suffered since the Great Depression, the S&P 500 dropped 14.7 percent in 1973 and 26.4 percent in 1974. The EAFE (Europe, Australia, Far East) Index fell 14.2 percent in 1973 and 22.2 percent in 1974.

By owning just domestic companies, U.S. investors may already be getting quite a bit of international diversification: about 80 percent of Coca-Cola's and McDonald's profits come from its foreign operations.

The table below covers the twenty-five-year period ending 12/31/96 (all figures are in U.S. dollars).

allocation	average annual return	largest 1-year gain	largest 1-year loss
100% stock	13.7% USA	41.9% USA	−24.5% USA
	3.9% global	40.3% global	−23.9% global
90% stocks/10% bonds	13.3% USA	38.4% USA	−21.4% USA
	13.4% global	37.0% global	−20.8% global
80% stocks/20% bonds	12.8% USA	35.0% USA	−18.3% USA
	12.9% global	33.7% global	−17.8% global
70% stocks/30% bonds	12.3% USA	31.5% USA	−15.2% USA
	12.4% global	31.6% global	−14.8% global

allocation	average annual return	largest 1-year gain	largest 1-year loss
60% stocks/40% bonds	11.8% USA	28.0% USA	−12.2% USA
	11.9% global	29.4% global	−11.8% global
50% stocks/50% bonds	11.3% USA	25.0% USA	−9.1% USA
	11.4% global	27.3% global	−8.7% global
40% stocks/60% bonds	10.7 USA	23.5% USA	−6.0% USA
	10.8% global	23.0% global	−5.7% global
30% stocks/70% bonds	10.2% USA	23.5% USA	−2.9% USA
	10.2% global	23.0% global	−2.7% global
20% stocks/80% bonds	9.6% USA	23.5% USA	−1.6% USA
	9.6% global	22.0% global	−1.2% global
10% stocks/90% bonds	8.9% USA	23.5% USA	−2.0% USA
	8.9% global	22.8% global	−1.8% global
100% bonds	8.3% USA	23.5% USA	−2.4% USA
	8.3% bonds	23.5% global	−2.4% global

Notes:
1. USA = 70% S&P 500 + 30% U.S. small-company stocks
2. Global = 50% S&P 500 + 30% EAFE Index + 20% U.S. small-company stocks
3. Bonds = 70% medium-term government + 30% U.S. T-bills

Appendix M
Stock Market Declines

If you are a relatively new investor, you may not have had first-hand experience with a bear market. Since corrections are a natural part of the stock market cycle, it is important to ask yourself how you would react. Would you panic or would you be patient? It is difficult to know for sure. Stock market fire drills do not really work, because it is one thing to ponder your reaction to a market meltdown—another to live through one with your financial goals at stake. However, a historical perspective may help you gain a better perspective and, more important, may help you remain patient.

The table below shows all of the periods when the U.S. stock market dropped 15 percent or more from 1953 through the end of 1998 (a "bear market" is defined as a drop of 20 percent or more; a "correction" is a decline of 10 percent or more). Of these fourteen down markets, the worst took place during the 1973–74 recession, resulting in the greatest loss since the Great Depression. Surprisingly, half of the 48 percent loss that took place during the 1973–74 decline was recovered within five months after the drop.

U.S. Market Declines of 15% or More [1953–1998]

bear year	% decline	# of down months	months to recovery
1953	15%	9	6
1956–57	16%	6	5
1957	20%	3	12
1961–62	29%	6	14
1966	22%	9	6
1968–70	37%	18	22
1973–74	48%	21	64
1975	15%	2	4
1977–78	18%	14	6
1978	17%	2	10
1980	22%	2	4
1981–82	22%	13	3
1987	34%	2	23
1990	20%	3	23
average	**24%**	**8**	**13**

One possible strategy to avoiding market declines is to sit on the sidelines until the volatility passes. According to a study by the University of Michigan, this is a bad idea. An investor who was on the sidelines during the best 1 percent of all trading days from 1963 to 1999 missed 95 percent of the market's gains.

These included investors who were sidelined in 1995 by the poor showing in 1994 for both stocks and bonds as well as those stock market investors who bailed out in 1996 because the 38 percent gain in 1995 made them nervous about a downturn. Those who bailed out in 1997 because the 23 percent gain in 1996 made them nervous missed a 29 percent gain in 1998!

Being in the market when it falls is not the greatest risk most stock investors face, it is being out of the market when it soars. The best strategy is to keep investing through any market environment.

The problem is that no one rings a bell when the market hits bottom. Similarly, you do not get any advance notice that the market is turning around. Stocks tend to gain significant ground in short periods; missing out on the first, brief phase of a recovery can be costly. For example, when the stock market took off in August 1982, ending years of mediocre performance, the market jumped 42 percent in just three months. From the October low of the 1987 crash to the end of December, just two months later, stocks rebounded 22 percent. And in the four months after the October 1990 Gulf War low, with the U.S. still mired in recession, the stock market shot up more than 30 percent.

Trying to get out of the market and get back in calls for two right decisions. There is no evidence that professional investors, market timers, brokers, financial analysts, or anyone else can get these calls right with any degree of consistency. One bad market timing call can seriously handicap lifetime performance.

The question then becomes, if stock prices fall hard, should you cut your losses and play it safe? Of all the options that investors have, this one may be the worst solution and the most devastating. An investment of $10,000 in common stocks, as measured by the S&P 500, on the day before the October 1987 crash would have fallen to $7,995 in a single day. Leaving the account intact would have resulted in a whopping 535 percent gain through June 30, 1998. Taking the $7,995 and reinvesting it in U.S. Treasury bills would have resulted in a gain of just 83 percent over the same period.

Appendix N
A Reason Not to Index

Appendix D showed a systematic withdrawal program (SWP) for Investment Company of America (ICA), a growth and income portfolio from the American Funds Group, starting with its first full year through the middle of 1998. Let us now look at two more examples of a SWP, comparing results from Washington Mutual, another growth and income fund offered through the American Funds Group with the S&P 500.

For this example, a different time frame (1/1/73 through 5/31/99) will be used, showing radically different results. Like the ICA example, it is assumed that a single $100,000 investment is made and that all capital gains and dividend payments are automatically reinvested into the fund. Also less money is taken out in this example (8 percent, or $8,000 per year).

As you can see, applying an SWP to the S&P 500 (or an index fund that matches the S&P 500) and a SWP results in the investor being flat broke by December 1996 (all of the $100,000 and its resulting growth has been depleted). Yet, by using professional management like that found with Washington Mutual (abbreviated as WM below), not only are the cumulative distributions greater ($208,000 versus $188,700), so is the remaining principal ($994,280 versus zero).

**Systematic Withdrawal Program Using a
Growth & Income Fund (Washington Mutual) vs. the S&P 500
$100,000 Invested in Each Portfolio on Jan. 1st, 1973**

date	cumulative withdrawal from WM	cumulative withdrawal from S&P 500	remaining value of Washington Mutual (WM)	remaining value of S&P 500
1/1/73	0	0	$100,000	$100,000
12/31/73	$8,000	$8,000	$79,280	$76,890
12/31/74	$16,000	$16,000	$57,460	$48,370
12/31/75	$24,000	$24,000	$74,830	$58,050
12/31/80	$64,000	$64,000	$89,980	$52,930
12/31/85	$104,000	$104,000	$170,740	$42,890
12/31/90	$144,000	$144,000	$260,020	$28,520
12/31/95	$184,000	$184,000	$503,180	$3,910
12/31/96	$192,000	$188,700	$596,530	$0
12/31/97	$200,000		$787,050	
12/31/98	$208,000		$931,140	
5/31/99			$994,280	

For the S&P 500, the average annual total return for this illustration was 6.0 percent (Jan. 1, 1973 through Dec. 15, 1996 when the money ran out) and 18.9 percent for the last ten years. For Washington Mutual Fund (WM), the average annual total return for this illustration was 12.9 percent (Jan. 1, 1973 through May 31, 1999) and 16.3 percent for the last ten years.

Two conclusions can be reached from this illustration. First, there is a benefit to professional management versus a passively managed portfolio such as the S&P 500 (which as an index fund is also considered to be a growth and income fund). Second, moderate gains or advances in some early years can make a great difference later on (compare the value of both portfolios at the end of 1974 and 1975 versus what happened in later years, such as 1980 and 1985, when the gaps become huge due to earlier gains by Washington Mutual).

Appendix O
Using Index Funds

The vast majority of mutual funds buy and sell securities based on the fund management's judgment about which securities are likely to provide the greatest return to investors, given any restrictions as described by the fund's literature or prospectus (e.g., "at least two-thirds of the portfolio will be invested in . . ."). An index fund, on the other hand, simply buys a large number, or all, of the securities listed in a particular index or market average—seeking to duplicate that index's or average's performance.

For most mutual funds, the "active" approach typically gives management latitude in managing assets. As a result, investors in these funds are often not entirely sure how their money is being invested at a given moment. Fund performance, which is dependent on the advisor's strategies and parameters as described in the prospectus (e.g., "U.S. large-cap growth stocks," "foreign bonds from mature economies," etc.), comes at a significant yearly cost: typically 1 to 2 percent or more of the value of the portfolio.

Indexing's "passive" approach is more objective and can be more predictable, with costs that are roughly half to one-sixth (expense ratios as low as 0.25 percent) the yearly cost. Perhaps a more important savings is the dramatically lower turnover rates that are common with index funds; the cost of buying and selling securities (trading costs plus the difference between the bid and the ask price) can easily be much greater than a fund's expense ratio. (Note: the expense ratio does not include the cost of acquiring or getting rid of securities.)

Active management does not mean you will outperform passive management, even during a market decline. According to Lipper Analytical Services, in five of the past seven downturns (ending 8/4/98), S&P 500 index funds held up better than actively managed U.S. stock funds.

Passive vs. Active Domestic Equity Mutual Funds During a Downturn

downturn	S&P 500 Index funds	active mgmt. general equity
7/17/98–8/4/98	–9.6%	–10.7%
10/7/97–10/27/97	–10.8%	–9.8%
2/18/97–3/31/97	–7.1%	–7.4%
6/5/96–7/24/96	–7.4%	–10.7%
2/2/94–4/20/94	–7.8%	–8.7%
7/12/90–10/11/90	–18.3%	–20.7%
8/13/87–12/3/87	–32.2%	–29.8%

By its very nature, indexing emphasizes broad diversification, minimal trading activity, and usually razor-thin costs. As a result, index investors benefit from a reduction of certain investment risks, the possibility of lower taxable distributions, and the ability to keep a higher percentage of investment returns.

Twenty years ago, index investing was available only to pension funds. Not until the Vanguard Group introduced the 500 Portfolio (which is identical to the S&P 500) in 1976 could individual investors index. Today, Vanguard remains the most recognizable name in indexing and offers a broad array of index choices.

Appendix P
Tax Basics for Mutual Fund Investors

This appendix provides you with an introduction to mutual fund taxation, including a list of necessary year-end tax forms and statements plus a discussion of mutual fund distributions. You will also learn about the four methods of calculating cost basis and capital gains or losses. Finally, the tax consequences of wash sales and gifts as well as inheritances will be covered.

Forms and statements

The following year-end tax forms and statements are sent to mutual fund shareholders in January and include information applicable to the preceding year:

- Annual statements list all account activity during the year, including purchases, redemptions, and fund distributions.
- Form 1099-B reports any redemptions or exchanges from your account during the year. You will need this information to complete Schedule D of your federal tax return; this information is reported to both you and the IRS.
- Form 1099-DIV reports the taxable ordinary income and capital gains distributed to your account(s) during the year; this information is reported to both you and the IRS.

It is a good idea to keep all of your annual statements and 1099 forms, even after you close your account(s). The statements may be needed to calculate cost basis and capital gains or losses. The IRS may request 1099 forms if you are audited.

Mutual fund distributions

Mutual funds distribute two types of income to their shareholders—ordinary income and capital gains. As an investor (shareholder), you have a choice of receiving distributions as cash or opting to have such distributions automatically reinvested in additional shares. Taxation is the same whether you receive such distribution(s) or reinvest such monies. Distributions declared in October, November, or December but paid in January of the following year are taxable as if paid on December 31st.

- **Ordinary income distributions:** A fund earns dividends and/or interest on the securities in which it invests. Once a fund subtracts its expenses from such income, the remainder is distributed to shareholders as ordinary income distributions. Ordinary income distributions, which are taxed at a maximum rate of just under 40 percent, also include any short-term capital gains earned by the fund (when the fund sells a security it has owned for less than a year for a profit).
- **Capital gain distributions:** When a fund makes a profit from selling its investments, it passes the profit on to its shareholders as capital gains distributions. Profits from the sale of securities held for more than a year qualify as long-term with a maximum federal tax rate of 20 percent.
- **Tax Exempt Dividends:** Interest from U.S. Government securities is exempt from state taxes. Interest from municipal bonds is exempt from federal taxes and is also exempt from state taxes in the state in which the bond was issued. Short-term capital gains distributions are treated as ordinary income for federal tax purposes.

Calculating capital gains and losses

When you sell or exchange shares of a mutual fund, the sale price is usually different from the original purchase price (*cost basis*) of the shares. When the sale price is greater, your profit is called a *capital gain*; if the sale price is less than the purchase price, your loss is called a *capital loss*. Although it appears straightforward, you may have had many different purchases, including your adding new money to the account, as well as reinvested dividends and/or capital gains. Furthermore, you might sell only some of the shares you own or make multiple sales at different times at various prices per share. To calculate a capital gain or loss for a particular sale, you must determine which shares were sold and how much you paid for those shares.

Four methods of calculating cost basis

In order to calculate your cost basis, you must first determine the purchase price for all of the shares you own in a particular fund. Over the year(s), you may have purchased shares at different prices and in differing amounts. In addition, any reinvested dividend and capital gain distributions are considered purchases and must be included in your calculations.

You may need all of your annual statements to ascertain every purchase made for a particular account. Once you have determined the purchase price for the different shares you own, you can determine your cost basis using one of the four acceptable methods: the FIFO method (First In, First Out), the Share Identification method, the Average-Cost single category method, or the Average-Cost double category method.

Deciding which method works to your advantage may require you to perform the calculations for each method before you make your first sale. Each method has advantages and disadvantages, depending on your tax situation. Your cost basis needs to reflect the price of all of your purchases, including any reinvested dividend and capital gains distributions.

Once you choose one of the four cost basis methods, you must use the same method for all of your accounts in a particular fund. You can use a different method for your other mutual fund accounts.

To illustrate the four methods for calculating cost basis, let us say that the numbers below represent your account activity in the XYZ Fund, through June 1999.

date	transaction	$ amount	share price	# of shares	share balance
11/2/98	purchase by check	$7,700	$11.00	700	700
11/30/98	reinvest dividends	$240	$12.00	20	720
1/9/99	purchase by exchange from other fund	$9,000	$10.00	900	1,620
6/27/99	purchase by check	$5,600	$14.00	400	2,020
	Total invested	$22,540			2,020 shares

On December 1, 1999 you have decided to sell 400 shares and expect to sell at a price of $13.00 per share, for a total sale of $5,200. Before you make this redemption (or exchange), you want to know whether it will result in a capital gain or loss. Based on this hypothetical example, we will calculate a cost basis using each of the four methods.

The FIFO method

Using FIFO, the first shares you sell are the first ones you bought. If you do not specify another method, the IRS will assume that you have used this method.

Applying FIFO to your account in the XYZ Fund, you are selling 400 of the 700 original shares you bought in November 1998. Your cost basis for those 400 shares is 400 multiplied by the $11 purchase price, for a total of $4,400. In this example, your sale of 400 shares resulted in a long-term capital gain (you held the shares for more than one year) of $800. Your capital gain would be reported as follows:

security description	purchase date	sale date	sales price	cost basis	loss	gain
400 shares of XYZ	11/2/98	12/1/99	$5,200	$4,400	—	$800

The Share Identification or Specific Shares method

This method allows you to choose which shares are sold, as long as you identify the shares *in writing before you sell them*. For each such redemption or exchange, you must send a dated letter to the fund identifying which shares are to be redeemed. The letter must specify the number of shares to be sold, the date the shares were purchased, and the purchase price of the shares.

While this method allows you to minimize or maximize gains and losses, it also requires you to keep written records confirming which shares were sold. You should keep a copy of all redemption letters; the IRS may request them. A number of mutual fund companies do not keep copies of redemption letters. Other funds stamp such letters with the date it was received and then return the original letter to the shareholder.

When choosing which shares to sell, investors can decide to redeem or exchange shares that have losses rather than shares that have gains. Capital losses offset capital gains dollar-for-dollar; there is no dollar limit. If, after offsetting capital losses with capital gains there is a remaining "net" loss, up to $3,000 per year of any remaining capital loss can be used to offset ordinary income (e.g., salary, bonuses, commissions, interest, dividends, redemptions from annuities). Any capital losses still remaining are then carried forward to the next year. You never lose your losses, they can be carried forward indefinitely.

In the XYZ Fund, you will have a capital loss if you sell the 400 shares you purchased in June 1999. Your cost basis for those 400 shares is 400 multiplied by the $14 purchase price, for a total of $5,600. Your sale of 400 shares resulted in a short-term capital loss of $400 (short-term because the shares were held for less than a year).

security description	purchase date	sale date	sales price	cost basis	loss	gain
400 shares of XYZ	5/7/989	12/1/99	$5,200	$5,600	$400	—

The Average-Cost methods

Both of the average-cost methods have special requirements: (1) you must state on your tax return, or on an attachment to your return, which method you have chosen; (2) *once selected, you must use the same method for all of your accounts in that particular mutual fund*; (3) you cannot later change methods for that account without permission from the IRS; (4) average-cost methods can only be used for mutual funds.

If you trade often, these two methods can be very labor intensive—every time you buy new shares at a different price (including the reinvestment of dividends, interest and/or capital gains), you must recalculate your average cost. However, if you have made regular, infrequent purchases over a long period of time, you may be able to use one of the average cost methods to your advantage.

Single Category method

This average cost method allows you to average the cost of all of your shares, regardless of the amount of time you have held them. On your tax return, you need to declare whether your holding period was short- or long-term. The IRS requires you to decide this on a FIFO basis. In our example, you bought your first 400 shares on November 2, 1998 (over a year ago); therefore you must declare a long-term capital gain.

For the XYZ Fund, your total cost, including reinvested dividends, was $22,540, and you owned a total of 2,020 shares. Your average cost is $22,450 divided by 2,020, or $11.16 per share. Your resulting cost basis for 400 shares is $11.16 multiplied by 400, or $4,464. In this example, your sale of 400 shares resulted in a long-term capital gain of $736.

security description	purchase date	sale date	sales price	cost basis	loss	gain
400 shares of XYZ	11/2/98	12/1/99	$5,200	$4,464	—	$736

The cost basis for the remaining shares in your account is now equal to the average cost you calculated ($11.16 a share). In the above example, 1,620 shares remain in the account after the sale; the purchase price of all 1,620 shares is now $11.16 (the average cost), regardless of the original purchase price. If additional shares are purchased in the future, you must recalculate your average cost. For example, if you purchased 500 additional shares at $12.00 per share, you would need to calculate a new average cost using 1,620 shares at $11.16 and 500 shares at $12.00.

Double Category method
This average-cost method requires you to calculate two average-cost bases: a short-term cost basis for shares bought less than a year ago, and a long-term cost basis for shares bought a year ago or more. Despite the extra work, some investors prefer this method because it allows them to choose whether their gains and losses are short- or long-term.

In the XYZ Fund, you have held 720 shares—your 700 original shares plus 20 shares bought on November 30, 1998—for more than a year. When you divide $7,940 (the total cost of these shares) by 720 (the total number of shares), you get an average long-term share cost of $11.03.

Additionally, you have held 1,300 shares—900 shares purchased on January 1999 and 400 shares purchased on June 27, 1999—for less than a year. When you divide $14,600 (the total cost of the shares) by 1,300 (the total number of shares), you get an average short-term cost of $11.23 per share.

Since you have made this separation, the IRS allows you to specify whether you are selling short- or long-term shares. However, *you must identify the shares in writing before you sell them.* For each redemption or exchange, you must send a dated letter to the fund, specifying the number of shares to be sold, the date the shares were purchased, the purchase price of the shares, and whether the shares are short- or long-term. If you fail to specify whether the shares are short- or long-term, their holding period will be determined by the IRS on a FIFO basis.

Suppose you decide you will sell your long-term shares. Your 400 shares at $11.03 give you a cost basis of $4,412. In our example, your sale of 400 shares resulted in a long-term capital gain of $788; if you had chosen to sell your short-term shares, your short-term capital gain would have totaled $708.

security description	purchase date	sale date	sales price	cost basis	loss	gain
400 shares of XYZ	11/2/98	12/1/99	$5,200	$4,412	—	$788

Special tax issue: Capital losses

For individuals and couples, a net capital loss on the sale of mutual fund shares, or any other security, can be used to offset income in two ways: (1) the loss can offset gains or (2) the loss can be deducted dollar-for-dollar against ordinary income (up to $3,000 whether you are married or single). Any unused capital losses may be carried forward to offset future income. In order to discourage loss-oriented selling, the IRS created several complex rules related to capital losses:

Wash sales

If you purchase shares of the same fund, including reinvested dividends, interest, and/or capital gains, within thirty days before or after you sell shares at a loss, the sale is considered a "wash sale." In this case, the shares purchased offset any realized capital losses on a share-by-share basis. The IRS does allow an adjustment to the cost basis of the purchased shares, compensating you for the disallowed loss.

Long-term capital gain distributions

If you hold mutual fund shares for six months or less and receive a long-term capital gain distribution during that period, any short-term capital loss you realized from the sale of those shares must be treated as a long-term capital loss to the extent of the capital gain distribution.

Losses after receipt of tax-exempt dividends

If you hold shares in a municipal or other tax-free mutual fund for six months or less and receive tax-exempt dividends (interest) during that period, any loss you realize from the sale of those shares will be reduced by the amount of the tax-exempt distribution.

Special tax issue: Inheritances or gifts

Your cost basis for inherited shares is usually the value of the shares on the day the decedent passed away. However, for gifts, your cost basis is the lesser of the value of the shares on the date the gift was made or the donor's cost basis, adjusted for any federal gift tax paid.

Appendix Q
A Benefit of Balanced Funds

Prudence can pay off. Even though stocks usually outperform bonds, there have been extensive periods of time when a balanced portfolio (30 percent to 70 percent in bonds and the balance in stocks) can be a better way to go than a pure stock portfolio (represented by the S&P 500 below)—especially when current income is needed.

The table below shows a systematic withdrawal program (SWP) for Income Fund of America (a balanced portfolio from the American Funds Group) versus a similar SWP using the S&P 500. Both withdrawal programs assume a one-time investment of $200,000 made on January 1st, 1974, annual withdrawals made at the end of each year, and a first-year withdrawal of $15,000 (7.5 percent of $200,000) that is then increased by 3.5 percent for each subsequent year (in order to offset the effects of inflation). As you can see, the balanced fund comes out ahead.

Systematic Withdrawal Program Using a Balanced Fund (IFA) and the S&P 500 $200,000 Invested in Each Portfolio on Jan. 1st, 1972

date	cumulative withdrawal from IFA	cumulative withdrawal from S&P 500	remaining value of IFA	remaining value of S&P 500
1/1/74	0	0	$200,000	$200,000
12/31/74	$15,000	$15,000	$165,240	$131,834
12/31/75	$30,525	$30,525	$208,287	$164,740
12/31/76	$46,593	$46,593	$265,307	$187,368
12/31/80	$116,691	$116,691	$248,709	$191,095
12/31/85	$219,029	$219,029	$488,588	$221,773
12/31/90	$340,574	$340,574	$632,843	$257,400
12/31/95	$484,932	$484,932	$1,067,108	$347,972
12/31/96	$516,905	$516,905	$1,197,075	$394,987
12/31/97	$549,997	$549,997	$1,428,937	$493,109
12/31/98	$584,247	$584,247	$1,529,268	$597,424
6/30/99	$584,247	$584,247	$1,594,321	$671,275

For the S&P 500, the average annual total return for this illustration was 11.6 percent (Jan. 1, 1974 through June 30, 1999) and 18.7 percent for the last ten years. For Income Fund of America (IFA), the average annual total return for this illustration was 13.5 percent and 12.1 percent for the last ten years.

Appendix R
Performance as a Contrary Predictor of the Future

The main reason I do not just use performance as a criteria for selecting "the 100 best" each year is that there is truly no relationship between past, present, and future returns. However, when it comes to risk measurement, past numbers are fairly, and often, quite similar to a fund's present risk profile.

A 1997 research report by the Smith Barney Consulting Group (302-888-4109) covering different periods ending Dec. 31, 1996, titled "Why Past Performance is a Poor Indicator of Future Performance" shows that top-ranked money managers tend to underperform in subsequent periods. The period covered for all of the tables below was from January 1, 1987 through December 31, 1996 and is based on the track records of seventy-two stock investment managers.

Average Change in Subsequent Performance

manager ranking	subsequent 1-year change	subsequent 2-year change	subsequent 3-year change	subsequent 4-year change
top quintile	− 9.3%	− 9.7%	− 10.4%	− 7.1%
2nd quintile	− 2.2%	− 2.8%	− 4.4%	− 2.8%
3rd quintile	+ 0.7%	+ 0.5%	− 1.7%	− 0.7%
4th quintile	+ 5.0%	+ 3.5%	+ 1.4%	+ 1.1%
5th quintile	+ 12.0%	+ 10.8%	+ 5.2%	+ 6.3%

Average 3-Year Annualized Returns

manager ranking	years 1–3	years 4–6
top quintile	+ 23.7%	+ 13.4%
2nd quintile	+ 19.1%	+ 14.7%
3rd quintile	+ 16.1%	+ 14.4%
4th quintile	+ 14.1%	+ 15.6%
5th quintile	+ 10.1%	+ 15.3%

Average 2-Year Annualized Returns

manager ranking	years 1–2	years 3–4
top quintile	+ 23.6%	+ 13.9%
2nd quintile	+ 18.0%	+ 15.2%
3rd quintile	+ 14.8%	+ 15.4%
4th quintile	+ 12.5%	+ 15.7%
5th quintile	+ 7.0%	+ 17.7%

Over the ten years studied (1987–1996), only fifteen managers remained in the top quintile for two successive two-year periods; twenty-seven managers fell from the top to the bottom quintile. Looking at all two-year periods, eleven out the seventy-two managers were in top quintile two successive (or more) times; twenty-eight fell from the top to the bottom quintile over two, successive, three-year periods.

The real conclusion of the Smith Barney study is not that good managers turn bad, but that investment style (growth vs. value, small cap vs. large cap, etc.) has a lot more to do with performance than most people think.

Appendix S
Stock Gains, Losses, and Averages

In the five calendar years ending December 1932, the S&P 500 had a cumulative loss of almost 49 percent. Although this is quite a depressing figure (particularly since similar losses took place during the 1973–74 recession), basing your stock market strategy on a couple of terrible periods is foolish.

To get a better feel for the likely range of returns you will experience, let us examine what happens when you throw out the worst 10 percent and best 10 percent of the years and then look at performance for the remaining 80 percent of the time. Here is what you would find, looking at rolling calendar year periods from 1871 through 1998 (all figures are from *Stocks for the Long Run* by Jeremy Siegel and the Institute of Business and Finance):

- For five-year periods (124 observations) and then eliminating the twelve best and twelve worst such periods, annualized returns ranged from 0.1 percent to 18.5 percent.
- For ten-year periods (119 observations), annualized returns ranged from 2.8 percent to 15.9 percent.
- For twenty-year periods (109 observations), annualized returns ranged from 5.3 percent to 13.8 percent.
- For thirty-year periods (99 observations), annualized returns ranged from 6.0 percent to 11.8 percent.

Note: If you earned 5.3 percent a year for twenty years, your money would grow 181 percent. If you earned 6.0 percent a year for thirty years, you would end up with 474 percent.

Looking at returns and variability from a different perspective, Jeffrey Schwartz, a senior consultant at Ibbotson, provides an even wider range of returns. According to his figures, since the end of World War II (throwing out the best 5 percent and the worst 5 percent of the years):

- Five-year returns vary from 2.5 percent to 22.7 percent a year;
- Ten-year returns vary from 4.0 percent to 20.4 percent a year;
- Twenty-year returns vary from 6.0 percent to 15.8 percent a year.

About the Author

Gordon K. Williamson, JD, MBA, MS, CFP, CLU, ChFC, RP is one of the most highly trained investment counselors in the United States. Williamson, a former tax attorney, is a Certified Fund Specialist and branch manager of a national brokerage firm. He has been admitted to the Registry of Financial Planning Practitioners, the highest honor one can attain as a financial planner. He holds the two highest designations in the life insurance industry, Chartered Life Underwriter and Chartered Financial Consultant. He is also a real estate broker with an MBA in real estate.

Mr. Williamson is the founder and Executive Director of the Institute of Business & Finance, a professional education program that leads to the designations "CFS" and "Board Certified" (800/848-2029).

He is also the author of more than twenty-five books, including: *Building & Managing an Investment Portfolio, Making the Most of Your 401(k), The 100 Best Annuities You Can Buy, All About Annuities, How You Can Survive and Prosper in the Clinton Years, Investment Strategies under Clinton/Gore, The Longman Investment Companion, Investment Strategies, Survey of Financial Planning, Tax Shelters, Advanced Investment Vehicles and Techniques, Your Living Trust, Sooner Than You Think, Getting Started in Annuities, Big Decisions—Small Investor, Building & Managing an Investment Portfolio,* and *Low Risk Investing.* He has been the financial editor of various magazines and newspapers and a stock market consultant for a television station.

Gordon K. Williamson is an investment advisory firm located in La Jolla, California. The firm specializes in financial planning for individuals and institutions ($100,000 minimum account size). Additional information can be obtained by phoning (800) 748-5552 or (619) 454-3938.